The New York Times

EASY TO NOT-SO-EASY CROSSWORD PUZZLE OMNIBUS VOLUME I

200 Monday–Saturday Crosswords from the Pages of *The New York Times*

Edited by Will Shortz

ST. MARTIN'S GRIFFIN ⚹ NEW YORK

The New York Times

EASY TO NOT-SO-EASY CROSSWORD PUZZLE OMNIBUS VOLUME I

ACROSS

1 Jacket
5 "___ the night before . . ."
9 Popular Ford auto, informally
14 Slangy denial
15 Cry before disaster
16 Singer Ford from Tennessee
17 Ceremonial act
18 Complains and complains and . . .
19 Good places for hen parties?
20 Voice amplifier on a pole
23 Like squashed insects
24 Edge
25 Negligent
29 Needle hole
30 Banking device, in brief
33 Correct, as text
34 Bullets, e.g.
36 "En garde" weapon
37 Do wondrous things
40 "Cogito ___ sum"
41 One who stands to gain a lot?
42 Matter of fact?
43 Strong cleaner
44 Fish steerer
45 Like some winter sidewalks
46 Ca++ or Cl−, e.g.
47 District
49 "You'll have to show me"
56 Once more
57 Verdi heroine
58 Crude group?
59 Greeting said with a tip of the hat
60 One-inch news story
61 District

62 "This way" sign
63 Muse's instrument
64 Conclusions

DOWN

1 Street's edge
2 Buckeye State
3 Hyundai or Honda
4 Unnamed ones
5 Invigorating drinks
6 Hit hard
7 Raging
8 Fair to middling
9 Computer whiz
10 Sweeper
11 Involved with
12 Ready to pluck
13 ___ Moines
21 Botch

22 Funnyman Richard
25 Force back
26 Nail filer
27 Make one
28 Facts
29 Kuwaiti chief
30 Tiptop, on a report card
31 Saws and laws have them
32 Netlike
34 So be it
35 New millennium year, or a part of 20-, 37- and 49-Across
36 Drapery color
38 Big zoo animal
39 Country album?

44 In the short term
45 Kind of seed on a roll
46 "Don't mind ___!"
47 Friendliness
48 Equestrian
49 Composer Stravinsky
50 Bryn ___, Pa.
51 Postal delivery
52 Leak slowly
53 Abreast of
54 Tear
55 Cold desserts
56 "So that's it!"

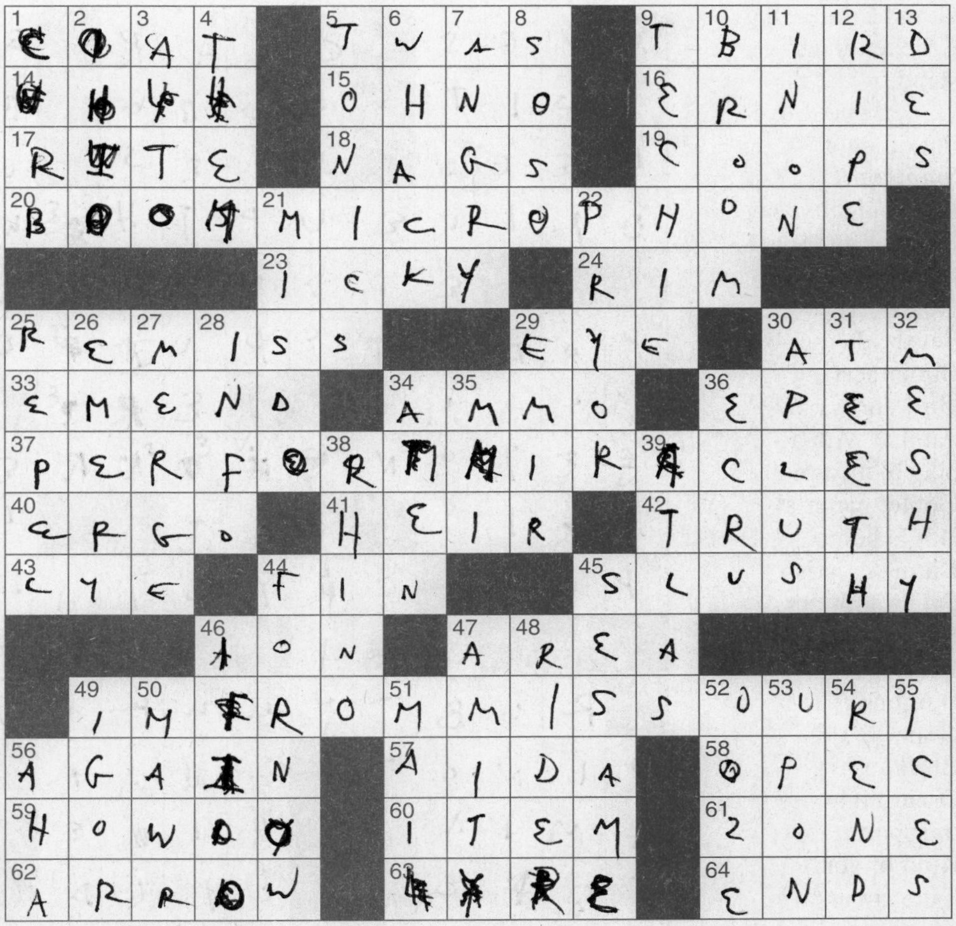

by Manny Nosowsky

The completed crossword grid (handwritten answers):

1 C	2 O	3 A	4 T		5 T	6 W	7 A	8 S		9 T	10 B	11 I	12 R	13 D
14 N	A	H	H		15 O	H	N	O		16 E	R	N	I	E
17 R	I	T	E		18 N	A	G	S		19 C	O	O	P	S
20 B	O	O	M	21 M	I	C	R	O	22 P	H	O	N	E	
				23 I	C	K	Y		24 R	I	M			
25 R	26 E	27 M	28 I	S	S			29 E	Y	E		30 A	31 T	32 M
33 E	M	E	N	D		34 A	35 M	M	O		36 E	P	E	E
37 P	E	R	F	O	38 R	M	I	R	A	39 C	L	E	S	
40 E	R	G	O		41 H	E	I	R		42 T	R	U	T	H
43 C	L	Y		44 F	I	N		45 S	L	U	S	H	Y	
			46 I	O	N		47 A	R	E	A				
	49 I	50 M	F	R	O	51 M	M	I	S	S	52 O	53 U	54 R	55 I
56 A	G	A	I	N		57 A	I	D	A		58 O	P	E	C
59 H	O	W	D	O		60 I	T	E	M		61 Z	O	N	E
62 A	R	R	O	W		63 L	Y	R	E		64 E	N	D	S

ACROSS

1 Hot chocolate containers
5 Bloke
9 Wire nails
14 "___ something I said?"
15 Timber wolf
16 Disprove
17 Toy block brand
18 Steps in human evolution
19 Place for a beach
20 Exasperate, as a motorist?
23 "So what ___ is new?"
24 Egyptian cobra
25 Toy gun noisemaker
28 Orkin target
31 Grand Coulee, e.g.
34 Crockett's last stand, with "the"
36 ". . . ___ he drove out of sight"
37 Summon electronically, say
38 Exasperate, as a neurologist?
42 Newsman Sevareid
43 Butter serving
44 Gird one's ___
45 Animal with a pouch, informally
46 Goblet material
49 Hog's home
50 Burnt ___ crisp
51 Bright thought
53 Exasperate, as a masseur?
60 Burgundy grape
61 Blacken
62 Oscar night transport
63 Kind of acid
64 Take cover
65 ___ about (approximately)
66 Full complement of dwarfs
67 Newspaper page
68 Lead-in for -aholic

DOWN

1 Not burning the mouth much
2 Cable subscriber
3 "Thank Heaven for Little Girls" musical
4 Where a cook cooks
5 Contract provision
6 Lottery equipment
7 Help in crime
8 Swanky
9 Shop without anything particular in mind
10 Summation
11 Cain's brother
12 Twofold
13 Train stop: Abbr.
21 John who sang "Rocket Man"
22 Moth-___
25 Basketballer
26 Oldsmobile model
27 Barbecue site
29 Track contests
30 April initials
31 California Gov. Gray ___
32 Ten-percenter
33 Not neat
35 Slip-on shoe, briefly
37 Old hand
39 TV's Winfrey
40 Not yea
41 Barkin or Burstyn
46 T-shirt material
47 Tongue-lashing
48 Loved to bits
50 Juicy steak
52 Burning
53 Icy coating
54 Harvard or Stanford: Abbr.
55 Reverberate
56 Horse trainer's aid
57 Bowery bum
58 Love, Spanish-style
59 Part of N.Y.C.
60 Faux ___

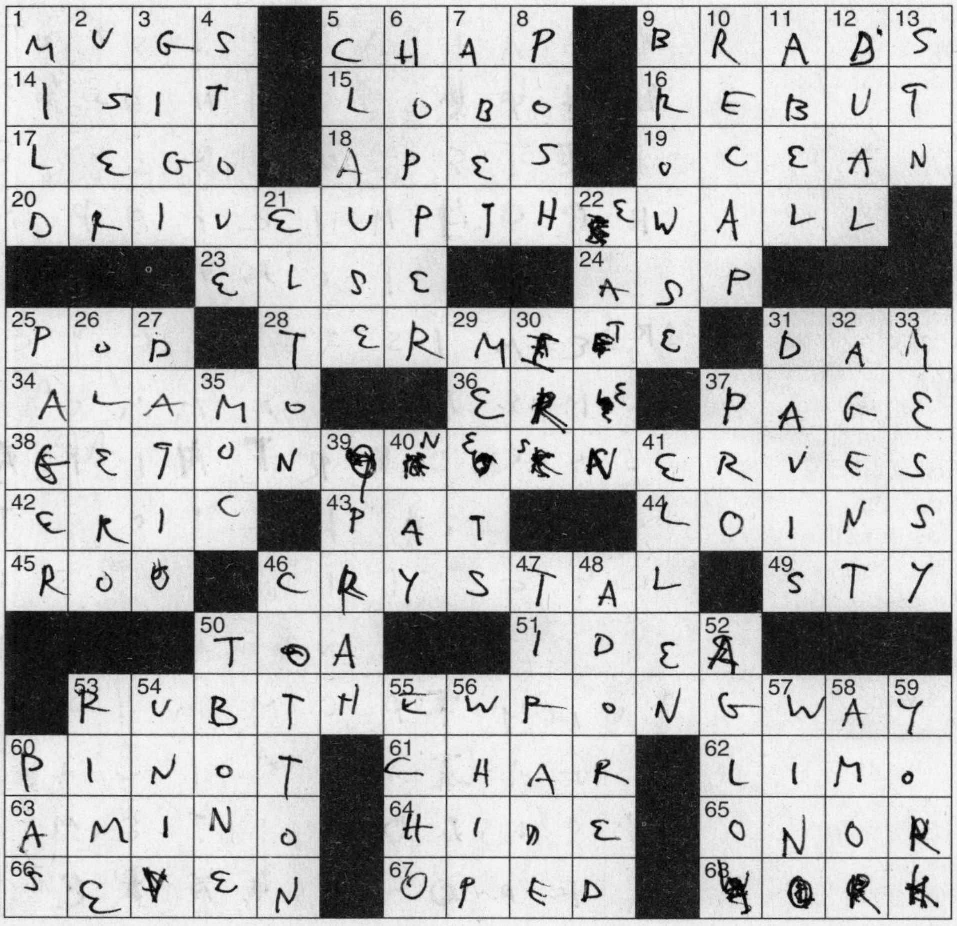

by Gregory E. Paul

Filled-in grid:

1 M	2 U	3 G	4 S		5 C	6 H	7 A	8 P		9 B	10 R	11 A	12 D	13 S
14 I	S	I	T		15 L	O	B	O		16 R	E	B	U	T
17 L	E	G	O		18 A	P	E	S		19 O	C	E	A	N
20 D	R	I	V	21 E	U	P	T	H	22 E	W	A	L	L	
			23 E	L	S	E			24 A	S	P			
25 P	26 O	27 D		28 T	E	R	29 M	30 I	T	E		31 D	32 A	33 M
34 A	L	A	35 M	O			36 E	R	E		37 P	A	G	E
38 G	E	T	O	N	39 O	40 N	E	S	N	41 E	R	V	E	S
42 E	R	I	C		43 P	A	T			44 L	O	I	N	S
45 R	O	O		46 C	R	Y	S	47 T	48 A	L		49 S	T	Y
			50 T	O	A			51 I	D	E	52 A			
	53 R	54 U	B	T	H	55 E	56 W	R	O	N	G	57 W	58 A	59 Y
60 P	I	N	O	T		61 C	H	A	R		62 L	I	M	O
63 A	M	I	N	O		64 H	I	D	E		65 O	N	O	R
66 S	E	V	E	N		67 O	P	E	D		68 W	O	R	K

ACROSS

1 Smelter's waste
5 The Amazon and others
9 Item a fisherman uses . . . or removes
14 Angel's headwear
15 Place for a keystone
16 Streaker in the night sky
17 VW or Volvo
18 Stride
19 Pizzeria fixtures
20 Tourist attraction in 31-Across
23 Sticky stuff
24 Wig, essentially
25 Clothing
28 Grief
29 Finder of secrets
30 Video producer, for short
31 City founded in 1718 by the Sieur de Bienville
36 Roof overhang
37 Sheeplike
38 Computer's core, briefly
39 Title holder
40 Length of yarn
41 Nickname for 31-Across
43 Hardly ordinary
44 Philosophical ideal
45 "Treasure Island" monogram
46 Prince Edward's earldom
48 Arctic phenomenon
50 Great Leap Forward leader
53 31-Across entertainment
56 Hotelier Helmsley
58 ___ avis
59 Put ___ words
60 Egyptian dam site
61 "Mystery!" host Diana
62 Legal claim
63 Patron saint of France
64 ___-eyed
65 Doily material

DOWN

1 Mine passage
2 Hillary's successor as first lady
3 Lengthen or shorten
4 Thug
5 "Sistine Madonna" artist
6 Many a Kurd
7 Take place
8 Where the Mets play
9 "Star Trek" engineer
10 Wish for
11 Some cultural artifacts
12 Author Deighton
13 S.A.T. org.
21 Mowing or raking, e.g.
22 Knocks
26 Four-star reviews
27 Polishing substance
28 Policy expert
29 Rudely ignore
31 Slangy negative
32 Steer clear of
33 Gently comes to a close
34 Canyon sound
35 Gibbon or gorilla
36 Rams' ma'ams
39 Looked at lustfully
41 It has a horn and charges
42 Early period in human history
44 Lone Star Staters
47 Mideast peninsula
48 Swing wildly
49 Slow, musically
50 Craze
51 Early Mexican
52 Ultraviolet ray blocker
54 Flubs
55 Jack's partner
56 Stripling
57 Opposite WNW

by Janet R. Bender

ACROSS

1 Helper: Abbr.
5 Hall-of-Fame pitcher Ryan
10 Light greenish-blue
14 Considerably
15 Swiftly
16 Spin
17 Jacob's twin
18 Great tempter
19 Mailed
20 Not just a fib
23 Linda Ellerbee's "___ It Goes"
24 Embarrassingly stuck
28 Winter Olympics vehicle
33 Suffix with schnozz
34 Surrounded by
38 "Lovely" Beatles girl
39 Like some classical columns
41 Cried one's eyes out
44 ___ de Guerre (French military award)
45 Nerd
46 Egyptian fertility goddess
47 Clamor
48 Long locks
51 Complete
53 Fairy tale monsters
58 Pugilist's weapon
63 Kiss
66 Tiny quantities
67 Running behind
68 Memo starter
69 Bathroom item
70 Molecule component
71 Temple area of Jerusalem
72 Problems with theories
73 Spigots

DOWN

1 One-celled blob
2 "Black-eyed" girl
3 Burn
4 Heavy footsteps
5 Zippo
6 Grp. that has energy users over a barrel?
7 Wash
8 Amino ___
9 ___ Fox, 1959 American League M.V.P.
10 Perplexed
11 "___ pasa?"
12 Large coffee maker
13 Pantry raider
21 Watch chain
22 Gandhi's land
25 Microbiologist Salk
26 Cover story?
27 Thanksgiving parade producer
29 Run-of-the-mill: Abbr.
30 Absolute nonsense
31 Places for muckety-mucks?
32 Dams make them
34 Start of kindergarten learning
35 County north of San Francisco
36 "___ say a word"
37 551, to Caesar
40 Kimono sash
42 Bit player
43 Barely make, with "out"
49 Hot dog topper
50 Drench
52 Playwright Henrik
54 Chopin's Polonaise No. 16 in ___
55 Lasso
56 Hinder, legally
57 Flower holders?
59 Plumb crazy
60 List-ending abbr.
61 Broad valley
62 Employs
63 Show ___
64 Prefix with sex
65 Theater sign

by Nancy Kavanaugh

ACROSS

1 Wall Street Journal visual, maybe
6 Interest figure
10 Tiny criticisms that are picked
14 Eagle's roost
15 Author of "A Death in the Family"
16 "And pretty maids all in ___"
17 Goal-oriented thing
19 Deadly poison
20 Suspect's story
21 Bottom of a sum
22 Lawyers' org.
25 Mealtime summoner
28 Royal home
31 Flower with a bulb
32 Where boxers box
33 Dairy Queen purchases
35 Part of a line outside a hotel
38 Illegal tender
41 Suffix with differ
42 Borders on
43 Line from the heart
44 Nasty criticism
45 Added support to
46 Plantation plant seedpod
51 "Who ___ we kidding?"
52 Parsley portion
53 Worker's demand
56 Rind
57 Robert De Niro title role
62 Uzbekistan's ___ Sea
63 Coup d'___
64 Blue eyes or baldness, e.g.

65 Turner and Cole
66 Shetland
67 Scattered seed over

DOWN

1 Tank filler
2 ___ Speedwagon
3 Missile's path
4 12-point type
5 Command to a dog
6 Torah reciter
7 Once more
8 Business card no.
9 Cave-dwelling fish
10 Bigwigs
11 Not just peeved
12 Melodious
13 "Great!"

18 Hitchhiker's wish
21 Film studio that made "Jerry Maguire"
22 Quickly
23 Member of the peerage
24 Alaska islander
26 Dress to the ___
27 ". . . ___ saw Elba"
29 Author Beattie
30 J. Crew publication
33 Merest remnant of a sandwich
34 Frequently, in poetry
35 Approximately
36 Take up, as a leg
37 Skate's bottom

39 Israel's Abba
40 Feathery wrap
44 Film photos
45 Buckwheat pancake
46 Channel for the politically aware
47 "Faust," e.g.
48 Chocolate bonbon, e.g.
49 Hymn player
50 Hymn singers
54 Police officers: Abbr.
55 River of Spain
57 Capitol V.I.P.: Abbr.
58 From ___ Z
59 Org. for many G.M. workers
60 Tell tall tales
61 Inc., in London

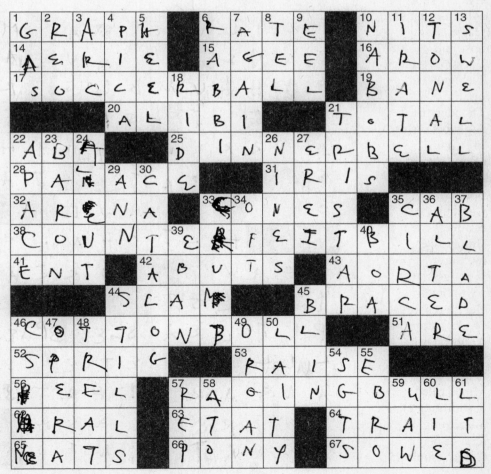

by Sarah Keller

ACROSS

1 Slave away
5 "Casablanca" heroine
9 Fat cat
14 "___ of Green Gables"
15 Windfall
16 Knock down a peg
17 Cynic's snort #1
19 Conservatives, with "the"
20 Bothered nigglingly
21 Roasting rods
23 No longer working: Abbr.
24 Joy's opposite
26 Cynic's snort #2
28 Miler Sebastian
29 Game show host Sajak
31 Lockup overseer
32 Tiebreakers, briefly
33 Thunderstruck
36 Alphabet enders, in Britain
37 Cynic's snort #3
40 Loverboy
43 Split country
44 Combustion residue
47 Brainpower measurer
50 What golfers try to break
51 Health resort
52 Cynic's snort #4
55 Annoy
57 "___ Abner"
58 Island where Minos ruled
60 Rise from a chair
61 Something to lend or bend
63 Cynic's snort #5
65 ___ Dame
66 Job to do
67 Neck of the woods
68 Strain
69 Aware of
70 Saucy

DOWN

1 Hot sauce
2 Drunkenly reveling
3 Belongs
4 "The Merry Widow" composer
5 Co. called "Big Blue"
6 Arcing shots
7 Like thick fog
8 1973 Rolling Stones #1 hit
9 Actress Mason
10 Kimono sash
11 Ban on talking
12 Led down the aisle
13 Correspondence
18 Heaven on earth
22 ___ Mahal
25 Desire
27 Economy, for one
30 Bulletin board affixer
34 You-know-___
35 Lawman Wyatt
37 Gas or oil
38 Kind of tide
39 Touch tenderly
40 Many a crop-duster
41 March 21 occurrence
42 Jock
44 Fred of "Top Hat"
45 Princess Diana's family name
46 Construction worker
48 Hush-hush
49 Two-lane topper
53 Brief brawl
54 Patriot Allen
56 Subway handhold
59 Sunrise direction
62 Flight board info: Abbr.
64 Fight stopper, briefly

by Nancy Salomon and Harvey Estes

ACROSS

1 Chooses, with "for"
5 Soup scooper
10 Follow orders
14 Pronoun in a wedding pledge
15 Kayak paddler
16 Boorish
17 Bees?
19 Rake ___ (get rich)
20 ___ nous (between us)
21 Podium feature
22 Giant Mel and others
23 Listen to again, as arguments
25 ___ Beach, S.C.
27 It's below the knee
29 Any "Seinfeld" episode now
32 Fly traps
35 Bluto's rival
39 Blubber
40 Egg cells
41 Foot, informally
42 Bring into play
43 Women's ___
44 Hereditary
45 Falling-out
46 Small handbill
48 Besides that
50 They're rough on golf greens
54 "Oh, what am I to do?"
58 Dressed
60 Particles in particle accelerators
62 A 10-, 11- or 12-year old
63 Take to the trail
64 Kind of contract
66 Continuously
67 Jungle vine
68 Border
69 Clutter
70 Put an ___ (halt)
71 Not a natural blonde

DOWN

1 "On the ___ hand . . ."
2 Call
3 The last amendment in the Bill of Rights
4 Woman with a future?
5 See 58-Down
6 Grad
7 Casual Friday wear
8 Like a four-leaf clover
9 Cousin of chloroform
10 Baltimore bird
11 Yellow flower
12 Blue-pencil
13 Hankerings
18 "You bet"
24 Wisconsin college or its town
26 Squirrel's home
28 Shootout time, maybe
30 ___ Major
31 No, in Moscow
32 "Little Red Riding-Hood" villain
33 "Who knows what ___ lurks . . ."
34 1989 Ricki Lake TV movie
36 School org.
37 Villa d'___
38 Give way
41 Michelin product
45 Iodine source
47 Tribal V.I.P.'s
49 Actor Green of "Buffy the Vampire Slayer"
51 Wedding walkway
52 Bring to the auto repair
53 Golfer Sam
55 Prepared
56 Join forces
57 PC key
58 With 5-Down, where reactions take place
59 Walk the earth
61 In the mail
65 Chinese ideal

by Gregory E. Paul

ACROSS

1 Affixed in a scrapbook, say
7 Julius Erving's nickname
10 Barbershop quartet part
14 ___ Shriver, sister of J.F.K.
15 Fish eggs
16 Navel buildup?
17 Announce officially
19 Nabisco cookie
20 Toothed tool
21 GRASS CUTTER WITH ZIP
23 Sympathetic pity
26 Astound
27 Shoulder muscle
29 Garage contents
31 "You betcha!"
32 Souped-up engine sound
33 April 1 prankster
36 Sunup
37 Wanders
38 Capital on a fjord
42 Winnie-the-Pooh's donkey friend
44 Run, as colors
45 Opposite ENE
48 Club ___ resort
49 Nation famous for tulips
51 Video game company
53 Letterman's nightly list
54 What the answer to each capitalized clue is
57 Sheep's cry
60 Florence's river
61 "The Battleship Potemkin" director
64 "Très ___" ("very well," in Paris)
65 Fuss
66 Secretary General before Kurt Waldheim
67 Memo starter
68 Family room
69 Bandleader Tito

DOWN

1 Livens (up)
2 Atmosphere
3 POST-BLIZZARD VEHICLE
4 Dickens's Tiny ___
5 Old French coin
6 Noted oracle site
7 Doesn't stand pat
8 Memorization method
9 Raspberry
10 Flower
11 Vent
12 Blessed event?
13 Mall units
18 WHAT A GOURMET ENJOYS
22 Mature filly
24 Make amends (for)
25 Male turkey
27 Home movie format
28 Pitcher's stat
29 "LASSIE ___" (1943 FILM)
30 Gore and Roker
34 Rowing need
35 Actress Esther
37 Deli loaf
39 ACTOR IN "PATRIOT GAMES" AND "GOLDENEYE"
40 Spy novelist Deighton
41 Peculiar
43 Give off
44 Lunch sandwich, for short
45 Sushi condiment
46 Recipe direction
47 Ring cycle composer
50 Cry of the police while pounding a door
52 River of Lyon
53 1980's–90's boxing champ
55 Use a book
56 Seek's opposite
58 "___ Too Proud to Beg" (1966 hit)
59 Poker stake
62 R-V link
63 "___ end"

by Peter Gordon

ACROSS

1 Head over heels (over)
5 Library microfilm
10 "Swiss Family Robinson" peaks
14 "Jeopardy!" host Trebek
15 Pewter or brass
16 With 28-Down, Abe Lincoln's bride
17 Sheet of ice
18 Two-door car
19 Soothsayer's clue
20 A long way (off)
21 Signals farewell at the beach?
23 Fencing call
25 Steal from
26 The shallowest Great Lake
27 Free rider
32 Under siege
34 Grumpy expression
35 Actor Wallach
36 "If only things had turned out different!"
37 Ballot parts that may be hanging
38 "Quit it!"
39 Prohibit
40 Cattle identifier
41 Earring sites
42 Human look-alikes
44 Helix
45 Long-distance letters
46 Bishop, e.g.
49 Rule about open meetings at the beach?
54 Nothing
55 Like many a DeMille film
56 ___ the Barbarian
57 32-card card game
58 Sicilian peak
59 When the mouse ran down the clock

60 Prefix with space
61 Office wagering
62 Comes in last
63 Jazzman Kenton

DOWN

1 Blunder
2 Poe's middle name
3 Author at the beach?
4 Paul Bunyan's tool
5 Veneer
6 Gershwin's "The Man ___"
7 Sleuth's find
8 Beer ingredient
9 They may be penciled in
10 One-celled being

11 Easter entree
12 The hunted
13 "Auld Lang ___"
21 Scribbled, old-style
22 Long, dismal cry
24 God of war
27 Reads, as a bar code
28 See 16-Across
29 Party pooper at the beach?
30 Skin lotion ingredient
31 Small dogs' cries
32 "Ali ___ and the 40 Thieves"
33 Verve
34 Fish that swims upstream

37 All-important
38 Make dirty
40 Opposite of neither
41 Theater chain founder Marcus
43 Scamp
44 Building machines
46 747, e.g.
47 Beauty's crown
48 Rocker ___ John
49 Ooze
50 ___ no good
51 Boy, in Bogotá
52 Say ___ (refuse)
53 Grandson of Adam
57 Carrier to Sweden

by Norma Steinberg

ACROSS

1 Moon shine
5 Trample (on)
10 Vile Nile creatures
14 "Super" star
15 Wood for a storage closet
16 Ark builder
17 "Roots" author ___ Haley
18 Jim Carrey's pet detective role
20 Angry natives go on them
22 Cruised the sea
23 German "Oh!"
24 Store department with jackets, ties and such
25 "The Dead Zone" novelist
30 Foxy
33 Thick soup
34 Bridge seat
35 Peg with a dent on top
36 Smell
37 Light bulb units
38 Volcanic flow
39 Fishing pole
40 New York canal
41 Instant Messenger user
42 Prior to, in poetry
43 Ralph Bellamy's master detective role
45 Tyne of "Judging Amy"
46 Mo. with most of Leo
47 Harebrained
50 Deep down
55 "White Fang" author
57 Song with trills
58 ___ vera
59 End of a hangman's rope
60 ___ a one
61 On a pension: Abbr.

62 "Oklahoma!" aunt
63 First word of Carroll's "Jabberwocky"

DOWN

1 Chew (on)
2 Singer Falana
3 Partner of "done with"
4 Bakery box liner
5 Reprove severely
6 Kind of support for a computer user
7 Lyrical verses
8 Dallas hoopster, briefly
9 Things kept under wraps?
10 Those "agin" it
11 Marvin Gaye music
12 Cut back
13 Roe source
19 Da ___, Vietnam
21 Reason for an ice pack
24 "Hey, ___!"
25 Way a fern reproduces
26 English royal house
27 Eat away at
28 Almost
29 Couric of "Today"
30 Like week-old doughnuts
31 Embankment
32 Long (for)
37 Burned at the steakhouse?
38 Emmy-winning Ed Asner role
41 Blue hue
43 British peer
44 Apparent sleepyhead
45 Hit with the fists
47 Not quite closed
48 Barn dance seat
49 Dundee denizen
50 One getting bags of fan mail
51 Bloodhound's asset
52 Take a card
53 Milano moolah
54 Pep rally cheers
56 Cambodia's Lon ___

by Sherry O. Blackard

ACROSS

1 London TV inits.
4 Opening bridge bid, informally
10 Take cover
14 Cotton State: Abbr.
15 Maria of the Met
16 Dilly
17 Wagon track
18 "Dallas," e.g., famously
20 India's first prime minister
22 Like households after daybreak
23 Spanish gold
24 Big rabbit features
26 One causing mayhem
28 "I Love Lucy," usually
33 Neighbor of Swe.
34 "A Confederacy of Dunces" author John Kennedy ___
35 Worked in a lumber mill
39 "Chestnuts roasting ___ open fire"
41 Lopez of "The Dirty Dozen"
43 Put on board
44 Charles's princedom
46 "Tinker to ___ to Chance"
48 Whopper
49 Many a "Twilight Zone"
52 Condition of affairs
55 Trickle (in)
56 "___ Wiedersehen"
57 When repeated, tells all
61 Modern correspondence
64 "Roots," e.g.
67 "The Murders in the Rue Morgue" writer
68 Italian money
69 Graceland, e.g.

70 U.F.O. crew
71 Sporting blade
72 Near ringer
73 Fink

DOWN

1 Building near a silo
2 Sky-colored
3 St. Patrick's, e.g.
4 Ill-fated, old-style
5 Shakespearean prince
6 Pen name of Charles Lamb
7 Gov. Landon and others
8 Tom Hanks's escape in "Cast Away"
9 Weekend wear

10 Sweetums
11 Fort Knox bar
12 Tractor maker
13 Oversight
19 The Ram
21 Actress ___ Dawn Chong
25 Poor name for a solid-colored dog
27 Voiced
28 Winter forecast
29 School in New Rochelle, N.Y.
30 Actress Sophia
31 "As ___ and breathe!"
32 Basic belief
36 Room decor
37 Falco of "The Sopranos"

38 Bucks and does
40 Spider's home
42 Eye part
45 Gumption
47 Villain, at times
50 Novelist Allende
51 Sparkler
52 Fine fur
53 Dutch bulb
54 Ere
58 Ponder
59 "Cómo ___ usted?"
60 ___ Lee of Marvel Comics
62 Smidgen
63 Just in case
65 Middling mark
66 Summer, in Montréal

by Gregory E. Paul

ACROSS

1 Beasts of burden
6 Tennis great Arthur
10 Kills, in mob slang
14 Kind of acid
15 Simba, for one
16 Jockey's whip
17 One who prays to Vishnu
18 Dog food brand
19 When said three times, a 1970 war film
20 Greek vowel
21 Manager's catchphrase
24 Spy novelist Len
26 Likely
27 Increases
28 They're integrated into microchips
33 Fettuccine, e.g.
36 Sandwich seller
37 It has a ball at the circus
38 Ottawa's prov.
39 "Alas!"
42 TV manufacturer
43 Soft ball material
45 ___ Major
46 Like some colognes
48 Towering over
50 "Antiques Roadshow" shower
51 "Charlotte's ___"
52 Potato chip accompanier
57 Saying about romance
61 Before, in poetry
62 Declare openly
63 Yield
64 Ancient Peruvians
66 Introduction to physics?
67 Oscar winner Guinness

68 Muse of lyric poetry
69 Hunted animals
70 Neck hair
71 Yeggs' targets

DOWN

1 Oohed and ___
2 Strike down
3 Egyptian peninsula
4 Terminus
5 Lefty
6 Memorable mission
7 Librarian's motto, perhaps
8 Arizona Indian
9 "The Dukes of Hazzard" spinoff
10 One that's armed and dangerous?
11 Limits of achievement
12 Duffer's cry
13 Fix, in a way
22 For what ___ worth
23 PC alternative
25 Disembowel
29 Rick's love, in "Casablanca"
30 Backboard attachment
31 Zigzag movement
32 Delight, slangily
33 Duck's home
34 Freshly
35 Poll that's just for fun

36 Actress Laura
40 Opposite of non
41 Personifies
44 Many an interstate
47 Admiral's org.
49 G-man's org.
50 Wrestling win
53 Family girl
54 Coffee before bedtime
55 Angry
56 Mexican moolah
57 Light source
58 Walkie-talkie word
59 Swindle
60 Composer Bartók
65 Pres. Charlton Heston's group

by Peter Gordon

ACROSS

1 Rustle, as cattle
6 Flexible, as an electrical outlet
10 The "E" in Q.E.D.
14 Mission priest
15 Mrs. Dithers, in "Blondie"
16 Spellbinder
17 Future architect's plaything
19 Nicholas, e.g.
20 Took the gold
21 Third col. on a calendar
22 Disneyland's locale
24 Give the green light
25 Minneapolis suburb
26 Elevator alternative
30 Uses stickum
34 Angry motorist's need
35 Big-ticket ___
37 Talent
38 Oil grp.
39 Linoleum layer
41 Make smooth
42 Napa Valley variety
44 Singer Seeger
45 Hammock's attachment
46 Like a lizard
48 "Monday Night Football," e.g.
50 Symbols of hardness
52 ___ Wednesday
53 Uzbek body of water
56 Like some stocks: Abbr.
57 Baton Rouge sch.
60 Headlight?
61 Future engineer's plaything
64 In awe
65 Sewing case
66 Sheeplike
67 "All ___ are off!"
68 Second baseman Sandberg
69 Died down

DOWN

1 Gush
2 Poi plant
3 Adam's arboretum
4 Rocket's trajectory
5 An initial, e.g.
6 Fraction of a field
7 Firms: Abbr.
8 Not look forward to at all
9 Tabby's teaser
10 Future artist's plaything
11 Demolish
12 Jai ___
13 Six years, for a senator
18 Think faster than
23 Collections of quotations
24 Future carpenter's plaything
25 Shoe features
26 Mall units
27 Debate subject
28 Gladiators' place
29 "Take ___ from me . . ."
31 Pageant crown
32 Someone ___ (not mine)
33 Ugly forecast
36 Dole (out)
40 Tell about
43 Darjeeling and oolong
47 Jenny Craig client
49 Like some property, after "in"
51 Parishioners
53 Captain of the Pequod
54 Fury
55 Oodles
56 1930's dust bowler
57 Tender ender?
58 "Auld Lang ___"
59 Kind of car
62 Sister Bertrille, e.g.
63 Flood control proj.

by Gregory E. Paul

ACROSS

1 Submarine detector
6 Bartender's "rocks"
9 Unexpected defeat
14 The Gem State
15 "The A-Team" star
16 Debonair
17 Settle a debt
18 Long, long time
19 Hungry
20 Running backs, often
23 In the past
26 Paved the way
27 Relative of "Darn!"
28 Cold, wind and sleet, e.g.
32 Tiny fraction of a joule
35 Student getting one-on-one help
36 Decay
37 Paraphernalia
38 Self-images
39 Astronaut's wear
41 As far as
42 Whistle blowers
43 Miner's quest
44 Attempts
45 Sp. woman
46 Carnival's setting
49 What flags do in the wind
51 Like avaunt and prithee: Abbr.
52 Test for coll. seniors
53 Hit the jackpot
58 "Common Sense" writer
59 Turf
60 Blood carrier
64 Painful stomach problem
65 Major-leaguer
66 Jurist Brandeis
67 College bigwigs
68 Desire
69 Borders

DOWN

1 Knight's title
2 Keats's "Bards of Passion and of Mirth," e.g.
3 Siesta
4 Captain with a whalebone leg
5 Formal pronoun
6 Marcos of the Philippines
7 Gator's cousin
8 Volcano in Sicily
9 Shylock
10 Language of ancient Carthage
11 Protection
12 Next-to-last fairy tale word
13 Slugger Williams and others
21 Peggy who sang "Fever"
22 Butler at Tara
23 Dessert, to a Brit
24 Extortionist
25 Oscar-winning Meryl Streep film
29 Not so much
30 More factual
31 ___ polloi
33 Like "American Beauty"
34 ___ Pointe, Mich.
37 Know-it-all
39 Lose it
40 ___ Lanka
44 Like most maps
46 Charlatans
47 Racer Jeff
48 Baseball stat
50 Fourth anniversary gift
53 Tater
54 Tall story
55 Cosby show
56 Drove like mad
57 Engine cover
61 Toupee
62 Backgammon impossibility
63 Donkey's cousin

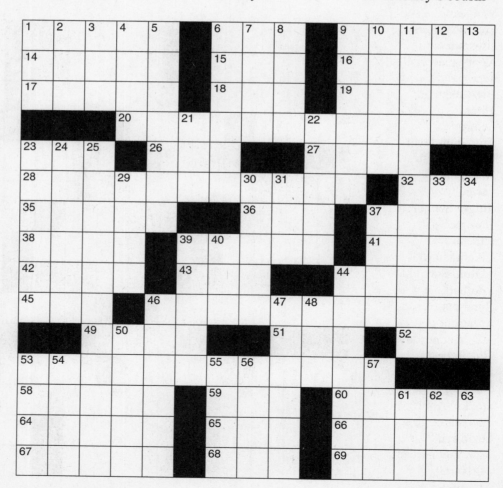

by Peter Gordon

ACROSS

1 Comic DeGeneres
6 Tear
9 Order of ale, perhaps
14 More than mislead
15 Relative of an ostrich
16 Moving swarm
17 Judges' seats
18 Notorious 1920's criminal
20 Champion's place
22 Ninny
23 Filmmaker Craven
24 Wide shoe spec
25 Masked critter
27 Cat's feet
29 Charming
32 Slow mover
35 Bit of grain
36 Film system with an extra-large screen
37 Champion's achievement
41 Military sch.
42 Well-put
43 Chops finely
44 Minsk's country
46 Doctors' charges
48 Rum drink
49 "___ Miniver"
50 VCR maker
53 Look at
55 Champion's reward?
59 Indolent indifference
61 Consoling phrase
62 Sci-fi film extra
63 Denials
64 Lorna of fiction
65 Susan of "All My Children"
66 Do not delay
67 Terminated

DOWN

1 Funny bone's locale
2 Jungle vine
3 Periods of penitence
4 Inscribe with acid
5 It usually smells
6 Decorates over
7 Ammonia compound
8 Hungarian sheepdog
9 Israel's Peres
10 "This weighs a ___!"
11 Designed for the workplace
12 "I had no ___!"
13 Kid's ball material
19 Trademarked plastic
21 Worshipers' seat
26 Prince of the dead, in ancient Egypt
27 Greek poet of yore
28 ___ Baba
29 When doubled, a guitar or horn effect
30 Place to lose yourself
31 Former partners
32 Sailor's mop
33 Delightful
34 Painkiller
35 Polo Grounds legend
38 Nothingness
39 Fam. doctors
40 Opposite of post-
45 Pasta choice
46 Least restrained
47 Computer key
49 Vineyard region of France
50 Patch the lawn
51 Old woman
52 Answered, on "Jeopardy!"
53 Airline to Israel
54 River into Korea Bay
56 ___ race (vie)
57 Conceal
58 School near Windsor
60 Instant

by Mel and Peggy Rosen

ACROSS

1 Pepsi or RC
5 Kuwaiti ruler
9 Stares open-mouthed
14 Birthstone after sapphire
15 Cheese nibblers
16 "My Fair Lady" lady
17 Courtroom figures
20 Winding road shape
21 Loch ___ monster
22 Lassos
23 Proofreader's mark
24 Tilling tools
25 Like fishers' hooks
28 Top 40 songs
29 Poem of praise
32 Command
33 Indian dress
34 Hertz rival
35 Ida Lupino, e.g.
38 Lawyers' charges
39 Topic of gossip
40 Because
41 Like octogenarians
42 Squalid neighborhood
43 Time of the year
44 Ooze
45 Candies that burn the mouth
46 "Is that your final ___?"
49 D.C. bigwigs
50 Low digit?
53 Last governor of New Netherland
56 Wear away
57 ___ Stanley Gardner
58 Company V.I.P.
59 Scattered, as seed
60 Requirement
61 Action before blowing out the candles

DOWN

1 Make do
2 Any symphony
3 Places for experiments
4 Entirely
5 Hosted
6 Central spot
7 Desserts that give chills
8 Striped official
9 Bottled spirits
10 Actors Robert and Alan
11 Artist Mondrian
12 Book after II Chronicles
13 Back talk
18 Recent med school graduate
19 Arousing
23 Parts with thorns
24 Ulysses S. Grant's real first name
25 Successful, in Variety
26 The Little Mermaid's name
27 Ran without moving
28 Sheik's bevy
29 Kilns
30 Music to do the hustle to
31 German industrial city
33 Ab strengthener
34 Opera songs
36 Edmonton N.H.L. team
37 Sleeping sickness carrier
42 Become enraged
43 Figured out
44 Ingmar Bergman, e.g.
45 According to ___
46 Earth rulers in a 1968 film
47 Imperious Roman
48 Put away
49 Like 24-karat gold
50 Hack's vehicle
51 Singles
52 Write on metal
54 Sawbuck
55 Make a seam

by Peter Gordon

ACROSS

1 Basic bit
5 Early invader of Europe
10 "Sesame Street" learning
14 Put money in the bank
15 Swahili for "freedom"
16 Buttonhole
17 Plow pullers
18 Sacred song
19 Medical breakthrough
20 Initially, after "at"
22 Fairy tale starter
23 With 42-Down, out-of-date
24 Second of two
26 Trumpeting
30 Vicinity
32 Two-bit
33 Thick carpeting
38 Half of half-and-half
39 Fragrant East Indian wood
40 Underground part
41 Illegal money, maybe
43 Spinning part
44 "Ma! He's Making Eyes ___"
45 Unruffled
46 Subject of a will
50 Actor Billy ___ Williams
51 Wild guess
52 Poker player's dream
59 Window ledge
60 Heavenward
61 Reason for a backrub
62 "That's ___!"
63 Common sense
64 Swing around
65 Freshman or sophomore

66 Fewest
67 52-Across is the best one

DOWN

1 Beginning
2 Subway alternative
3 Completed
4 The "M" in Y.M.C.A.
5 Take a header
6 "Get ___ of yourself!"
7 "Swan Lake" skirt
8 Greek war god
9 Cruel
10 Fancy tie
11 Not too tactful
12 "Odyssey" sorceress

13 Have the wheel
21 Winston Churchill, politically
25 Backrub response
26 Money for the poor
27 Cook, as pasta
28 Humdinger
29 Quizzes
30 Dateless
31 Was sorry about
33 Jack Horner's find
34 Egg on
35 Smidgen
36 Ill-gotten goods
37 To be, in Toulouse
39 Nevertheless
42 See 23-Across
43 Atoll protector

45 Vote for
46 "How I Spent My Summer Vacation," maybe
47 Stadium entrance
48 Actress Shire of "Rocky"
49 Less inept
50 Rat Pack member Sammy
53 Mitch Miller's instrument
54 Lotus position discipline
55 Place for mascara
56 Pac Ten school
57 Give the cold shoulder
58 Listen to

by Gregory E. Paul

18 MONDAY

ACROSS
1 Big galoot
4 Cave dweller
7 Where L.A. is
12 Medical insurance abbr.
13 Andy's partner in old radio
15 Sixth-grader's age, maybe
17 Dance craze of the 90's
19 Beethoven's "Moonlight ___"
20 Start of a playground chant
22 Exaggerated 50's car feature
23 Volcanic fallout
24 Magician's cry
27 Give a speech
30 Lungful
31 A.P. or Reuters, informally
33 Honolulu's ___ Stadium
37 Old Glory
41 Arrangement
42 "What ___ God wrought?"
43 Old Testament boat
44 Like some ancient Mexican architecture
46 A large quantity
49 Rainbow's shape
52 Tiny country in the Pyrenees
54 Basic lunch
60 In jeopardy
61 Got situated
62 Grosse ___, Mich.
63 ___-do-well
64 Summer D.C. clock setting
65 TV's O'Donnell
66 E.R. workers
67 Power (up)

DOWN
1 Resistance units
2 Amo, amas, ___
3 Central points
4 Speak to gruffly
5 Midwest university site
6 Having melody and harmony
7 Noted small-plane maker
8 Much
9 TV host with bandleader Eubanks
10 Ex-Mrs. Trump
11 Celebrations
14 Sitcom set in a junkyard
16 Old Rambler manufacturer
18 Opera parts
21 Most desperate
24 Bridge declaration
25 Bar mitzvah, e.g.
26 Part of Q.E.D.
28 Unhealthy part of cigarettes
29 Yale student
32 Under control
34 October's birthstone
35 Roll call response
36 Questions
38 Piña colada ingredient
39 Baden-Baden, for one
40 Less solvable
45 Bronx Bomber
47 Selects from the menu
48 Sunrise
49 "Now!"
50 Helicopter part
51 Unusual objet d'art
53 Rowed
55 Spare items
56 ___ spumante
57 Roman way
58 Relinquish
59 Modern RCA offering

by Peter Gordon

ACROSS

1 Faint from surprise
6 Manger contents
9 Big fissure
14 Snake charmer's snake
15 Juice drink suffix
16 Line from the heart
17 Officer in charge of a ship's rigging, informally
18 State west of Mont.
19 Part of a ranch herd
20 Proofreader's asset
23 Slanted type: Abbr.
26 Head-turning letter turner
27 Annapolis sch.
28 Sit in jail
30 High tennis shot
32 Violinist's asset
36 Cumberland ___
39 Gallic goodbye
40 Nile viper
41 Songstress Lena
43 Govt. old-age insurer
44 Reporter's asset
47 Place to lay money on horses: Abbr.
48 Pussy
49 Camping stuff
52 Sheeplike
56 ___ d'oeuvre
57 Possible title for this puzzle
60 German wine valley
61 Neighbor of Leb.
62 Called balls and strikes
66 Long-limbed
67 Kind of feeling
68 Myopic Mr. ___
69 Blackthorn fruits
70 Big inits. in electronic games
71 Bridges

DOWN

1 Chem. contaminant
2 Place for a pit stop in London
3 Delivery docs, for short
4 Real
5 Wacky
6 Port city north of Tel Aviv
7 Annex
8 Thirst (for)
9 24 cans
10 Jacuzzi product
11 Precincts
12 Ale holder
13 One Mrs. Trump
21 At any time
22 Surrealist Salvador
23 "Don't get any funny ___!"
24 Little hoppers
25 Skylit rooms
29 Everest, for one
31 Earth tone
33 Pas' mates
34 Bring into play
35 Tanning lotion letters
36 ___-Roman wrestling
37 Nobelist Sadat
38 Annoyers
42 Known, geographically speaking
45 Long, thin musical instrument
46 Store door sign
47 Halloween hue
49 Little women
50 Lucy's landlady on "I Love Lucy"
51 Pal
53 Churchillian symbol
54 Unit of Time
55 "Hogwash!"
58 Things on rings
59 Totals
63 Links org.
64 Unit of time
65 Parties

by Nancy Salomon and Bob Frank

ACROSS

1 Louisville Sluggers
5 Computer text can be written in this
10 Gen. Bradley
14 Suffix with buck
15 Water pipes
16 Pink, as a steak
17 Fishing hook
18 Unlikely dog show winners
19 Cry of shock
20 "Shhh!"
23 Radio station in a 1970 Paul Newman title
24 Frozen water: Ger.
25 See 28-Across
28 With 25-Across, three-time Masters champ
31 Timeless Christmas wish
35 Booth Tarkington novel
37 Barber's obstacle
39 Soup container
40 "Shhh!"
44 "There! ___ Said It Again" (old song hit)
45 Pot's partner
46 2 or 3, to 6
47 Pigeon's perch
50 Mobil product
52 Happening place
53 Naval initials
55 This, in Havana
57 "Shhh!"
63 Hair roller result
64 "Don't Cry for Me, Argentina" musical
65 Not just a star
67 Heloise offering
68 Expert group
69 Meanie
70 ___-bitsy
71 Icy rain
72 Putin's refusal

DOWN

1 Word with punching or sleeping
2 Many a Mideasterner
3 High-protein food
4 Computer games, e.g.
5 Bullets and such
6 Places to wear towels
7 Part of N.Y.C.
8 "What's gotten ___ you?"
9 Any Time
10 Ultimatum phrase
11 Travelers to Bethlehem
12 "I don't give ___!"
13 Scarlet
21 Henry VIII's house
22 Yank (off)
25 Grow moldy
26 Chutzpah
27 Brought to a close
29 Classic name in insurance
30 ___-jongg
32 Urgent
33 Leslie of "Gigi"
34 ___ nous
36 Potato chip accompaniment
38 Striped shirt wearer
41 Complain, complain
42 Hindu social group
43 Special time
48 Word that precedes a sentence?
49 180° from WNW
51 Sofa
54 Stair parts
56 Commandment verb
57 Throw in the towel
58 Vases
59 Many a toy train track
60 Shop-opening time
61 On pins and needles
62 Sped
63 Windy City, for short
66 Disappoint, with "down"

by Gregory E. Paul

ACROSS

1 Under a stopwatch
6 Beech or birch
10 Part of a film's credits
14 Move up
15 Captain's position
16 Aware of
17 Design with looped string
19 Sport ___ (modern vehicles)
20 Top-of-the-chart number
21 Telescope part
22 Gains again, as strength
24 Vineyard container
25 Breathe hard
26 Tennis or table tennis
28 Sweetbrier
32 Like snow
33 Group at school athletic events
34 Two-masted vessel
35 "___ We Got Fun?"
36 Obstinate ones
37 Stuff (in)
38 Word after bump or jump
39 7:5, e.g., at a horse race
40 Secluded valleys
41 "Mona Lisa" painter
43 Praises
44 Satiate
45 Nasty remark
46 Fancy floor, maybe
49 Like a candidate for hair transplant
50 Boy
53 Western writer ___ Wister
54 Duplicate
57 Sell
58 Tract
59 Wipe clean
60 Singer Nelson of 30's–40's film
61 Acrobats' security
62 Big name in rental trucks

DOWN

1 Sandwich that crunches
2 Persian Gulf land
3 Small amount
4 Road curve
5 Announce
6 ___-you note
7 Cincinnati team
8 Right-angled extension
9 Stones in crowns
10 Place to golf
11 Prepay, with "up"
12 One-dish meal
13 Fling
18 Siesta
23 Football lineman
24 Carnival treat
25 Larches, e.g.
26 Bootblack's job
27 Varicolored horse
28 "The Great ___ Pepper" (1975 movie)
29 Propelled a boat
30 Tchaikovsky ballet characters
31 They line some old streets
32 Siren's sound
33 Pal
36 From Rabat
40 Mathematics writer Martin
42 Muhammad ___
43 "Le Roi d'Ys" composer
45 Rum-soaked cakes
46 "Get out of my seat!"
47 Due
48 E-mail option
49 Writer Harte
50 Trunkful
51 Church nook
52 Salon employee
55 "You ___ here"
56 Boo-hoo

by Joan Yanofsky

ACROSS

1 Fool
5 Partner of born
9 Attack
14 Work hard
15 Continental currency
16 "Midnight Cowboy" role
17 Sicilian spouter
18 "Q ___ queen"
19 Sound off
20 Carouse
23 "O ___ Mio"
24 Letter writer's afterthoughts
25 Defective
28 Send another way
31 Gorilla
34 Out of whack
36 Hit the slopes
37 Parting of the heavens, maybe
38 Reprimand
42 The "O" in S.R.O.
43 Telephone button that lacks letters
44 Burn balm
45 Dissenting vote
46 Red giant in Scorpius
49 Suffix with musket
50 Spell-off
51 Gen. Robert ___
53 Passive-aggressive response
61 Like a Three Stooges routine
62 The Platters player
63 Spill the beans
64 Out of port
65 Hymn word
66 Lohengrin's inamorata
67 Popular name in fruit juices
68 Used to be
69 Derrière

DOWN

1 Escalate, with "up"
2 Smidgen
3 Maxi's opposite
4 They're made with the help of maps
5 John, Paul, George or Ringo
6 Ball carrier
7 ___-Lackawanna Railroad
8 Word said with a hand-slap
9 Shop without buying
10 Makes, as money
11 Celeb
12 Direction from which el sol rises
13 Pigeon-___
21 Midsection
22 Eye-related
25 Breakfast sizzler
26 Microwave maker
27 Ripsnorter
29 Milo of "The Verdict"
30 Instrument that's strummed
31 Enough
32 Pet complaint
33 Join
35 Underhanded
37 "Are you a man ___ mouse?"
39 Trio trebled
40 Blasting stuff
41 Selling point
46 Trojan hero
47 Close-fitting coat
48 Figure skater Zayak
50 Poet William Rose ___
52 Hot coal
53 Thailand, once
54 Get ___ shape
55 Which words to read in 20-, 38- and 53-Across to get a warm welcome
56 Winter break
57 "The ___ of the Ancient Mariner"
58 She, in Vichy
59 Rocket org.
60 Chairlift alternative

by Gregory E. Paul

ACROSS

1 Corp. heads
5 Less numerous
10 "The Thin Man" pooch
14 Light greenish-blue
15 Bluto's dream girl
16 Cowboy boot attachment
17 Road grooves
18 Whitman's dooryard bloomer
19 Eat like a bird
20 The Beatles' 1965 calendar anomaly
23 Trio after R
24 Ninny
25 Children's author/illustrator Maurice
27 Lip-___
29 6/4/01, e.g.
31 ___ Jima
32 "I'm impressed!"
34 Kimono tie
35 50-Down and others
36 Bing Crosby's 1934 calendar anomaly
40 Scam victim
41 Twosome
42 Classic Pontiac
43 Aardvark morsel
44 Exacts revenge on
45 "Bride or groom?" asker
49 Monkey Trial name
51 Roofing sealant
53 Pie ___ mode
54 Donny Osmond's 1973 calendar anomaly, with "The"
58 Closet buildup
59 Singer Bonnie
60 Was philanthropic
61 Nabisco cookie
62 Stan's slapstick partner

63 Change for a five
64 Actor Richard
65 Taxi ticker
66 Director Gus Van ___

DOWN

1 Gentle touch
2 Fairness
3 Have superior firepower over
4 Miss Universe's wrap
5 Creates origami
6 Inventor Howe
7 Cunning
8 Gabor and Perón
9 Finding new actors for
10 Colorado skiing mecca
11 More swift
12 Put somewhere out of sight
13 "Raiders of the Lost ___"
21 Nevada resort
22 Itsy-bitsy
26 W.B.A. stats
28 Ice cream holder
29 Karate schools
30 Atty. grp.
33 Eludes
35 New Mexico art colony
36 Critical point
37 Northern Manhattan dweller, e.g.
38 Zealot
39 180-degree maneuver
40 "___ Boot" (1981 war film)
44 Vaseline, for one
46 Capital on the Florida Strait
47 Toward midnight
48 Least cooked
50 Sri Lanka export
51 Comedienne Fields
52 Succeeding
55 Chaucer piece
56 Sword handle
57 Self-involved ones
58 Something to do in a suit

by Patrick Jordan

ACROSS

1 Open, as a toothpaste tube
6 Mare's meal
10 Price
14 Oyster's prize
15 Aberdeen native
16 Killer whale
17 Today's slide rule
19 Unkind
20 Busch Stadium team: Abbr.
21 Sunbeam
22 Oolong brewers
24 Foot the bill
25 Silents star ___ Bara
26 Stopping at nothing
30 Pie nuts
34 Butter look-alike
35 Use a library
37 Sen. Thurmond
38 "At once!"
39 Binge
41 "Whip It" rock group
42 Typo
44 Money drawer
45 ___ the beginning (present from the start)
46 Daytona 500 acronym
48 Elizabeth II, to Elizabeth I
50 Alpha's opposite
52 Sort
53 Bottle cork
56 Jackie's second
57 Home of the Knicks: Abbr.
60 Sun dancer
61 Today's telex
64 Merle Haggard's "___ From Muskogee"
65 Falco of "The Sopranos"
66 Steel girder
67 Kind of pressure
68 Bridle strap
69 Hammer's partner

DOWN

1 They come in bars: Abbr.
2 Not having a hair out of place
3 Telephone
4 Path of a football pass
5 Like mice and geese
6 "___ can you see . . ."
7 Misbehave, with "up"
8 Molar, e.g.
9 "Sophie's Choice" star
10 Today's record
11 Cookie with a creamy middle
12 "Go away!"
13 Turns bronze
18 Strata
23 Fruit juices
24 Today's mimeograph
25 Catherine the Great, e.g.
26 Al of the Indians
27 The "U" in UHF
28 Eye drops
29 Aug. follower
31 Boxing site
32 Former CNN show "Evans & ___"
33 Walloped, old-style
36 Crème ___ crème
40 New York city where Mark Twain lived
43 Wheelchair access
47 Illicit cigarette
49 Draw out
51 A+ or C−
53 Home ec's counterpart
54 Use a 47-Down
55 Sheriff Taylor's son
56 Evangelical's cry
57 Demeanor
58 Fly in the ointment
59 Rubies and such
62 Midnight, on a grandfather's clock
63 "The Sopranos" network

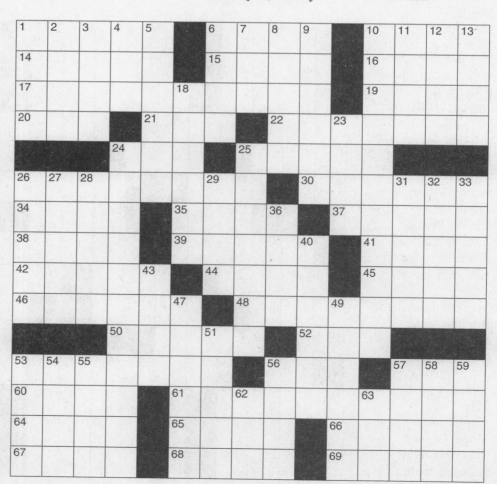

by Gregory E. Paul

ACROSS

1 Leader until 1917
5 Dinner for Dobbin
9 Said, old-style
14 Starring ___
15 Radar screen image
16 Football's Merlin
17 Impresses greatly
18 Actress Anderson
19 In the cards
20 1915 Lillian Gish film, with "The"
23 Filming site
24 Tiny member of a colony
25 Deuce follower, in tennis
26 Member of Old MacDonald's farm
27 Nobelist Wiesel
28 Brit. playwright
31 Dummkopf
34 Opening stake
35 Do some manicuring
36 1997 Roberto Benigni film
39 Liberals, with "the"
40 Over-50 grp.
41 What is more
42 Home for a 26-Across
43 Ian Fleming villain
44 Imitate
45 Steinbeck family name
46 "___ to Billy Joe"
47 Agt.'s take
50 1978 Peter Ustinov film
54 Carried
55 Post-It
56 ___ Velva
57 Hot temper
58 At all
59 Wishes undone

60 Spars
61 "I double-___ you!"
62 Hand over

DOWN

1 Grouches
2 "Ooh-la-la!"
3 On one's toes
4 Take five
5 Stretched figure
6 Up in the air
7 ___ Fey of "Saturday Night Live"
8 Rob Reiner's mock rock band
9 Pushover
10 Unadorned
11 About

12 Razor-sharp
13 Cutoff point
21 Port-au-Prince is its capital
22 Flowery "ta-ta"
26 Shelley, for one
27 When to say "Feliz Año Nuevo"
28 Knack
29 Bad photo
30 Actress Ward
31 Misfortunes
32 Reduced in calories
33 In doubt
34 Walked out on
35 Idée ___
37 Jazz singer Vaughan

38 Home on the range
43 Motherly sorts
44 Cling (to)
45 Attorney General Reno
46 Bewhiskered animal
47 Huff
48 Tipped off
49 Lolita, e.g.
50 Lady of Spain
51 Bits of work
52 Bossa ___
53 Nonuniformed police officer
54 Collision sound

by Sherry O. Blackard

ACROSS

1 Brass =
   copper + ___
5 Map out
9 Long for
14 Jacob's twin
15 Music of India
16 Place for a
   boutonniere
17 Nerd identifier #1
20 Sailor's assent
21 Expected,
   as payment
22 Bit of current
23 Drug ___
   (government
   position)
24 Air conditioner
   meas.
25 Casino
   employee
28 Hold
29 "All the
   Things You ___"
   (Kern tune)
32 Poe bird
33 Goatee's
   location
34 Gravity-powered
   vehicle
35 Nerd identifier #2
38 Enliven, with "up"
39 ___ splicing
40 Jigsaw
   puzzle unit
41 Fast plane: Abbr.
42 Religious
   offshoot
43 West Pointers
44 Algebra and trig
45 Basic Web site
   info, for short
46 Fashion designer
   Giorgio
49 Soybean product
50 Sci-fi vehicle
53 Nerd identifier #3
56 Jazz instruments
57 Tiny bit
58 ___ of Sandwich

59 Praiseful
   poem penner
60 Genesis garden
61 "Goodness!"

DOWN

1 Actress Catherine
   ___-Jones
2 Brit's exclamation
3 Back of the neck
4 Billiards stick
5 Antebellum
6 Paint coat
7 Got older
8 Remind too often
9 Refuse to talk
10 Talks hoarsely
11 Church area
12 Zig or zag

13 "What ___ is new?"
18 Egg quantities
19 Mexican-
   American, e.g.
23 Office worker
24 Illegal inducement
25 Lozenges
26 Icicle supports
27 Head off
28 War of 1812
   treaty site
29 "Tiny Alice"
   playwright
30 Don't just
   stand there
31 Rims
33 Prague native
34 Loses control
   on ice, e.g.

36 Phrase of
   understanding
37 Opposite of
   transparent
42 Most sensible
43 Lounging robe
44 Whips up
45 Civil War historian
   Shelby
46 Lhasa ___ (dog)
47 Thoroughfare
48 Roman 1,111
49 Walked (on)
50 Salt lake state
51 Something
   to fill out
52 Paris airport
54 Mincemeat dessert
55 Corporate V.I.P.

by Stanley Newman

ACROSS

1 Black, in poetry
5 Actress Best and others
10 "The ___ thickens"
14 Besides
15 Tiny bit
16 Greasy
17 Food item served in a basket
18 Therefore
19 Barber's motion
20 Hanna-Barbera cartoon dog
22 Humorist Martin
23 Taina who was one of Les Girls, 1957
24 Picked up, as an hors d'oeuvre
26 Fragrance
30 Restaurant activity
32 Prance about
34 Prefix with classic
35 Adam and Eve's place
39 ". . . happily ___ after"
40 Bombay believer
42 1957 Harry Belafonte hit
43 Bruce or Laura of Hollywood
44 Bambi's aunt
45 Fries with a little butter
47 Properly pitched
50 Indigent
51 Persian, now
54 Hamelin pest
56 Longest river of Europe
57 Heroic action
63 "Diary of ___ Housewife"
64 ___ Lama
65 Like the Sahara
66 Address preceder
67 Observe Yom Kippur, e.g.
68 Even-steven
69 Driving is hard when this is driving
70 Fender flaws
71 Makes a choice

DOWN

1 Corn units
2 Voting group
3 Capital on a fjord
4 ___ contendere
5 Gas additive
6 Excavating machine
7 Prefix with second
8 Confronted
9 Call on
10 Unwanted stamp on mail
11 Lid or lip application
12 Complexion tone
13 Prepared a manuscript
21 Stand
22 One of 100 in D.C.
25 Religious
26 Scored 100 on
27 Rip-roaring success
28 Above
29 Lawn moisture
31 Kofi of the U.N.
33 Sorority letter
36 Palm fruit
37 Viewed
38 Prying
41 Flood
46 Opposed to
48 Entertainer Peeples
49 Wandering
51 Several Russian czars
52 Livy or Pliny
53 Movie with John Wayne as Davy Crockett, with "The"
55 Astrological ram
58 College in North Carolina
59 Defense org. since 1949
60 Understanding
61 Go easy on the calories
62 Bettor's figuring
64 Pop

by Sarah Keller

ACROSS

1 Barn's place
5 The "t" in Nafta
10 Hockey shot
14 Inter ___
15 Paint the town red
16 Angelic ring
17 Picnic pastime #1
19 Missing from the Marines, say
20 N.B.A.'s Shaquille
21 Location
22 Deep ___ bend
23 Automatic phone feature
25 Came to earth
27 Scissors cut
29 Electric bill listing
32 Grease job
35 It goes side-to-side
39 "Treasure Island" author's inits.
40 One ___ million
41 Picnic pastime #2
42 Egypt's King ___
43 Sum (up)
44 Lads' partners
45 Out of harbor
46 Swain
48 Wild guess
50 Undamaged
54 Madden
58 Perform in a glee club
60 Huntley of 50's–60's NBC news
62 Passé
63 "Till we meet again"
64 Picnic pastime #3
66 Spellbound
67 School assignment
68 "Green Gables" girl
69 Completely unconscious
70 Lawn mower name
71 Picnic, e.g.

DOWN

1 Party handout
2 Without help
3 Ticked off
4 Listlessness
5 Audition, with "out"
6 Civil War side
7 Profit
8 Mississippi ___
9 Oscar-winner Burstyn
10 Dairy Queen orders
11 Picnic pastime #4
12 Shaving gel additive
13 Barbershop emblem
18 Pizzazz
24 Follower of Virgo
26 "You Don't Bring Me Flowers," e.g.
28 Major-leaguers
30 Rubber cement, e.g.
31 This, south of the border
32 Bluffer
33 Nullify
34 Picnic pastime #5
36 Mensa figures, for short
37 Cost of belonging
38 P. C. Wren novel "Beau ___"
41 Become obstructed
45 Isaac's father
47 Hold rapt
49 & & &
51 Was hurting
52 Picked
53 To the point
55 Perform penance
56 Davis of "Thelma & Louise"
57 1950's Detroit dud
58 Without women
59 "Othello" villain
61 Old Russian royal
65 CBS logo

by Gregory E. Paul

ACROSS
1 Pepsi, e.g.
5 Bit of parsley
10 Tuxedo shirt fastener
14 Its capital is Muscat
15 Vestige
16 Carson's late-night successor
17 Agitated state
18 Man of many words?
19 Mystery writer Ambler
20 Italian for "pick me up"
22 Intelligence
24 Ice cream treat
25 Public square
26 Secretarial work
29 Guards
32 Arduous
33 Most likely ones to be invited
34 ___ and aah
35 Boxer Laila ___
36 Italian for "to the tooth"
38 Delta rival
39 What an air ball doesn't touch
40 Begin's co-Nobelist in 1978
41 Twosome in the gossip columns
42 Parkland birds
44 Olympic prizes
46 Do a do-si-do
47 Red Rose
48 Big name in toy trains
50 Italian for "beautiful singing"
54 "___ it rich?"
55 Poetry Muse
57 Copy cats?
58 Catcher Tony
59 Capital near Casablanca

60 "You said it, sister!"
61 Puffy Combs's first name
62 Prepared to pray
63 Signals agreement

DOWN
1 Price paid
2 All: Prefix
3 Lion's den
4 Alka-Seltzer, for one
5 Yo-yo necessity
6 Nonpoetic writing
7 Brand of sauce
8 Italian ___
9 Beats it
10 Vulgar person
11 Italian for "baked earth"
12 Military subdivision
13 Physicians, briefly
21 Tues. preceder
23 Photo finish
25 Word processing command
26 Choreographer Twyla
27 New Haven student
28 Italian for "first lady"
29 Prayers
30 Sauna item
31 Hoaxes
33 Confuse
36 In unison

37 Supreme Court worker
41 Creative person
43 Card game also called sevens
44 Member of the 500 home run club
45 List abbr.
47 Corolla part
48 "Loose ___ sink ships"
49 Fortuneteller's phrase
50 Title pig in a 1995 film
51 Jules Verne captain
52 ___ the line (obeyed)
53 Has
56 Dashed

by Peter Gordon

ACROSS

1 Small hindrance, as in plans
6 Actor Guinness
10 Small-circulation publication for fans
14 Fighting
15 Much of Eur. is in it
16 Geraint's love
17 "Swan Lake" piece
20 Road curve
21 Actress Dawber and others
22 Watergate scandal figure Chuck
23 Davenport
24 First 007 flick
25 Brunch dish with spinach
31 Schedule
32 Judge
33 Teachers' org.
34 Certain retrievers, for short
35 Khaki-like color
37 Taverns
38 From ___ Z
39 Explorer Hernando de ___
40 Paris newspaper, with "Le"
41 Window covers
45 1994 Jodie Foster title role
46 God
47 Maniacal
50 Coffee, slangily
51 Old Ford
54 Charlemagne's domain
57 Electron's place
58 Labor
59 Hammerin' Hank
60 Townshend of the Who
61 Loch ___
62 Some dental records

DOWN

1 Walking stick
2 Blvds. and rds.
3 "___ a Teen-age Werewolf"
4 Blueprint
5 Ask for a hand?
6 Ox or fox
7 Side muscles, for short
8 Hippocrates' H
9 Tangible
10 Wild-eyed one
11 Hostels
12 One-named singer/model filmed by Andy Warhol
13 Apple of temptation site
18 ___ riot (comedy review)
19 "Death be not proud" writer
23 Certain NCO's
24 Big bore
25 Gladden
26 Cameroon neighbor
27 Hunter in the night sky
28 ___ of itself
29 They're hardly hip
30 Facility
31 Serb or Croat
35 Essentially amount (to)
36 Bibliography abbr.
37 007
39 Direct
40 Disney studio
42 Pepsin, e.g.
43 False fire?
44 Score before 15
47 Fellow
48 Learning by flashcards, e.g.
49 Often
50 Shakes up
51 Italian money
52 "Troilus and Cressida" setting
53 Trophy rooms
55 A Stooge
56 Average

by Ethan Cooper

ACROSS

1 Lump
5 Emeralds and diamonds
9 Kind of decongestant
14 "___ Croft: Tomb Raider" (2001 movie)
15 On
16 "La Bohème," e.g.
17 Consumer
18 Unaccompanied
19 Mail a payment
20 Source of continual suffering
23 Lamprey ___
24 Colorant
25 Kind of pliers
30 Hospital capacity
34 Off-road traveler: Abbr.
35 Saturate
36 Turn in a chair
38 Material for uniforms
40 Dog's "hand"
42 Overhead
43 Where rods and cones are
45 Boston ___ Orchestra
47 Young goat
48 Panache
49 Features of some women's shoes
52 Important loan info, for short
53 Carpet alternative
54 Possible title for this puzzle
63 Flip over
64 Run away
65 Inkling
66 LaBelle or LuPone
67 "The Thin Man" dog
68 Doctor's action to a newborn's bottom
69 T. S., the poet
70 Grizzly
71 Use a keyboard

DOWN

1 Market oversaturation
2 Whip
3 Popular cookie
4 Like a prison window
5 Classic Italian astronomer
6 Thames school
7 Pre-stereo
8 Uses money
9 Like Eric the Red
10 Gorillas and chimps
11 Big rig
12 Parched
13 Running behind
21 South Africa's Mandela
22 Looks at
25 Mother-of-pearl
26 Neighbor of Lucy and Ricky
27 Madonna title role
28 Short snooze
29 Cousin of a giraffe
30 Baby's tie-on
31 Elicit
32 Man with horns
33 Toys attached to ropes
37 Prepare for dinner
39 Writer Anaïs
41 Stir-frier
44 Poisonous snakes
46 Annually
50 Like some inexpensive homes
51 Altruist's opposite
52 I.R.S. agent's task
54 Fool
55 Milky gem
56 The Abominable Snowman
57 Aware of
58 In any other way
59 Prefix with morphosis
60 Lazily
61 Kind of tide
62 VCR insert

by Nancy Kavanaugh

ACROSS

1 Basic gymnastics move
5 Overcharge, informally
10 Christmastime
14 Choir attire
15 Gold medal, e.g.
16 Satan's work
17 Finished
18 Friend to Franco
19 Not bold
20 Apology #1
23 ___ nous
24 Years and years
25 Actress Tomei
28 Manet and Monet
32 Treasure chest
33 Chutzpah
35 "Yoo-___!"
36 Apology #2
40 Scooby-___ (cartoon dog)
41 Online marketplace
42 "Pagliacci," e.g.
43 Handle
46 Norwegians' neighbors
47 My ___, Vietnam
48 Whitish
50 Apology #3
56 Opposite of "for here"
57 Response to a general
58 Name of five Norwegian kings
60 Old Russian autocrat
61 What makes il mondo go round?
62 Fairy tale villain
63 Sharpen
64 Asocial type
65 Slightly off-color

DOWN

1 To's partner
2 It "makes the world go round"
3 Nimble mountain animal
4 See
5 California peak
6 Promising one
7 Japanese cartoon art
8 Theater box
9 As Miss Manners would do it
10 San'a native
11 Part of the eye
12 Some Pinocchio pronouncements
13 Actress Sommer
21 Al of Indy
22 Auction offering
25 Highest peak in Crete: Abbr.
26 Knight's "suit"
27 Moving machine part
28 Treaty co-signer
29 Rip up
30 Yankees manger Joe
31 Some beans
33 Scoff at
34 Lawyers' org.
37 Prefinal tournament
38 Farmer in the spring
39 Symbol of welcome
44 2000 candidate
45 Aye canceler
46 Generous one
48 Burning desire?
49 Steeple
50 What a wool shirt can do
51 Clown's name
52 New York archbishop Edward
53 Man, in Italy
54 Gold-medal gymnast Korbut
55 Drug agent
59 Effeminate

by Bernice Gordon

ACROSS

1 Bright-colored
6 Planes in the news
10 Beat but good!
14 Ice Capades locale
15 Dentist's request
16 Actress Skye
17 Just under the wire
19 Forfeit
20 Old-fashioned popular novel
22 Shades of blue
24 Elbow's place
25 Hot temper
26 Muscle spasm
27 Prima donnas
30 Gourmand
32 Centers of activity
34 "i" finisher
35 Termite's relative
36 Trivial
41 Goof up
42 Gun, as an engine
43 Travel across a tarmac
45 One who's diplomatic and urbane, astrologically
48 Cuba's Castro
50 Big success
51 Altar words
52 Agcy. with loans for homeowners
54 Money back
56 Navy petty officer
60 "Render ___ Caesar . . ."
61 Places for cheese
64 Change for a five
65 Places
66 Delight in
67 Outlasted, with "out"
68 Leave in, to an editor
69 Harvests

DOWN

1 Kilmer of "At First Sight"
2 Belfast grp.
3 Explorer Amerigo
4 Prefix with stellar
5 Going to hell
6 PlayStation maker
7 Tater
8 Aquarium favorites
9 Curl one's lip
10 Like jokers
11 Walk, slangily
12 Hesitant
13 Kitchen gadget
18 One who knows the scoop
21 Modify
22 Part of A&P: Abbr.
23 Utah's ___ National Park
28 Tennessee athlete, for short
29 Company that introduced Donkey Kong
31 Going ___ (fighting)
33 Cake decorator
35 Unfavorable
37 Macaroni & Cheese maker
38 Composer Rorem
39 Hindu prince
40 Sign above a door
44 Suffix with Manhattan
45 Tavern supply
46 "Beats me"
47 Sailed
48 Rad
49 A, B or C
53 Rope fibers
55 Swiss capital
57 Valentine bouquet item
58 Remote button
59 Helper: Abbr.
62 Old man
63 The "S" of CBS: Abbr.

by Sherry O. Blackard

ACROSS

1 Port on
  Osaka Bay
5 Fess up
10 "Hey, you!"
14 "Since ___ You
   Baby" (1956 hit)
15 Satchel on the field
16 Exit location, often
17 Mall locale
19 Germany's ___
   von Bismarck
20 Umpire's decision
21 Slept like a hen
23 Manila envelope
   feature
26 Amtrak
   transportation
27 Tooth problem
30 Means of escape
32 Stoop parts
35 Month after Av
36 One with an
   allover tan
38 ___ culpa
39 Beyond tipsy
40 Sites for
   skirmishes
41 Night school subj.
42 Broadbrim, e.g.
43 Marcos, the shoe
   collector
44 Golden rule
   preposition
45 Mooring place
47 Susan of
   "L.A. Law"
48 John with an
   outrageous
   wardrobe
49 "Cómo ___
   usted?"
51 Sordid
53 Like the
   best towels
56 Apple variety
60 Diva's delivery
61 Not doing much
   disciplining
64 Take five

65 Type size smaller
   than pica
66 Summers in Rouen
67 Stadium near Shea
68 Katmandu's land
69 Enraptured

DOWN

1 Fuzzy fruit
2 Neighbor
  of Yemen
3 Porgy's mate
4 Unlikely to cheat
5 Breathing problem
6 The U.N.'s ___
  Hammarskjöld
7 Cambridge sch.
8 Prince in
  a Borodin opera

9 Pavarotti, e.g.
10 "To your health!"
11 Suit ender
12 Satisfy fully
13 Walked over
18 Sans purpose
22 Brewery kilns
24 Now poor,
   as relations
25 Places to splash
27 Indian metropolis
28 Political pawn
   González
29 Squid's cousin
31 Color, hippie-style
33 Pasta topper
34 Locale for this
   puzzle's theme
36 Pierre or Henri, e.g.

37 Mme., in Madrid
40 Please, in Potsdam
44 Joyce masterpiece
46 What you will
48 Big birds
50 Rockies resort
52 Israeli hard-liner
   Sharon
53 Mrs. Roosevelt
54 Assayers' stuff
55 The "T" of TCI
57 Webmaster's
   creation
58 Roulette bet
59 Reason to cram
62 Fictional sleeper
63 Boston subway
   inits.

by Sarah Keller

ACROSS

1 Zebras on the gridiron
5 Examine, slangily, with "out"
10 Puppy sounds
14 He sang about Alice
15 Imitated a crow
16 "The ___ Love" (R.E.M. hit)
17 Comical Highlanders?
20 Belfry spots
21 Yellow parts
22 Harris and Bradley
23 Former frosh
25 Acts like a mother hen
29 Clear soup
33 Prank
34 Biblical name for Syria
35 Bumper sticker letters
36 Proofreaders from Prague?
40 Cause for overtime
41 "Stalag 17" extras
42 Like much of Poe's work
43 Pass receiver
46 Your parents' music
47 Wished undone
48 Part of T.G.I.F.: Abbr.
49 Brilliance
52 Give comfort to
57 Beachgoers from northern Spain?
60 Naysayer
61 Company that merged with BP, 1998
62 Be dependent

63 Capone's nemesis
64 Spud
65 Carpet layer's calculation

DOWN

1 Tramp's attire
2 Part of Q.E.D.
3 Go on the lam
4 Dover ___
5 Dresses down
6 Sidewalk eateries
7 Birds in barns
8 Prankster's projectile
9 Univ. e-mail ending
10 Part of a pirate's refrain
11 Like J.F.K. Airport

12 Cheat, in a way
13 They're dubbed
18 Address
19 Pulls a fast one on
23 Takes wing
24 "This one's ___"
25 Almanac stuff
26 Open, as a jacket
27 Girder composition
28 [not my error]
29 Three, they say
30 Early New Zealander
31 Donny's sister
32 Comforts
34 "I bid you ___ farewell"

37 Graf ___
38 Really enjoy
39 Flushed
44 Basra residents
45 "Swan Lake" attire
46 Demosthenes, e.g.
48 Thief's customer
49 Israel's Abba
50 Chaplin prop
51 D-Day craft
52 Knee-slapper
53 Hospital fluids
54 Terminal man?
55 Hold sway
56 "Orinoco Flow" singer
58 Polish off
59 Diminutive, in Dundee

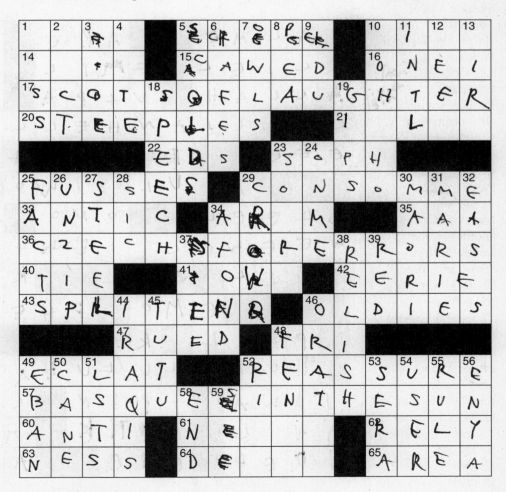

by Nick Grivas

ACROSS

1 ___ d'Or (award at Cannes)
6 Mimic
9 To ___ (without exception)
13 Eero Saarinen's architect father
14 Actor Jannings
15 1953 Leslie Caron film
16 God, to a Muslim
17 Wine valley in California
18 Skin lotion ingredient
19 "The Little Foxes" playwright
22 Shoebox marking
23 Sign on a door
24 Top-notch
25 Haleakala National Park site
27 ___ Jima
29 Cart part
32 Lennon's widow
33 Hull projection
37 Nightgown wearer of rhyme
41 In good health
42 Part of many e-mail addresses
43 Nancy Drew author Carolyn
44 Comic Philips
45 "Boy, am I tired!"
47 "Murphy Brown" bar owner
50 Cabbage's cousin
52 Buddy
55 City whose language uses only the 12 letters found in this puzzle
59 Hawkeye's home
60 ". . . hear ___ drop"
61 Lousy car
62 Shade of blue
63 Brother
64 Syrup flavor
65 Carol
66 Compass dir.
67 "Gil Blas" novelist Lesage

DOWN

1 Artist Rembrandt ___
2 Kate's TV roommate
3 Northern French city
4 Ground-up corn
5 Designed for all grades
6 "___ and the Night Visitors"
7 Oil conduit
8 Israeli airline
9 San Antonio landmark
10 La Scala's city
11 Unaccompanied
12 Never, in Nürnberg
14 Boredom
20 Kwik-E-Mart owner on "The Simpsons"
21 ___-tzu
25 Whimper
26 The Greatest
28 "Holy cow!"
29 http:// follower
30 TV's "___ Haw"
31 Snaky fish
32 Deep-frying need
33 Sensed
34 Barely make, with "out"
35 German article
36 "Crooklyn" director
38 Hasty escape
39 Regard
40 50's prez
44 "Xanadu" grp.
45 Coin sound
46 When repeated, a snicker
47 Receiver button
48 Actor Mandel
49 Fully
51 Dress cut
52 Argentine plain
53 Garlicky mayonnaise
54 Sheets and stuff
56 Crippled
57 Soprano Gluck
58 Prosperity
59 Actor Ziering

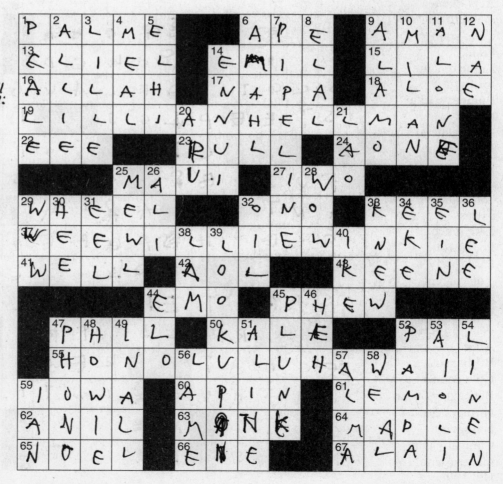

by Peter Gordon

ACROSS

1 The Marines, e.g.
6 Mafia bosses
10 Venus de Milo's lack
14 Take as one's own
15 Guinness who was knighted
16 "Star Wars" princess
17 Game
20 Submissions to eds.
21 What the booby prize winner scored
22 "Money ___ object"
23 Purim honoree
25 Yellow-ribboned tree
27 N.B.A.'s Erving, informally
29 Space race acronym
30 Rules maven
32 Squeeze (out)
33 Wedding guide
36 Hosted, as 3-Down
38 Game
41 Chinese dumpling
42 Best
43 "What Kind of Fool ___?"
44 Wrinkled fruit
46 "___ there?" (part of a knock-knock joke)
50 Gen-___
51 Martini maker
52 Tomorrow, in Tijuana
54 Roman wrap
56 Director DeMille
59 "Oy ___!"
60 Game
63 Was in the hole
64 Disrobe
65 Writer Joyce Carol ___
66 Means justifiers
67 "Check this out!"
68 Exxon alternative

DOWN

1 It opens in a public square in Seville
2 Forsyth's "The ___ File"
3 Friars Club events
4 Mail order abbr.
5 Edwardian or Victorian
6 Gillian's role on "The X-Files"
7 An 88, e.g.
8 Child's wish for Christmas
9 Biol. or chem.
10 Whittier poem "___ Well"
11 Dancer's partners
12 Beethoven's Ninth is in one
13 Give in to gravity
18 ___ Lingus
19 At a feverish pace
24 Hangout
26 Sealskin wearer, maybe
28 Pa Clampett
30 The Beatles' "And I Love ___"
31 Bean on the screen
34 Makeshift
35 Artist Matisse
37 Queen topper
38 Where you're from
39 Having a pressing need?
40 What's what in Spain
41 Car wash option
45 What many brothers are also
47 Must
48 "I'll be right there!"
49 States as fact
52 Russian space station
53 Big name in kitchen foil
55 Mount Olympus dwellers
57 Baby blues
58 Kentucky Derby prospect
60 A Stooge
61 Across the street from: Abbr.
62 Stage hog

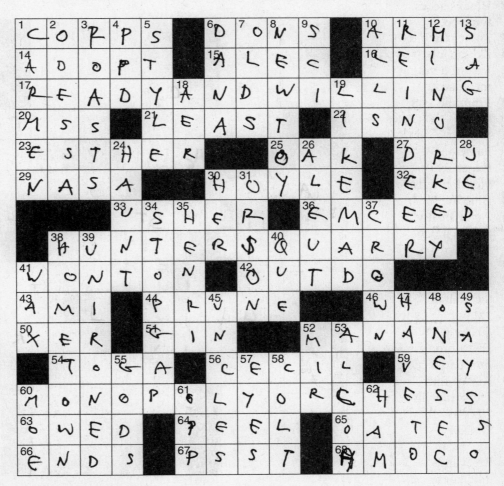

by Nancy Salomon

ACROSS

1 Extremely thrilled
5 Sites of some pillow fights
10 Urban renewal target
14 Skating jump
15 Member of a W.W. II wolf pack
16 Cry of pain
17 Hair wave
18 Apple gizmo
19 Blindingly bright
20 Plays in a zoo?
23 Cheekiness
24 Spinner
25 World leader from 1959
28 Blocks access to a zoo?
33 Put a match to
34 Do the job
36 Part of a voting machine
37 From the U.S.
39 Coach
41 It has a home page
42 Expensive violin, briefly
44 Bluefins
46 Actor Beatty
47 Settles a debt in a zoo?
49 Get along
51 Fifth sign of the zodiac
52 "May I ___ silly question?"
53 Has a promising future in a zoo?
59 Ray of film
60 Prefix meaning "sacred"
61 Passably
64 ___ Strip
65 Relevant, in legalese
66 Vicinity
67 Transport dating from the Stone Age
68 Keyed up
69 Cry at a bakery

DOWN

1 Breach
2 Feller in a forest
3 Origin, as of an idea
4 Not quite
5 Leaves a zoo quickly?
6 Some orchestra members
7 Actor Calhoun
8 Fannie ___ (securities)
9 Layers
10 General outlines
11 In ___ of
12 Knowing about
13 Recuperate
21 Drug dealer's nemesis
22 Wallpaper unit
25 Hug
26 "We ___ please"
27 Rudder's spot
28 Take notice
29 School started by Henry VI
30 Sheep-related
31 Held a party for
32 One of the Corleones
35 Ballet wear
38 Monopoly property
40 Emphasizes forcefully in a zoo?
43 Rick who sang "Disco Duck"
45 Literary pen name
48 "As if I care"
50 Wyatt Earp, for one
52 Lots of lots
53 Supermarket supplies
54 Traveler to Tel Aviv
55 Tool related to a 2-Down
56 White House worker
57 Seabird
58 Noted loser by a whisker
62 Census datum
63 ___ bran

by David J. Kahn

ACROSS

1 Wedding entertainers
5 Wine containers
10 Like fine wine
14 "Your turn," to a 5-Down
15 Cheerless
16 Trout's home
17 Leon Uris's "___ 18"
18 On "E"
19 "You got that right!"
20 Sherlock Holmes in "The Woman in Green"
23 When to return from lunch, maybe
24 "___-hoo!"
25 ___ Beta Kappa
28 Hankering
29 Place holders
33 Alien landings, telepaths, etc.
35 Computer key
37 Italian dearie
38 Betty Haynes in "White Christmas"
43 First czar of Russia
44 Like sauerkraut and strudel
45 Ingredient
48 Bankrupt
49 Great respect
52 Antlered animal
53 Batman and Robin, e.g.
55 Old-timer
57 Blanche Devereaux in TV's "The Golden Girls"
62 Close to closed
64 Gentleman callers
65 Small dog, informally
66 Isinglass
67 Egg size
68 Makes angry
69 Labor leader I. W. ___
70 Ceased
71 Mailed

DOWN

1 Its port is known as the Gateway to India
2 Pilot
3 Ozzie or Harriet
4 Sink feature
5 Many a trucker
6 ___ mater
7 Back-to-school time: Abbr.
8 Oscar winner Bates
9 V.I.P.'s seating locale
10 Fed chairman Greenspan
11 Coach's strategy
12 Squeeze (out)
13 Cub's home
21 Gershwin's "___ Eat Cake"
22 Response to a punch in the stomach
26 Roll call response
27 Mary Higgins Clark's "Before ___Good-Bye"
30 In the manner of
31 Chunk in the Arctic Ocean
32 Eye sores
34 James Dean or Marilyn Monroe
35 Job for a body shop
36 Beige
38 Widespread
39 White House office shape
40 Company picnic activity
41 K-O connection
42 Like some old buckets
46 Flowery verse
47 Gang fight
49 Stick (to)
50 Undermine
51 Frank's partner in the comics
54 "Wavy waste," to Thomas Hood
56 ___ lazuli
58 Russia's ___ Mountains
59 Cutup
60 Downhill racer
61 Canned
62 G.P.'s grp.
63 Sloop's sail

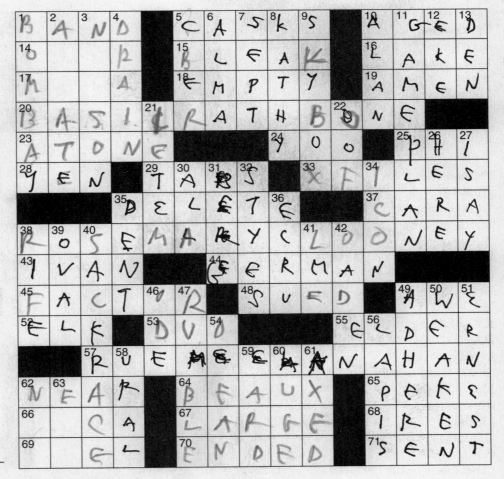

by Sherry O. Blackard

ACROSS

1 Warsaw Pact land
5 1990's Philippine leader Fidel
10 What "m" is in F = ma
14 Singer Turner
15 Off from the center
16 Amo, amas, ___
17 Label on some sportswear
18 1985 Glenn Close film
19 Cuban boy
20 Track star Carl
22 Main point
23 What might follow catch or latch
24 Y
27 See 41-Down
29 Storekeeper's stock: Abbr.
30 Et ___ (footnote abbr.)
31 Campus locale
33 Large shoe specification
35 Self-mover's rental
40 Y
44 "Mission possible" group?
45 "___ you nuts?"
46 Jazzman Herbie
47 "___ likely!"
50 British rule in colonial India
52 Rebel Turner
53 Y
59 Rat's learning place
60 Lined up
61 Maine forest sight
64 Musical work
65 Russian writer Maxim
67 Don Juan's mother
68 Go-___
69 "The door's open!"
70 Lightly burn
71 Farm mothers
72 "Ta-ta!"
73 Poet ___ St. Vincent Millay

DOWN

1 Electricity or water: Abbr.
2 42 Long, e.g.
3 Six-sided figure
4 Pilot's communicator
5 Dodge product
6 Without questioning or debate
7 Add, as an ingredient
8 Writers for old literary columns
9 Boil
10 Large estate
11 ___ acid
12 December drop-in
13 Prepared to sing the national anthem
21 ___ Lanka
25 Was positive
26 Prefix with lateral
27 Swimming pool shade
28 Stage actor Alfred
32 Focus of a genome study
34 Early 60's singer Little ___
36 Order with eggs
37 Left
38 Armbone
39 Gave for a while
41 Prefix meaning 27-Across
42 Cursor mover
43 Derrière
48 Oil-rich Indians
49 Seat of power
51 Toast topper
53 Light up
54 Sweet fruit
55 Sky-blue
56 They may go out on a limb
57 Strong suit
58 Clamor
62 Rapper Combs
63 Poet Pound
66 It may be money in the bank: Abbr.

by Michael Shteyman

ACROSS

1 "A Jug of Wine, a Loaf of Bread - and Thou" poet
5 Fruits by a partridge
10 Kind of palm
14 Noose material
15 1973 #1 Rolling Stones hit
16 "___ the night before . . ."
17 The answer is . . .
20 Twinkies maker
21 White-haired fellow, maybe
22 Where a brood is raised
23 Visible
24 Berth place
27 Conversationalist
32 Inquires
36 Whizzes
38 Skater Harding
39 With 62-Across, the question is . . . (!)
42 Like "E pluribus unum"
43 Ship of 1492
44 Dumb ___ (stupidheads)
45 Minimovies
47 Items in a 22-Across
49 Elevator man
51 Storybook bear
55 Went down the easy way
59 With ice cream
62 See 39-Across
64 Lee or Musial
65 "___ a Symphony" (1965 hit)
66 Like overused gym clothes
67 Cause for a lawsuit
68 Cry of a blamer
69 Dines

DOWN

1 Symphony performer: Abbr.
2 Idiot
3 Strike ___ (what models do)
4 Takes five
5 Dog's "dogs"
6 Son of Seth
7 Cabinet Dept.
8 Part of a roof
9 Hush-hush
10 Phaser setting, on "Star Trek"
11 Impressed
12 [I'm shocked! Shocked!]
13 Peak in Greek myth
18 Math groups
19 Covered with wool
23 Homo sapiens, for example
25 Syllables meaning "I forgot the words"
26 Sammy Davis Jr.'s "Yes ___"
28 Lion, for MGM, e.g.
29 Fort ___ (gold site)
30 Fictional Jane
31 They're caught on beaches
32 Punch tools
33 Ex-head of Iran
34 The Green Hornet's valet
35 Awaken
37 Participated in a choir
40 Completely
41 "___, you're it!"
46 Attempt to mediate
48 Small fight
50 Gem State
52 Love, in Livorno
53 Lecterns
54 Fix to suit
55 Price
56 Knowing about
57 Leaving a small opening
58 Dispatched
59 21-Across of 6-Down
60 It's plucked
61 Peepers
63 Abbr. after some military names

by Steven Dorfman

ACROSS

1 Still in contention
6 Artist Chagall
10 Turns sharply
14 Enticed, with "in"
15 Essayist's alias
16 List ender
17 One bringing up the rear
19 Basilica's center
20 Warbler Yoko
21 Italy's shape
22 Left port
24 Hollywood's Ken or Lena
25 Prefix with vitamin
26 Pop artist Johns
29 Surgeon's asset
32 Think tank nuggets
33 20-mule team load
34 Postal motto conjunction
35 Unwelcome mail
36 Sills selections
37 Actor O'Shea
38 Wriggly fish
39 Rower's craft
40 Prickly plants
41 Sweepers' utensils
43 Made into mush
44 3 and 2, e.g.
45 Seine feeder
46 Abbott, to Costello
48 Cool-sounding rapper
49 Barely make, with "out"
52 Help in a heist
53 Vegas V.I.P.
56 "Hud" Oscar-winner
57 AOL patron
58 "___ in your mouth, not . . ."

59 Pound a Selectric
60 Fill to the gills
61 Theme of this puzzle

DOWN

1 Guthrie the younger
2 Usurer's offering
3 ___ facto
4 Fido fixer
5 All you can eat
6 Juicy fruit
7 Touched down
8 ___ Tin Tin
9 Pauses in speech
10 Nadir's opposite
11 Boardwalk confection
12 Collapsed under pressure
13 Winter toy
18 Roulette color
23 Football's Karras
24 Fall birthstone
25 Piece of cave art
26 Were in accord
27 "So long, Pierre!"
28 Offers for a song
29 Besmirches
30 Nick of "Cape Fear"
31 R2-D2 or C-3PO
33 Main impact
36 Ornate leaf, or a design patterned after it
37 Mule's mother
39 Railway siding
40 International airport section
42 Flute sound
43 Liner's landing
45 Earthy hue
46 Pessimist's word
47 Toe the line
48 "This is the thanks ___?"
49 Jazz's Fitzgerald
50 Etta of the comics
51 Gael's tongue
54 "This ___ test"
55 Albanian currency

by M. Preston Sherwood

ACROSS

1 Dump hot coffee on
6 Disdainful remark
10 Hook with a handle
14 Turn to mush
15 Not fooled by
16 Stadium shape, maybe
17 Set straight
18 Not that
19 Noggin, in Nantes
20 Share the role?
22 Got 100 on
23 Crow's-nest site
24 Up to, in ads
25 Round Table title
27 "The West Wing" star
29 Radio static, e.g.
33 Designer Pucci
37 Ecstatic
39 "From my perspective," archaically
41 The "B" in G.B.S.
42 Barbara of country
44 Dangerfield who doesn't get any respect
45 Eucharist spot
46 63-Across and others
48 Minded junior
50 Seek the hand of
51 "I did it!"
55 Took one's turn
58 Provided electricity for the john?
61 ". . . ___ before the deadline"
62 "Boola Boola" collegians
63 Quotable Yankee
64 1972 Kentucky Derby winner ___ Ridge

65 What's more
66 Taking advantage of
67 June 6, 1944
68 Sharp as a tack
69 V-formation fliers

DOWN

1 Something beyond your control
2 Mea ___
3 Seed covers
4 Kosher, so to speak
5 Fender blemish
6 TV dinner fare
7 Asthmatic's device
8 Culinary directive
9 Inviters
10 Bought drinks for everyone?
11 With, to Maurice
12 Kismet
13 Skedaddled
21 Where a telecommuter works
26 Emcees' lines
27 "High ___" (Bogart classic)
28 Put the collar on
30 Persia, now
31 Like the Gobi
32 Whirling current
33 Austen novel
34 One of three squares
35 Ain't correct?

36 Walked the mongrel?
38 "End of story!"
40 Stallone, to pals
43 Building with just a few floors
47 Continues
49 Playful pinch
51 The ones here
52 Lofty perch
53 Sews the hose
54 "Time is money," e.g.
55 Scrabble formation
56 Author Bagnold
57 Bygone Chevy
59 "Winnie ___ Pu"
60 "Snug as ___ . . ."

by Ed Early

ACROSS

1 "Stars and Stripes Forever" composer
6 "Miss ___ Regrets"
10 Simple payment method
14 Stand at a sitting
15 Ernst's art
16 Conductor Klemperer
17 Cause, as havoc
18 Big bovines
19 ___ Bator
20 Start of a quip
23 "___ by Starlight"
26 Squeezers
27 Quip, part 2
32 Out of whack
33 Monte of Cooperstown
34 Letterman's network
37 TKO callers
38 Response to a bad pun
39 Dinghy or dory
40 Have a go at
41 Wind-borne soil
42 Keyed up
43 Quip, part 3
45 Stern with a bow
48 Camden Yards player
49 End of the quip
54 Arguable
55 Harp's cousin
56 Up to
60 Cause to yawn
61 Bad day for Caesar
62 Yogi was behind it
63 Risked a ticket
64 Symbol of redness
65 Church council

DOWN

1 Give a darn?
2 Sculler's need
3 Put to work
4 Like some stockings
5 Acid neutralizers
6 Bloodhound's clue
7 Subway alternative
8 Notion
9 Ratted, in mob lingo
10 Kissin' kin
11 Bodybuilder Charles
12 Gawk
13 Sharpens
21 Sought office
22 Tied up
23 Eligible for Mensa
24 Circus chairperson?
25 Uplift spiritually
28 Personnel manager, at times
29 Irregularly notched
30 "Halt, salt!"
31 Paris potable
34 Modern home
35 Swiss city on the Rhine
36 Cordwood measure
38 ___ long way
39 In a kindly manner
41 Centers of activity
42 Trouser cuffs
43 Like tavern peanuts
44 ___ polloi
45 Pentameter parts, maybe
46 Nosy sort
47 Be gaga over
50 Smooth-talking
51 Fictional "Mr."
52 Elder or alder
53 Arboreal abode
57 Beach bum's shade
58 "Who am ___ say?"
59 Wielded the baton

by Michael S. Maurer

ACROSS

1 Boa or babushka
6 Pueblo dweller
10 "Jurassic Park" beast, briefly
14 Hebrew scroll
15 Not "fer"
16 Suffer from
17 Author Jong
18 Fax or FedEx
19 Kind of page
20 Comedic actress who's able?
23 Mo. containing U.N. Day
24 Acted shrewish
28 Sergeant with badge 714
32 Sauce brand
34 Tokyo, to shoguns
35 Gab, gab, gab
36 Character actor who's able?
38 Workplace watchdog org.
39 Like a designated driver
40 First word of Virgil's "Aeneid"
41 R. & B. singer who's able?
43 Salad oil holder
44 Kenan's Nickelodeon pal
45 Help for the stumped
46 Zombie, before revival
47 Get steamed
49 Jazz style
50 German philosopher who's UNable?
57 Legal wrong
60 Galway Bay's ___ Islands
61 O.K.
62 The whole shebang
63 Insurer's calculation
64 "Totally cool!"
65 Bishop of the Rat Pack
66 Green Hornet's aide
67 France's patron saint

DOWN

1 Goblet feature
2 Mrs. Dithers
3 Bone-dry
4 440 or 10K
5 Alternative to a conventional mortgage
6 ___ a clue (is lost)
7 Double curve
8 Flamingo color
9 Imperiled
10 Revealing swimsuit
11 You can take it or beat it
12 First lady
13 Signed like an illiterate
21 Frigid
22 Herr's home
25 Prepare for action
26 Classic "Tonight Show" tomahawk tosser
27 Be generous
28 Monks' habits
29 Fraternity hopeful
30 Not just puff
31 Football Hall-of-Famer ___ Walker
32 Morocco's capital
33 Sermon closer
36 Most common papal name
37 "It Must Be Him" singer Vikki
39 Evidence at an auto accident
42 "Excuse me"
43 "Rodeo" composer Aaron
46 Miler Sebastian
48 Swank
49 Confidence game
51 Met song
52 Illustrator Thomas
53 Artist Paul
54 King of comedy
55 Denier's words
56 "Terrible" time
57 ___ Mahal
58 Ear: Prefix
59 ___ v. Wade

by Peter Abide

ACROSS

1 Rah-rah
5 Pays to play
10 Fraternal org.
14 It smells
15 Trigger, to Roy Rogers
16 50-and-up org.
17 Black and white #1
19 Stair unit
20 Tickle pink
21 No-goodnik
22 Work units
23 Adding kick to
25 Even if, for short
27 Daze
30 Broom ___ (comics witch)
33 Tear carrier
36 "So that's it!"
37 Clamorous protest
38 Busy mo. for a C.P.A.
39 Black and white #2
41 "Wheel of Fortune" buy
42 Did an old locomotive job
44 Señora Perón
45 Son of Aphrodite
46 Book after Daniel
47 Testing
49 Lip-___
51 Convertible, informally
55 Time to crow
57 Sticks up
60 Fish in a way
61 Switch end
62 Black and white #3
64 Ernie's TV pal
65 Unfolds
66 Rock on the roll?

67 Marquis de ___
68 Home to the Masai
69 Caustic alkalis

DOWN

1 Show backer
2 "Ta-da!"
3 Hayes who sang "Never Can Say Goodbye"
4 One who's down in the mouth?
5 Roadie's burden
6 Preparer for a flood
7 Bring to proper pitch
8 Make beloved
9 Drag one's feet
10 It may produce a run in
11 Black and white #4
12 Neighbor of Calif.
13 Omar of "Scream 2"
18 Campsite sight
24 Michael Jordan, notably
26 Plugugly
28 ___ Beta Kappa
29 Many a John Wayne flick
31 First Bond flick
32 Roll call calls
33 100-meter, e.g.
34 ___ no good
35 Black and white #5
37 How the ecstatic walk

39 Detach gradually
40 Princeton greenery
43 Kick off the convention
45 White House Easter event
47 Athlete of the Century Jim
48 Peacekeeping grp.
50 Shepherd's staff
52 Hungarian wine
53 Martini tidbit
54 Nolo contendere and others
55 Ball belles
56 Neighborhood
58 "It's ___ real!"
59 PlayStation maker
63 The Gray: Abbr.

by Sherry O. Blackard

ACROSS

1 Seemingly forever
5 Heaps and heaps
9 Really big shows
14 Proverbial heirs
15 Kind of wolf
16 Untagged?
17 Hatcher of "Lois & Clark"
18 Bausch & ___
19 Laughfests
20 1955 role for 49-Across
23 Food in bars
24 "Nashville" director Robert
28 1972 role for 49-Across
33 Slender blades
34 Crones
35 First-rate
36 Con's place
37 Needle
39 Some transfusions
40 You can believe it
41 Campaign news
42 Bringing ruin (to)
43 1951 role for 49-Across
47 More chic
48 Witch's feature
49 Star of this puzzle, born 4/3/24
55 Spills the beans
58 Brain wave
59 Beat-up
60 Coin equivalent of a sawbuck
61 They're sometimes put on
62 Pre-med course: Abbr.
63 Fall blossom
64 Fishnet, e.g.
65 Fluctuate wildly

DOWN

1 Tsp. and tbsp.
2 Social misfit
3 Like a King novel: Var.
4 Read through quickly
5 Ready to go
6 Tastelessly affected
7 "Dinner's ___"
8 Wyo. neighbor
9 Signs up
10 ___ Claire, Que.
11 Lance of the bench
12 Op. ___ (footnote abbr.)
13 D and C, in D.C.
21 Baba and others
22 Barracks boss
25 Choral compositions
26 Arctic coat
27 Katmandu native
28 Stop it
29 Decides one will
30 Sports artist LeRoy
31 Poolroom need
32 W. Hemisphere grp.
37 "___ is human"
38 Bridge guru Culbertson
39 Put in the bank
41 Crowd favorite
42 Klinger player on "M*A*S*H"
44 Light-footed
45 One side in baseball negotiations
46 Terre Haute's river
50 Neeson of "Nell"
51 Comics pooch
52 Fudge, e.g., to a dieter
53 Strong cart
54 Not fooled by
55 Co-star of Betty, Rue and Estelle
56 Part of U.N.L.V.
57 Ten-percenter: Abbr.

by Nancy Salomon and Sherry O. Blackard

ACROSS

1 Hope/Crosby's "Road to ___"
5 Festoon
9 Played charades
14 A ___ apple
15 Kind of phone
16 Where Fiats are made
17 Actress Talbot
18 Up to the task
19 Host of TV's "Cosmos"
20 "Star Wars" character
23 Pittsburgh-to-Buffalo dir.
24 Actor Ryan
25 Lasso
27 Recording studio apparatus
31 Celestial object
34 Leatherworker's tool
37 In love with oneself
39 Mrs. Gorbachev
40 Puerto Rican-born golf champion
44 Ginza locale
45 See 47-Across
46 Fannie ___
47 Weapons that 45-Across
49 Irving Berlin's "Blue ___"
52 Angry states
54 Actress Davis
58 Place to relax
60 "Queen of Outer Space" star, 1958
64 The "W" in R.W.E.
66 Dick Cheney, e.g.
67 No brainiac
68 Squirrel's nugget
69 Actress Miles
70 Responsibility
71 Them, essentially
72 1914 battle line
73 "Peer ___"

DOWN

1 Earl Scruggs's instrument
2 Kind of flu
3 Unit of petrol
4 Stuck
5 Battle memento
6 Jim who wrote "MacArthur Park"
7 "___ want for Christmas . . ."
8 Senator in space
9 Ship on which W.W. II ended, 9/2/45
10 Call ___ day
11 Element found in flashbulbs
12 Spirit
13 Unit of force
21 "When We Were Kings" subject
22 Keystone character
26 Smelting byproduct
28 Last Pope Gregory
29 They're often lent
30 Causes to bring out the National Guard
32 On the briny
33 Demolish
34 Substitutes (for)
35 Hit upside the head
36 Adores
38 Fargo's locale: Abbr.
41 Greenish blue
42 Things in view
43 Diamond stat
48 Peter, Patrick and Paul: Abbr.
50 McMuffin ingredient
51 Pirate
53 Streetwise
55 Companion magazine to Jet
56 "___ intended"
57 "Give it ___!"
58 Park lake denizen
59 Flamenco guitarist ___ de Lucia
61 Zorro's marks
62 Dried up
63 On ___ with
65 Actress Joanne

by Kevin McCann

ACROSS

1 Daffy
5 Put up
10 S on a dining table
14 Oodles
15 Most arias
16 Paris's home, in myth
17 Novelist Morrison
18 Duck aside?
20 Cooling off
22 August 1 birth
23 Disentangle
24 Four-in-hand, for one
26 Résumé info
28 Alphabetizes, e.g.
30 Fixes a seam, say
35 Where a star might lead?
38 Not completely
39 Resort near Snowbird
40 Verges on
42 Words said with a nod
43 Kind of nut
45 Not outspoken
47 Witness
48 Burn soother
49 British sports cars
51 Hive material
55 Bowl over
59 "___ the season . . ."
61 One in a black suit
62 Small estate?
65 Money guru Greenspan
66 Verve
67 The "U" of UHF
68 Muse of history
69 Quaver or semiquaver
70 Shakespeare's theater
71 Pull down

DOWN

1 Majorette's need
2 Single-handedly
3 Mixer
4 Kindling?
5 Abbr. on a shingle
6 Inspiration for "Wheel of Fortune"
7 Nobelist Wiesel
8 Quik ingredient
9 "Come, come"
10 Zap
11 "I smell ___"
12 Sets of points
13 Small fry
19 Outcome of many a chess promotion
21 School with historic playing fields
25 Pressing one's suit?
27 Steak defect
29 ___ Tower
31 Kitchen rack?
32 Proficiency
33 Little chirper
34 "Keep it in"
35 Ladder danger
36 Miscellany
37 ___ von Bismarck
41 Bring back in
44 McGwire specialty
46 Currier's partner
50 Jet engine problem
52 When doubled, a Washington city
53 Firefighter Red
54 Element in arc lamps
55 Brother's word?
56 Venus de ___
57 Sci. class
58 Basketball defense
60 Keen about
63 Make a face
64 Norma Webster's middle name

by Greg Staples

ACROSS

1 Words on
 a book jacket
6 Roberts of
 "The Mexican"
11 Campaign
 contributor, maybe
14 Postal scale unit
15 Furious
16 Building add-on
17 Lawyer's wear?
19 ___ king
20 Bewitch
21 Entirely
22 Big hairstyles
24 Rotating part
 under the hood
25 Poles with footrests
26 One sharing
 Iranian money?
32 Old-fashioned tie
33 Hosiery shade
34 "My word!"
38 Ambulance supplies
39 Winged
40 "Star Trek"
 navigator
41 To be, in 49-Down
42 Navigator's position
43 Takes on
44 Journal entry?
47 Join the army, say
50 Supped
51 Instrument with
 hammers
52 Silk-producing city
55 Points scored
 for a safety
58 Critical
 campaign mo.
59 One who's
 tempting NBC's
 Williams?
62 Psi's preceder
63 Grocery part
64 Showing awe
65 Mother ptarmigan
66 They're shown
 to a novice
67 Wrongs

DOWN

1 Not just one
2 Tackle box item
3 Computer operating
 system developed
 by Bell Labs
4 Electronics brand
5 City of Ulster
6 She tumbled
 after Jack
7 Russia's ___
 Mountains
8 Indolent
9 Suffix on names
 of 57-Down
10 Make bubbly
11 Necklace item
12 Mete out
13 '02 or '03, e.g.
18 Road caution
23 Warm place on a
 winter's night
24 Neared, with "on"
25 Surprise greatly
26 Fall tool
27 Egyptian deity
28 New Testament
 book
29 Part of a voting
 machine
30 How to respond to
 an insult
31 Lady's mate, in a
 Disney film
35 Wise one
36 A Baldwin
37 Do some
 housecleaning
39 At the drop of ___
43 Position of pressure
45 Weather map line
46 Emulate Dennis
 Miller
47 Period in history
48 Suitable place
49 See 41-Across
52 Speech problem
53 Harvard rival
54 Washington bills
55 Nicholas II was the
 last one
56 "Jesus ___" (shortest
 verse in the Bible)
57 See 9-Down
60 Brazilian city,
 familiarly
61 In the past

by Tyler Hinman

ACROSS

1 Helpful hints
5 Head off
10 Greater likeliness to win
14 High draft rating
15 Home of La Scala
16 "Hercules" TV spinoff
17 Homework excuse #1
20 River embankment
21 Additionally
22 Pretentious, as a display
23 Breastbone
25 News item for a scrapbook
27 Wide-brimmed hat
29 401(k) alternative
32 Financial predicament
36 Dos preceder
37 Nike rival
39 Homework excuse #2
42 Bob Marley's music
43 S.A.T. administrator
44 Composer Schifrin
45 Easter egg application
46 Winter Olympics races
49 Radio-active driver
50 Newscast segment
55 Sunny farewell
58 Civil War side: Abbr.
60 Tabriz resident
61 Homework excuse #3
64 Prissy
65 Corporate department
66 Big copper exporter
67 Flow slowly
68 Dental records
69 Get ready, for short

DOWN

1 Works hard
2 Arm of the sea
3 Annoy
4 "60 Minutes" reporter
5 Bordeaux beau
6 Popular antioxidant
7 Carolina college
8 Like an "eeny meeny, miney, mo" selection
9 AOL Time Warner network
10 Bring to bear
11 Red ink
12 Bearded beasts
13 Like falling off a log
18 Till compartment
19 Bob, e.g.
24 Tiny Tim's instrument
26 "I have no idea!"
28 Certain mushroom
29 Flash of inspiration
30 Commuter line
31 Concerning
32 Stony
33 Toe the line
34 Winter Olympics vehicle
35 Joule fraction
38 Feeling off
40 Chatterbox
41 Groucho, in "Monkey Business"
47 William Tell, e.g.
48 Remarked
49 Eat like a horse
51 "Tubby the Tuba" lyricist Paul
52 Misanthrope
53 Become accustomed (to)
54 Tear to shreds
55 Word on a fuse
56 Orpheus's instrument
57 Garfield's foil
59 Nintendo competitor
62 XX times VIII
63 Overhead trains

by Stanley Newman

ACROSS
1 Hired sleuths, slangily
5 Fay of "King Kong"
9 King's domain
14 "I smell ___!"
15 Top-notch
16 Chair designer Charles
17 Costa ___
18 Wade through mud
19 Taking habitually
20 Web browser's aid
23 Weather map lines
24 Ebert's former partner
28 ___ rule
29 Dog in Oz
31 "Hallelujah, ___ Bum"
32 Spaceman of serials
36 Singer Orbison
37 Took public transportation
38 Fall flat
39 Be overly fond
40 Bauxite, e.g.
41 Dry cleaner's supply
45 Microwave
46 Miniature racer
47 Holiday quaff
48 Involve
50 They get the lead out
54 T.V.A. function
57 Patriots' Day month
60 Onion, for one
61 Gofer
62 "___ Foolish Things"
63 "Dies ___"
64 Secured, as a deal
65 Theme of this puzzle
66 Makes doilies
67 Neighbor of Vietnam

DOWN
1 Foot bones
2 Indians with poisoned arrows
3 Chocolate source
4 Sci-fi locale
5 Cleaning cloth
6 What cast members fill
7 Bartlett's abbr.
8 Vault cracker
9 What a class might have
10 Softens
11 "What ___, chopped liver?"
12 Grid Hall-of-Famer Dawson
13 Chop suey additive
21 Simplest form of payment
22 Analogy words
25 Russian ballet company
26 Ham it up
27 Cake part
29 Country star Travis
30 Baltic Sea feeder
32 Stopped in one's tracks
33 Navigational aid
34 Masterful
35 What wavy lines mean, in comics
39 It's chased in futility
41 Frying pan
42 ___ Alto
43 Dresses after bathing
44 Reaction to bad news
49 "___ Called Wanda"
50 Showy display
51 "All My Children" regular
52 Drive in Beverly Hills
53 Flexible Flyers
55 Post mortem bio
56 ___ mater (brain cover)
57 The Braves, on scoreboards
58 ___ Beta Kappa
59 Coffee order: Abbr.

by Mark P. Sherwood

ACROSS

1 Partiality
5 Word with sand or speed
9 Easy one for an infielder
14 Expunge, with "out"
15 Israeli dance
16 Island southwest of Majorca
17 Like a Dali watch
18 "Not on ___!" ("No way!")
19 "Final answer?" asker
20 Go ballistic
23 Fine fiddle
24 Butcher's hardware
28 Poe classic, with "The"
33 Future fungus
34 Sharpshooter Oakley
35 Verne hero Phileas
39 Dogcatcher's catch
41 Jamboree shelter
42 On the ball
44 Makes simpler
46 1930 Vincent Youmans song
50 Cochise portrayer Michael
51 Great Lakes tribesmen
54 Toaster's words
59 "Stormy Weather" composer
62 Shade giver
63 Miser's pronoun
64 Friars Club event
65 Catches some rays
66 Military sch.
67 Marinara alternative
68 The "o" in Reo
69 Back talk

DOWN

1 Politico Abzug
2 "Talk turkey," e.g.
3 Draws a bead on
4 Tampa neighbor, informally
5 Comparison word
6 Justice's garb
7 Hawkish god
8 Garden walkway
9 Carnivorous fish
10 Following orders
11 Overeat, with "out"
12 Commando's weapon
13 Mas' mates
21 Removes a squeak from
22 ___ out a living
25 Barn topper
26 Actress Moran
27 Undo a change
29 CD predecessors
30 ___ pole
31 Orderly formation
32 Rover's restraint
35 ___ morgana (mirage)
36 Hollywood's Ken or Lena
37 Tiara inlays
38 Ali moniker, with "the"
40 Vote for
43 Where the Raptors play
45 Snick and ___ (thrust and cut)
47 Vote against
48 Soap operas, e.g.
49 Glass ingredient
52 Lab heaters
53 Tool buildings
55 Director Preminger
56 River to the Caspian
57 Tear apart
58 Pianist Dame Myra
59 Dada founder
60 Fish eggs
61 ___ Cruces, N.M.

by Jon Delfin

ACROSS

1 Taurus or Aries
5 Louis of the F.B.I.
10 Fat-free?
14 Restaurant chain initials
15 Baseball Hall-of-Famer Combs
16 Scarlett's home
17 Bob Dylan, né ____, 5/24/41
20 Hilton rival
21 Journalist Sawyer
22 Penultimate fairy tale word
23 Radar screen image
25 Wine expert, maybe
28 Stadium harassment
29 Rocker Ocasek
32 Part of Q.E.D.
33 Dallas suburb
34 Musician Brian
35 Bob Dylan-penned hit of 1965
39 Luau treat
40 Van Gogh home, for a time
41 First of a famous sailing trio
42 Have title to
43 Polygraph detections
44 You may have a hand in it
46 Husky's tow
47 Trapper John's post
48 Wax eloquent
51 Chemists' knowledge
55 Bob Dylan's birthplace
58 Israel's Abba
59 Steaming mad
60 Son of Aphrodite

61 Mailed
62 Fragrant compound
63 HUD, for one: Abbr.

DOWN

1 Snobs put them on
2 "I think I goofed"
3 Soliloquy start
4 Gilbert and Sullivan specialty
5 Put in leg-irons
6 Stubble remover
7 Leprechaun land
8 Freddy Krueger's street
9 Skirt's edge
10 Do a full monty

11 Tibetan holy man
12 1979 hostage site
13 Lion's tresses
18 Carry on
19 The Wizard of Menlo Park
23 Sty dwellers
24 Burt's ex
25 Metronome setting
26 Item in a quiver
27 Lustrous fabric
28 Rhythm's partner
29 Mail, as payment
30 Nonsensical
31 Barbarian of pulp tales
33 Propelled, as a gondola

36 Xylophone striker
37 Mold-ripened cheese
38 Showed great interest
44 Eliot's miser
45 "Woe ___!"
46 Movie double's task
47 ___ Cristo
48 Keatsian works
49 Bumpkin
50 Shepard in space
51 Via Veneto car
52 Handed-down history
53 On
54 Orient
56 Hurry
57 "___ Doubtfire"

by John D. Leavy

ACROSS

1 Operatic voices
6 Bankroll, e.g.
9 "Dancing Queen" pop group
13 Take under one's wing
14 Eager
16 Exerciser's target
17 Film starring 60-Across, 1941
19 Mentor
20 A few chips, perhaps
21 Glory (in)
22 Passion
23 Prince of Monaco
25 "Give ___ rest!"
27 "i" completer
28 Film starring 60-Across, 1952
33 Bricklayer
36 Dayan of the Six-Day War
37 French article
38 Film starring 60-Across, 1932
41 Actor Stephen
42 "À votre ___!"
43 Like most clocks in April and October
44 Film starring 60-Across, 1954
46 It's off la côte de France
47 Swab
48 "The fatal egg by Pleasure laid": Cowper
52 Coffee, in a beanery
55 Ring exchange site
58 Clairvoyant
59 Don Juan's mother
60 Actor born in May 1901
62 Nightly comic
63 Pinza of "South Pacific"

64 Sports replay technique
65 Two-screen cinema
66 Hither's partner
67 Fall flower

DOWN

1 Elephant of children's lit
2 Turkish city
3 Sir Georg of the Chicago Symphony
4 Magnificence
5 "Was ___ blame?"
6 Eucharist bread
7 Tel ___
8 Dreadful
9 Knitted blanket
10 Azure
11 Vamp Theda
12 Touch on
15 Tickle pink
18 Worry
24 "The Bald Soprano" playwright
26 Math statement
28 Football coach Lou
29 Capri, e.g.
30 Not theirs
31 "This one's ___!"
32 Hatching place
33 Baseball's Throneberry
34 Without ___ (pro bono)
35 ___ Basin, German coal region
36 Restaurant card

39 Wood distortion
40 Spray cans
45 Woman warrior
46 Thermometer fill: Abbr.
48 Cotton alternative
49 Move, as plants
50 "If You Could ___ Now"
51 Wrong move
52 Send a Dear John letter
53 Freshly
54 "___, vidi, vici"
56 Never getting off one's duff
57 Threesome
61 Explorer Johnson

by Frances Hansen

ACROSS

1 Besides
5 "Cómo ___ usted?"
9 City near Düsseldorf
14 They hang around
16 Accustom: Var.
17 Southern lights
19 Take the conn
20 Noted monologuist
21 Hwys.
22 W. Hemisphere grp.
24 Scope
26 Window bases
29 "Mon Oncle" star Jacques
31 It comes before a dropped name
34 29 for copper, e.g.: Abbr.
35 Choo-choo's sound
37 Lowest in importance
39 Game you can lose only once
42 Fastening devices
43 Labor
44 Roger of "Cheers"
45 Cardinal's insignia
46 Those, to José
48 Choker
50 Out of port
52 Scull propeller
53 Der ___ (Konrad Adenauer)
55 Musical Horne
58 Having no chips left to bet
63 Explosive stuff
66 Sleeping perch
67 Most minuscule
68 Queen ___ lace
69 "What ___?"
70 J.F.K. arrivals

DOWN

1 "What a pity!"
2 Boor
3 Dam's counterpart
4 Oklahoma Indian
5 Detergent brand
6 What some pups grow up to be
7 50/50 test choice
8 Org.
9 Poetic adverb
10 Marching band drum
11 Brunei and Oman, e.g.
12 Toledo's lake
13 1987 role for Costner
15 Actor Flynn
18 Perfectly
23 Wirehair of film
25 Small brook
26 Daring feat
27 Attic covering, maybe
28 Found's partner
29 Pamplona runners
30 Yours: Fr.
32 Cosmetician Lauder
33 Hot seasons in Québec
34 They might be fine
36 Aware of
38 Architect Saarinen
40 "Gotcha"
41 It parallels the radius
47 Brining need
49 Tough tests
51 Feel
52 Hall's singing partner
53 Razor brand
54 "Dianetics" author ___ Hubbard
56 One-named artist
57 Winter air
59 Pitcher Tiant
60 Directors Ang and Spike
61 M.I.T. part: Abbr.
62 Captures
64 "___ a girl!"
65 Point value in Scrabble of every letter in this puzzle

by Peter Gordon

ACROSS

1 What you pay
5 Mideast theocracy
9 Mustard choice
14 English painter John ___
15 Crèche trio
16 Put up
17 "The Wild Bunch" director
19 Fergie, formally
20 Rorschach test stuff
21 Martini's partner
22 Go out with
23 Varnish resin
25 Ballet bend
27 Soccer standout Hamm
30 Stengel's Yankees, e.g.
33 Pulls the plug on
35 Gossamery
37 "Finally!"
38 Jacob's first wife
41 Theme of this puzzle?
43 Frighten away
44 In high spirits
46 ___ Gay
48 Mind teaser
49 Not good at schmoozing
53 Euro forerunner
54 Pull an all-nighter
57 Scene
58 Canterbury can
60 Nouveau ___
63 Pendulum's path
64 Shi'ite's deity
66 Big Indian
68 "Swell!"
69 Skip by
70 Go out with
71 With 45-Down, C_2H_5OH
72 Ready to pluck
73 From the U.S.: Abbr.

DOWN

1 Made a mimeo of
2 Forthright
3 Make queasy
4 1990's sci-fi series "___ War"
5 "___ Angel" (Mae West film)
6 Séance noises
7 Visibly horrified
8 It meant nothing to Nero
9 Feast finale
10 "Dies ___"
11 Book before Lamentations
12 Mozart's "L'___ del Cairo"
13 Ultimate in degree
18 From Kilkenny
24 Potato option
26 Some potatoes
28 ___ many words
29 Regarding
31 Lab worker, perhaps
32 Vote of support
34 ___-Lorraine
36 Ham holder
38 Angler's purchase
39 "Beowulf," for one
40 First king of Jordan
42 Santa ___ winds
45 See 71-Across
47 What "-phile" means
50 Stuck
51 Compound of gold
52 Dirty old man
55 Jouster's garb
56 Dolphins' home
59 Like Cheerios
61 Pentium product
62 Can't stomach
64 Actress Sue ___ Langdon
65 Court do-over
67 Toothpaste-endorsing org.

by Alfio Micci

ACROSS

1 Delhi dress
5 Bloke
9 String bean's opposite
14 Take note of
15 City on the Tiber
16 Can't stomach
17 Song for Lily Pons
18 Manual reader, say
19 Where you might find a 7-Down
20 Ale on the top shelf?
23 Lady of León
24 Clay, now
25 Radio V.I.P.'s
28 Botheration
30 Cracker-requesting bird
33 Jason's ship
37 Malevolent
40 Supreme Ross
41 Packard of Hewlett-Packard, say?
44 Like a 10
45 Apple's apple, e.g.
46 Gusto
47 One who'll give you a hand
49 Lunch hour
51 W. C. Fields persona
52 "Shoot!"
55 Bad thing to bear
60 Smart goat?
64 Public spat
66 Goose egg
67 X and Y, maybe
68 Take to the soapbox
69 Pizzazz
70 Show respect to a judge
71 Lord of poetry
72 Eye sore
73 Subway Series team

DOWN

1 Persian potentates
2 Lofty home
3 Be in charge
4 Coeur d'Alene's home
5 Nader, notably
6 Parasite's place
7 Amorphous creature
8 Jeopardy
9 Yom Kippur ritual
10 Up to the job
11 Junky
12 "Auld" land
13 Hematite, for one
21 Chapter in history
22 Stiff's omission
26 Olympic track gold medalist Marion
27 Kick off
29 Oxeye window shape
31 Org. concerned with tooth care
32 Cracker name
33 H_2SO_4 and such
34 Place for a fast buck
35 Ursa Major
36 Birthstone after sapphire
38 "How was ___ know?"
39 Building block brand
42 Ringside cheer
43 Like the dinosaurs
48 Squealer
50 Before, to bards
53 Analyzes, with "up"
54 Prepared to be dubbed
56 Render harmless
57 The Old South
58 Partygoer
59 Twisty turns
61 Golden rule word
62 Suffix with nine, but not ten
63 Civil War side, with "the"
64 Weep
65 Weep

by Tyler Hinman

ACROSS

1 Burrito filler
5 Send out
9 Brown ermine
14 Bowser's bowlful
15 Sari wearer
16 Blood carrier
17 Shipping method
18 Pay to play
19 Out-and-out
20 1965 Beatles #1 hit
23 Santa ___ winds
24 Rocky hill
25 Light-footed
29 Shakespeare's Sir Toby
31 It has a low pH
34 Cousin of a puffin
35 Start of long-distance dialing
37 Friendly
40 A nod could express it
43 48-card game
44 "What a good boy ___!"
45 Giant Hall-of-Famer
46 Altar site
48 Mystery writer's award
52 Skull-and-crossbones stuff
55 Jazzman Adderley
57 Cause of wrinkles
58 Part of a Pope poem
62 Scroll in an ark
65 Yankee nickname
66 Baptism or bris
67 Orléans's river
68 The avenging Mrs. Peel
69 Once more
70 Having secret marks, maybe
71 Reach across
72 Result of downsizing

DOWN

1 Toper's total
2 "Seinfeld" gal
3 Like DeMille films
4 Coffeehouse music
5 Poetry Muse
6 "Om," e.g.
7 Keen about
8 Echelon
9 King Fahd, for one
10 Family emblem
11 Food scrap
12 Scarfed down
13 La Brea goo
21 Like Archie Bunker's humor
22 Mrs. Gandhi
26 Rum cake
27 Slow period
28 ___ out a win
30 Chanel of fashion
32 Dynamic Duo's garb
33 Babysitter's handful
36 Odorless gas
38 Arrives à la the Iceman
39 Rah-rah
40 Former Yugoslavian president
41 Lock opener?
42 Chalet site
43 Half of a store-owning duo
47 Something inexplicable
49 Street girl
50 Playing marbles
51 Takes more Time?
53 It may be glassy or icy
54 Marveled aloud
56 Like 60% of the world's people
59 Whiskeys
60 Easy win
61 Russia's ___ Mountains
62 Special touch, in brief
63 A winning combination in today's puzzle theme
64 Purge

by Stephen Windheim

ACROSS

1 Not just a hit
6 Jeff MacNelly comic
10 Uncertain
14 Vena cava neighbor
15 Raise a red flag
16 "The Lion King" lion
17 Special soldier
19 Result of using the wrong film speed, maybe
20 Dusk, to Donne
21 Prod
22 Stirred up
24 Hoosegow
26 Uncle Miltie
27 Boat maneuverer
28 Villain in a western
31 Where the Blue Nile and White Nile meet
34 Butchers' offerings
35 Spanish treasure
36 Not now
37 "You Light Up My Life" singer Boone
38 It's slipped in a slot
39 Ages and ages
40 Tijuana cash
41 When procrastinators don't do things
42 Wave with a foaming crest
44 ____-Magnon
45 Second family of the 1990's
46 Put on hold
50 Office building area
52 Like a sad sack
53 ____ bonne heure (very well): Fr.
54 Future Derby runner, maybe
55 Texas state flower
58 Chip in
59 O.K. Corral shooter
60 Where the deer and the antelope play
61 Film critic Rex
62 28-0, e.g.
63 Gallows reprieves

DOWN

1 Wise guys
2 Fancy mushroom
3 Sacramento's Arco ____
4 Sault ____ Marie
5 Children's game
6 Talk a blue streak?
7 Granitelike
8 Bauxite or magnetite
9 Plea
10 How stores buy things
11 Lie
12 Chimney part
13 Harvard ____
18 Transvaal settler
23 Mythical monsters
25 Complain
26 Yaks away
28 Some jazz
29 Strauss's "Mein Herr Marquis," e.g.
30 Award for "The Producers"
31 Bouillabaisse
32 Comment after an accident
33 Put down
34 Arizona sights
37 May-____ romance
38 "Rad!"
40 Andean land
41 Small quakes
43 Slaved away
44 Great Lakes fish
46 Caught some Z's
47 She's on TV for a spell
48 Mournful piece
49 Promgoers
50 From a distance
51 Inflection
52 Wizard
56 Thai neighbor
57 ____ King Cole

by Randall J. Hartman

ACROSS

1 "Gee whillikers!"
5 Deviate
9 Terra ___
14 Judge
15 Switch ending
16 Thai or Taiwanese
17 Suffix with fabric
18 Valley girl?
19 Mad
20 Alaska
23 High-ranking clergyman
24 ___ Fables
28 "Snow White and the Seven Dwarfs"
31 Biblical tower site
34 Home, informally
35 A, in Aachen
36 Dumbfounded
37 "___ say . . ."
39 Judge's seat
40 Org. governing two conferences
41 Japanese soup
42 Funny hitting sounds
43 The Clermont
47 Aloft
48 Supporter
52 What 20-, 28- and 43-Across each turned into
55 Cassette contents
58 Goes kaput
59 How many a product is advertised
60 Idolize
61 ". . . or ___!"
62 Lone Star State sch.
63 Windblown soil
64 Famed loch
65 Prepare a salad

DOWN

1 Hold
2 Horse opera
3 "Uncle Tom's Cabin" writer
4 Proclaimed
5 Grazing lands for gnus
6 Up
7 Massage deeply
8 It can be used to walk the dog
9 Ultraliberals
10 Arbitrary parental "explanation"
11 Eve's beginning
12 Month after avril
13 Additionally
21 Stairwell item
22 Catch, as a bronco
25 Western New York town
26 Toy piano sound
27 Does a film editor's job
29 ___ the line
30 Thus far
31 Canada's ___ National Park
32 Terrible
33 Mideastern dancer's asset
37 Burn lightly
38 Donkey
39 Three-fingered saluter
41 1820 White House residents
42 Group
44 Princeton team
45 Fixate (on)
46 Scoundrels
49 Fifty minutes past the hour
50 Adlai's running mate
51 Answers an invitation
53 Gulf of ___ (entrance to the Red Sea)
54 Mah-jongg piece
55 Prince in the comics, for short
56 Altar declaration
57 Female hare

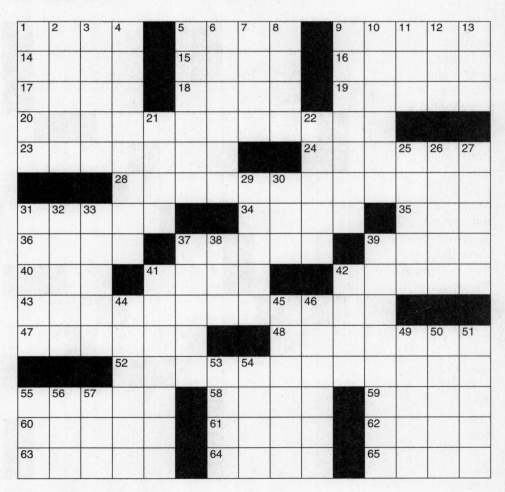

by Patrick Merrell

ACROSS

1 Check point?
5 Like Swiss cheese
10 Tartan garb
14 Iris's place
15 Dean Martin song subject
16 Eligible for service
17 "So long"
19 Pull the plug on
20 Much of the surface of Mars
21 Carried
22 Most Foreman wins, informally
23 "Farewell"
26 Purplish red
30 Aria
31 Essay page, for short
32 ". . . and ___ a good-night"
34 Nile slitherer
37 International writers' org.
38 "Adieu"
40 Strong alkali
41 Approx. number
42 Textile trademark
43 Carry on
44 Mussolini, e.g.
45 Crucial element
48 "Toodle-oo"
52 ___ Xing
53 Campaign speech, e.g.
54 Way-out
58 Colonel or corporal
59 "Until next time . . ."
62 Nosh
63 "The Story of ___ H"
64 Give as an example
65 Do in
66 Ruth ___ Ginsburg
67 Was able to answer on a test

DOWN

1 Kind of stop
2 With: Fr.
3 ___-do-well
4 Traveled like an Inuit
5 Most vigorous
6 Gen. Bradley
7 "___ luck!"
8 Bard's "before"
9 "So's ___ old man!"
10 Where 48-Down fought in 1999
11 Words from an emcee
12 Actress Téa
13 Come to a point
18 Lots
21 Scarlett O'Hara, e.g.
24 Of service
25 ___-poly
26 Wear a long face
27 Bronx Zoo houseful
28 Lady's escort
29 Act of Contrition reciter
33 Poem of praise
34 Greenspan of the Fed
35 Lip-___
36 Tampa-St. ___
38 Obese's opposite
39 Predatory whale
43 Not the most refined fellow
44 Mule's father
46 More nimble
47 Musical chairs goal
48 European group
49 To no ___
50 Buttinsky
51 Made a request
55 Prefix with drama
56 Yardage pickup
57 Villa d' ___
59 Bar bill
60 Orthodontists' org.
61 Fine-grained wood

by Fred Piscop

ACROSS

1 Filch
6 Cook's canful
10 Burn a bit
14 Garbage can insert
15 S-shaped curve
16 Swear words?
17 Blazing
18 It has "county" and "city" inside
20 Software test version
21 "Tiger Lilies" novelist Sidney
22 Kipling classic
23 Urge forward
25 Speak evil of
27 Kuwait's peninsula
29 Subway entrance
30 It has "round" inside
31 Curiosity victim
32 God with a hammer
36 Prepared to be dubbed
37 Zilch
38 Tick off
39 Thompson of "Pollock"
40 Hall & Oates, e.g.
41 It has "bare" inside
42 Prepare for competition
44 Show the ropes to
45 Avian messengers
48 Diviner's deck
49 N.Y.C.'s Park, e.g.
50 Tackle box gizmo
52 Saws with the grain
55 It has "can" and "tin" inside
57 Gem surface
58 Toledo's lake
59 Tenn. neighbor
60 Geographical "boot"

61 Turned blue, perhaps
62 Inheritance factor
63 Fax forerunner

DOWN

1 Bacon portion
2 Bachelor's lack
3 Welcomed as a brother
4 It has "amble" and "ramble" inside
5 Bard's before
6 Milk train, e.g.
7 Literary conflict
8 Payment
9 Mark for misconduct
10 Hoodwink

11 Japanese verse
12 Web site?
13 What 11-Down doesn't do
19 Caspian feeder
21 Sinker material
24 Stout serving
26 It has "rot" and "die" inside
27 Commodious boats
28 Gossipy Barrett
29 It has "son" inside
33 Dissenting, to the church
34 Place for a roast
35 Monopoly payment

37 Dennis, to Mr. Wilson
38 Henry VIII's sixth
40 Ballroom activity
41 Tusked animal
43 Parks in 1955 news
45 Waited for baby?
46 Poacher's haul
47 One to rub out?
48 ___ Haute, Ind.
51 Like good hamburger meat
53 Soccer icon
54 Charon's waterway
56 Mack of early TV
57 Athletic

by Gayle Dean

ACROSS

1 Jazz lick
5 Item on a to-do list
9 Intriguing bunch
14 Letters on a cross
15 Widemouthed jug
16 Use a soapbox
17 The big house
18 Churn
19 Gets a lift
20 Nickname for Leona Helmsley
23 Keats praised one
24 Harper's Bazaar illustrator
25 Second shot
30 Make beloved
32 Piled up
33 In no particular key
36 Take seriously
37 Interstate divider
41 Like some exhausts
42 Trump Castle employee
43 Neighbor of Georgia
46 Lure into crime
50 Dynamo part
51 Empty spaces
53 "___ Gang"
54 "People Are People" rock group
57 ___ dish (lab vessel)
61 This, in Tijuana
62 "Jake's Thing" author
63 Doughnut-shaped
64 Kind of collar
65 Riga resident
66 Take potshots (at)
67 Fresh-mouthed
68 Guesstimate phrase

DOWN

1 Suggestive
2 Sequentially
3 Quaker
4 Send packing
5 It's another day
6 In flight
7 Gunk
8 Curly cabbage
9 Eye bank donation
10 Meyers of "Kate & Allie"
11 Good, in the 'hood
12 Broke a fast
13 Brown of renown
21 Poet's "below"
22 It stays by your side
26 Summer top
27 Out of port
28 Wail like a banshee
29 Announcer Hall
31 Aerie hatchling
32 Soprano Gluck
34 Nothin'
35 Yeoman's yes
37 On the disabled list
38 "___ Camera"
39 Seuss's Horton, for one
40 Not the brightest bulb on the tree
41 Courtroom V.I.P.'s
44 "Ixnay!"
45 Spleen
47 B & B patron
48 Financial checks
49 Magic word
51 "Beau ___"
52 Oscar contender
55 "Don't make a ___!"
56 Saint-___ (French seaport)
57 Quart divs.
58 Seemingly forever
59 Part of TNT
60 Dead letters?

by Sarah Keller

ACROSS

1 Does origami
6 Antenna type
10 LP flaw
14 Give or take
15 Bat's navigation aid
16 Sonata finale
17 New Boy Scout
19 Assayers' samples
20 54-Across logo
21 Brownie ____ (things to earn)
22 Afternoon socials
23 Pedestal topper
24 Protect, in a way
26 Lakefront home feature
31 Bummed around
32 ____-Rooter
33 Wing it, musically
36 Tabloid fliers
37 Maps out
39 Miss Horne
40 Norm: Abbr.
41 Julia's Oscar-winning role
42 Add a lane to, say
43 1969 Shirley MacLaine musical
46 Hidden away
49 Mother of Helen of Troy
50 Pulitzer winner James
51 Give confidence to
54 Letterman's network
57 Wrestling hold
58 Torturer's tool
60 Niagara River source
61 "I dropped it!"
62 Classic toothpaste brand
63 Word that can follow the ends of 17-, 26-, 43- and 58-Across
64 Like Santa's cheeks
65 Off-the-wall

DOWN

1 Lot in life
2 Old wedding vows word
3 Like a recluse
4 Fizzler
5 Blended family member
6 Desecrate
7 PC pictograph
8 Totally gone
9 Stressful spots
10 Rob Roy need
11 "M*A*S*H" setting
12 Think tank nuggets
13 No longer in vogue
18 Dig (for)
23 Currier's partner
25 Sgt., for one
26 "Besides that . . ."
27 Flat floater
28 Shirt with a reptilian logo
29 Type of goose
30 Countless years
33 ____ Knight
34 Work without ____ (take risks)
35 A zillion
37 Shark or T. rex
38 Tell a whopper
39 Milano moolah
41 Merino mother
42 Gets wet up to the ankles
43 Israeli money
44 All thumbs
45 Tarragon or chervil
46 Biblical spy
47 Ancient marketplace
48 Beany's TV friend
52 "Get lost!"
53 Has a late meal
54 Pluto or auto ending
55 Needing straightening
56 Swing in the breeze
59 PC "brain"

by Mark P. Sherwood

ACROSS

1 NaCl
5 "Waiting for Lefty" playwright
10 Adventure hero Swift
13 Jai ___
14 Detective's skill
15 Lie in the sun
16 Like some mirrors
18 ___ interview
19 Rage, e.g., onstage
20 Ratfinks
22 It's a long story
25 Veg out
26 Splatter protector
29 Louisiana senator, 1948–87
34 Veg out
36 Something to gloss over?
37 Moses' older brother
38 Looped handle
39 Bochco TV drama
42 Vamp Theda
43 Nobelist Bohr
45 C.S.A. state
46 Rebounds per game, e.g.
47 WKRP, e.g.
51 MS. markers
52 Pisa dough
53 Hot pot or pepper pot
55 Do Zen
59 "Out!"
63 Tennis great Lendl
64 Depictions of fruits, say
67 Bog
68 The Jetson boy
69 Theater schlepper
70 Animal with horns
71 Witherspoon of "Legally Blonde"
72 Devout

DOWN

1 Call at home?
2 Dubya, to Yale
3 Composer Schifrin
4 Flipper freezers
5 Grand ___ Opry
6 Slip into
7 Omelet base
8 Pro football's Bald Eagle
9 Group of fish
10 Curbside call
11 Tom Joad, for one
12 "Miracle" team of 1969
15 Transistor developers
17 King of tragedy
21 Earthen pot
23 Web-footed flier
24 Nepal's locale
26 "That's all, folks!" voice
27 Ancient Aegean Sea region
28 City on the Rhine
30 Water balloon sound
31 Emulate Demosthenes
32 Org. that "tracks" Santa
33 Airborne pests
35 Highland/lowland separator
40 Schooner fillers
41 Witch's blemish
44 Gill opening
48 Pencil's end
49 Act the snitch
50 Auction off
54 Raise, as an anchor
55 Charades, essentially
56 Wickedness
57 Like some turkey meat
58 Land of Molly Bloom
60 Woodstock hairdo
61 Bridal accessory
62 Catch sight of
65 ___ Alamos, N.M.
66 NaOH or KOH

by Randall J. Hartman

ACROSS

1 ". . . why ___ thou forsaken me?"
5 Swimmer's unit
8 Steak order
13 Doo-wop group member
14 Wyo. neighbor
15 "Two ___" (Sophia Loren film)
16 One with forked tongue
17 "Annie ___" (winner of two Oscars)
18 ___ bond (link between two particles of opposing charge)
19 "Two Gentlemen of ___"
21 Two or more 25-Acrosses, geologically: Var.
23 Suffix with percent or project
24 A penny has two of them
25 Historic time
27 Second-stringers
29 Two-___ conversion (touchdown follower, sometimes)
31 ___-totter (toy for two)
35 Mil. address
37 Western tribesmen
39 ___ double (bet in which two winners must be picked)
40 High-five sound
41 Pooped
43 Prefix with commute or conference
44 Of a pelvic bone
46 "Who ___ Turn To?"
47 The two Begleys
48 Two-way ___ (psychology lab fixture)
50 Nine-___ (short golf course)
52 Govt. investigator
54 Blushing
55 One of two in the play "Shylock Returns"
58 Orch. section
61 Like two ___ in a pod
63 Two-___ (yawl or brig, e.g.)
65 Pseudonymous "Under Two Flags" author
67 Isl. of Australia
69 Don Ho's "___ Bubbles"

70 Combination of two or more sets, in math
71 Two-dimensional extent
72 911 responders
73 Fresh-mouthed
74 Johnnie Cochran's field
75 A real pain

DOWN

1 Split in two
2 Little green man
3 The two in a binary celestial body
4 Pamplona runner
5 Mauna ___
6 ___ breve (2/2 time, in music)
7 The two on a battery
8 Either of two matched pieces of furniture
9 Response to an ump, maybe

10 Former science magazine
11 "Chapter Two" playwright Simon
12 Suffix with refer or prefer
14 Two-wheeled vehicle of old
20 Recent: Prefix
22 Two-___ rally (bit of baseball excitement)
26 Bit of high jinks
28 Two-___ (Corvette, e.g.)
29 Warhol's genre
30 Synagogue scroll
32 Connected, as two musical notes
33 Pipe elbows
34 Corned beef holder
35 "___ want for Christmas . . ."
36 Twosome

38 Man of Málaga
40 Scrooge player Alastair
42 Choice between two unfavorable options
45 Two, in a proverb
49 ___ Dawn Chong
51 Writer LeShan
53 Brazilian seaport
55 Two at ___ (in couples)
56 Put in one's two ___ worth
57 Motel meeting, maybe
58 ___ -chef (number two person in a kitchen)
59 Fish in a melt
60 Reformer Jacob
62 "Two Mules for Sister ___" (Clint Eastwood film)
64 Two-___ (ballroom dance)
66 Two, in Tijuana
68 Use a Singer

by Fred Piscop

ACROSS

1 Big blowout
5 Little dent
9 Candidate's concern
14 1977 movie in which Bo Derek's leg is bitten off
15 Snack item since 1912
16 Rover
17 Statement from actor Rob's debtors?
19 Hot trend
20 Rock's Brian ___
21 Disney's Ludwig ___ Drake
22 Make more attractive
24 Dr. Dre, for one
26 Columbia Pictures founder
27 Monochromatic rock?
33 Up to snuff
36 Junior, to Senior
37 Holy ___
38 Plunders
40 Took in
42 College bigwigs
43 Water channel
45 Slalom track
47 Lotion ingredient
48 Aged, unemotional shrew?
51 Pointer's word
52 "A Hard Day's Night" director
56 Reports by phone
60 Hail, to Caesar
61 Stowe girl
62 Self-evident truth
63 Question from an uncertain Osiris?
66 It may be about a yard
67 Casing
68 Prelude to a duel
69 First name in rock since 1970
70 Put up
71 A zillion

DOWN

1 Shady spot
2 Kind of football
3 Lois Lane exclusive
4 Turn left
5 Del Rio of film
6 Tend to pressing business
7 Just out
8 Keeps at it
9 Hopping mad
10 "Encore!"
11 Latin I word
12 A crystal ball user has it
13 Worry-free locale
18 Roulette bet
23 Put an edge on
25 Like some justice
26 Dispute
28 Words in a dedication
29 Radial surfaces
30 Viva-voce
31 Dessert, say, to a dieter
32 Limerick language
33 Besides
34 Weevil's target
35 Garish
39 Followers of Robert Bruce
41 PC key
44 Like some schoolbook publishers
46 What you're doing now
49 Coffee accompaniment, maybe
50 Wine sediment
53 Colleague of Edison
54 Perrier alternative
55 Hoarse
56 Soup and sandwich spot
57 Jump on the ice
58 Kind of trap
59 Nuts
60 Speller's phrase
64 Reggae relative
65 Doctrine

by Richard Silvestri

ACROSS

1 Like many
   a wrestler
6 Balance
   sheet item
10 One of a
   great quintet
14 ___ Rogers
   St. Johns
15 Alice's
   chronicler
16 Beasts in a span
17 Purple shade
18 Plowman's need
19 Cutlass maker,
   briefly
20 Start of a quip
   about middle age
23 "Star Wars"
   walkons
24 Kachina
   doll makers
25 Embellish,
   in a way
28 It may be
   upside-down
31 Fireplace
35 Org. with a
   much-cited journal
36 Needing patches
37 Micromanager's
   concern
38 Middle of the quip
41 Grand
42 It's insurable
43 Ike's command,
   once: Abbr.
44 Small songbirds
45 Blackthorn fruit
46 Ruse
47 Blame bearer
49 Smoker or diner
51 End of the quip
58 Steinbeck hero
59 Scads
60 When repeated, an
   Ivy League tune
61 Social introduction?
62 Baltic port
63 Packing heat

64 "___ here long?"
65 Object of blind
   devotion
66 Aggressive sort

DOWN

1 Java neighbor
2 Tinker with,
   in a way
3 Fish lacking
   ventral fins
4 Full of holes
5 Spinnaker's place
6 Extremely,
   informally
7 ". . . ___ saw
   Elba"
8 Cheerful
9 Old TV sidekick

10 Investigate
11 Linchpin's place
12 Reebok competitor
13 Pulver's rank: Abbr.
21 Accompanist?
22 Pricing word
25 Bochco TV drama
26 Love affair
27 Place to practice
   driving
29 Class in which
   posers are presented
30 Small hill
32 Court
   attention-getter
33 Be still, at sea
34 N.F.L. great Hirsch
36 Smith's partner
37 Cause for a recall

39 Kipling classic
40 Earth Summit site
45 Stone-faced
46 Monk's home,
   maybe
48 Arcade name
50 Chance to swing
51 Calisthenics
   improve it
52 Motive for
   some crime
53 Full of energy
54 List ender
55 Win big
56 Virginia's
   Robert ___
57 Arp movement
58 Front end of a
   one-two

by Alan Arbesfeld

ACROSS

1 Cracker toppers
6 "Dirty" activity
10 Director's call
13 Javelin, for one
14 Having a strong resemblance
15 Botanist Gray
16 Nurse's office supply
18 Difficulty, to the Bard
19 Like a gardener's pants
20 Stellar
22 "Rocky II" climax
24 Links unit
25 Light reflection ratio
28 Bomb squad worker
30 Modeling medium
31 Believing that the universe has a soul
35 Thunder Bay's prov.
36 Place to put the feet up
38 Lennon's love
39 Uncages
41 Semicircular recess
42 Theater name
43 Victim of hair loss?
45 Austen heroine
47 Water current in the same direction as the wind
50 Windy one
52 Gun manufacturers
56 Mentalist Geller
57 Millionaire makers
59 Cacophony
60 Capone rival
61 Plume source
62 Legal conclusion?
63 Jump over
64 Places for forks

DOWN

1 Amount of trouble?
2 Bristol's county
3 Head overseas
4 Penetrated
5 Put on board
6 Mole, maybe
7 A little squirt?
8 "I Cain't Say No" musical
9 Minus
10 Redheads
11 Bar order, with "the"
12 Spreadsheet section
14 Start of a magician's cry
17 Pitcher Hideo ___
21 Jefferson or Edison: Abbr.
23 Whodunit start
25 Roll call misser
26 Hermitic
27 Bean counter's concern
29 Bargain basement unit
31 In total agreement (with)
32 Dissenting votes
33 ___ many words
34 Filmdom's Ethan or Joel
36 Relative of "Hurrah!"
37 Shop area
40 Nebr. neighbor
41 Explorer Vespucci
43 Fool
44 Quite the fan
45 Schumann work
46 Slugger in 1961 news
48 Bother
49 Suffix in nuclear physics
51 Adm. Zumwalt
53 University founder Cornell
54 Marsh plant
55 Members of a fast fleet
58 Prefix with angular

by David Ainslie Macleod

ACROSS

1 Ship's complement
5 Atlas feature
10 Call's mate
14 Lifesaver
15 Yankees manager Joe
16 Nobelist Wiesel
17 Tech sch. grad
18 Beginning of a quote by W. C. Fields
20 Paparazzo's purchase
22 Place for the undecided
23 Hawaii County's seat
24 Military assaults
26 Quote, part 2
30 Napoleon, notably
31 Debatable
32 It'll take your breath away
35 Easy stride
36 Settle, in a way
38 L.B.J. in-law
39 Coast Guard off.
40 Outstanding
41 Cliffside dwelling
42 Quote, part 3
45 Got bored stiff
49 Bond foe
50 Galloping
51 Astronomer Copernicus
55 End of the quote
58 It towers over Taormina
59 It may be belted
60 Asian capital
61 Actor ___ Patrick Harris
62 ___ 'acte
63 Midway alternative
64 Kind of case

DOWN

1 Word in French restaurant names
2 Betting setting
3 Thus
4 Unwelcome sight on an apple
5 ". . . is fear ___"
6 "Later!"
7 Sp. ladies
8 Go off
9 Holiday in 60-Across
10 Feature of a miter joint
11 Film role for Kate Nelligan
12 "Odyssey" enchantress
13 Conservative Alan
19 Note in the C minor scale
21 Long sentence
24 Ancient colonnade
25 Mariner's cry
26 Typographer's strike
27 Neurotransmission site
28 Sounds in pounds
29 Drive forward
32 Five-time Wimbledon champ
33 Big Apple award
34 "Not on ___!"
36 1960 Olympics site
37 An OK city
38 Like perfume
40 Half of a 45
41 Part of A.D.
43 Slate.com employee
44 Comics character with an "R" on his sweater
45 Pen
46 Like many kitchens
47 Nautical direction
48 Banks hold it
51 Notable caravel
52 Suit to ___
53 Colleges, to Aussies
54 It may be shaken
56 Sorority chapter
57 Baby's cry

by Jon Delfin

ACROSS

1 Short haircut
4 Check out, so to speak
8 Deaden
14 Bush spokesman Fleischer
15 Stationery quantity
16 Grim one?
17 Treat for a pup
19 Pooh pal
20 "That's ___ ask!"
21 Thin toast
23 Something to pick
24 Singer Sumac
26 Nevada senator Harry
27 The Internet's ___ Drudge
28 Baseball's first Hall-of-Famer
31 Introduction to economics?
33 Suffix with president
34 New England state sch.
36 Floppy disk?
40 Makes aware
42 1993 Earp portrayer
43 Groups within groups
44 Letters on many black churches
45 "Shoot!"
46 Simple chord
48 Prepares for a crash
50 Actress Russo
53 Deliberate affront
55 Theater admonition
56 "Xanadu" rock band
57 Painter Matisse
59 No room to swing ___
62 Tout's tidbit
65 W.W. II missile
67 Summary
68 Stick ___ in the water

69 Soccer standout Hamm
70 Smear
71 Foxx of "Sanford and Son"
72 Cold comment?

DOWN

1 Cake with a kick
2 Pitcher Hershiser
3 Copper's bopper
4 Trombonist Kid ___
5 Idea's beginning
6 "Headliners & Legends" host
7 Hammer and sickle, e.g.
8 Tidbit for a bird feeder
9 Superwide
10 Nonpro?
11 "Once ___ Honeymoon" (1942 film)
12 Reason for a raise
13 Quarterback Favre
18 Long ride?
22 1967 seceder
25 Addict, e.g.
27 Shaded growth
28 Rapid blinks, maybe
29 Manchurian border river
30 Where to have a banger
32 Staircase parts
35 Cuckoo

37 Scavenge, in a way
38 Otherwise
39 Fraternal group
41 Family of patrons of the arts
47 "The Sport of the Gods" author
49 Fictional whaler
50 Get-well center
51 Bond on the run
52 Prominent
54 Savage sort
58 Classic shirt brand
60 Gulf States bigwig
61 Winter lift
63 Chorus syllable
64 Hosp. section
66 The end, to 'Enry

by Kent Lorentzen

ACROSS

1 Stored, as honey
6 Name prefix meaning "son of"
9 Make provision (for)
14 Where drachmas were once spent
15 "Son ___ gun!"
16 Sponger
17 Start of an idle question
20 Many namesakes: Abbr.
21 State tree of New Jersey
22 "Psst! Pass ___!"
23 ___ Affair
24 Baseball's strikeout king
26 Scharnhorst admiral
29 Yokels
31 Decline
34 Big name in philanthropy
37 Bologna's place
39 Question, part 2
41 Pressure, in a way
42 Surmounted
43 Person who knows the drill?: Abbr.
44 Slingshot item
46 Much binary code
47 Joint tenant's place?
48 Way to stand
50 Spanish ayes
53 Brings out
56 Cross shape
59 End of the question
62 Deborah of "Days of Our Lives"
63 Sign of aging
64 Prepare for reuse, perhaps
65 Parable's message
66 Old pronoun
67 No longer in

DOWN

1 Muslim pilgrimage
2 Operatic prince
3 R.S.V.P. part
4 East ender?
5 Holstein's home
6 Anticipation or sadness, e.g.
7 Onetime Michael Jackson do
8 Trans Am rival
9 "Aladdin" prince
10 Red Square figure
11 Riga resident
12 ___ Rios, Jamaica
13 Declaration of Independence starter
18 Shriner topper
19 Go into free-fall
23 Hard-to-combine gas
25 Up and about
26 Burn
27 Skinned
28 "Aunt ___ Cope Book"
29 Massenet's "Le ___"
30 Deceived
31 Name in 2000 headlines
32 Ecological community
33 Deadly poisons
35 Irregularly notched
36 Made tame
38 Cravat's cousin
40 "___ seen enough!"
45 Guinness adjective
47 Paramecium propellers
48 Its tip may be felt
49 Set, as a price
50 Chang and Eng's homeland
51 ___ -European
52 Mark for life
54 Jazz home
55 Shrewd
56 Precisely
57 Nave neighbor
58 Played for a sap
60 Net location
61 La-la starter

by Robert Dillman

ACROSS

1 Pocahontas's husband
6 Invitation to duel, perhaps
10 Close to closed
14 Intense hatred
15 Tabula ___
16 Ankle-length skirt
17 Nearing the hour
18 James Bond beauties?
20 Titan orbits it
22 St. ___ (spring break spot)
23 Drop in on
24 Bar choices
26 Feather's mate
27 Where to order un thé
30 Luau staple
32 Back from dreamland
37 ___ above
38 "Alfred" composer
40 Cameos, e.g.
41 Marine creatures with unneeded limbs?
44 Masked critters
45 L.B.J. son-in-law
46 Barrie pirate
47 Buchholz of "The Magnificent Seven"
48 H.S.T.'s successor
49 Kickoff preceder
50 Absorbed, as a loss
53 Part of UHF: Abbr.
55 Pole worker
58 Kind of stand
60 Statement of the obvious
64 Emulate Prometheus?
67 Veep John ___ Garner
68 Word processor command
69 Custard concoction
70 "___ Marner"

71 Scraped (out)
72 Itches
73 Winter Palace residents

DOWN

1 Goes bad
2 Concert halls
3 Suit jacket buildup
4 2004 Olympics stars?
5 Atlanta university
6 A.A.R.P. members
7 Reindeer herder
8 So far
9 Elbows, but not knees
10 Horner's last words
11 Shakes up
12 Linchpin's place
13 Court order?
19 Actor Depardieu
21 Sherpa's home
25 More tender
27 Come down with
28 Allergy season sound
29 Uproar
31 ___ we trust
33 Least desirable wharves?
34 Something to remember?
35 "Dinner at Antoine's" author
36 They're common in Mississippi
39 Treble clef lines
42 What you will
43 Thumb-raising critic
51 Chewy candy
52 Send to Siberia
54 Surrealist Max
55 In ___ (actually)
56 Security lapse
57 Half a sawbuck
59 OPEC member
61 "To Live and Die ___"
62 Permanent marker?
63 Quantico cuisine
65 Zodiac's start, in England
66 U.S.N.A. grad

by Karen Hodge

ACROSS

1 White House nickname
4 Reaches a peak
10 Be a nag
14 Pother
15 Milk-related
16 Western Hemisphere abbr.
17 1984 Democratic keynoter
19 ___ doble (Spanish dance)
20 Come forth
21 Commit to another hitch
23 Small pointer
24 Have status
25 "Catch a Falling Star" singer
27 Queen, maybe
28 Throughway
30 Walk-ons, e.g.
31 Not averting one's eyes
33 Blatant deception
35 With 36-Across a depiction of Jesus
37 See 35-Across
37 On a branch, maybe
40 Do Little?
44 "___ man with seven wives"
45 Sailed through
46 Something to flip
47 Chief steward
50 Adriatic seaport
51 Rocker Brian
52 Break up with, and not nicely
53 Numbskull, to a Brit
55 Nice evening
57 Hypes a movie, perhaps
59 Word in many college names
60 Concern of 43-Down
61 "___ Rosenkavalier"

62 Margarine
63 Farmer, at times
64 Nus, to us

DOWN

1 Shooters' needs
2 Unyielding
3 Hot Lips portrayer
4 Plunger's target
5 Derby
6 Euro forerunner
7 On disk
8 Track official
9 Use elbow grease on
10 Salary limit
11 #1 hit for Jimmy Dorsey, 1941
12 Began again
13 Ask for a hand?
18 Choler
22 Cheops construction
25 Beeped
26 Barbizon School painter
28 One of two Plantagenet kings
29 Back then
32 Page 1, 3 or 5, e.g.
33 Harpo's interpreter
34 Directive to James
37 Olive stuffer

38 Common temple name
39 Exult
41 Apple-pie order?
42 Radial makers
43 Staff of Life
45 Fuse unit
48 Guys, slangily
49 Samuel Lover's "Rory ___"
50 Prickly seedcase
53 Game ending
54 On ___ with
56 Howe'er
58 Bummed

by A. J. Santora

ACROSS

1 Inventory's place
6 Opposite of baja
10 Singer Redding
14 University in Beaumont, Tex.
15 Wagered
16 Polite encl.
17 Like rams and lambs
18 Iris's locale
19 Religious image: Var.
20 Figured out a British royal
23 Word with drum or trumpet
24 Good times
25 Inventor Otis
27 Make way
31 Daisylike bloom
32 PC key
33 Capp and Green
35 Hoped-for low number: Abbr.
36 Invoiced a British royal
41 Fictional detective ___ Pym
42 The Reagan boy
43 Geologist's measure
44 Food of the gods
47 Aide's job
52 Crosses the threshold
54 G-man: Abbr.
55 Land's end
56 Discarded a British royal
60 Celestial hammerer
61 Area code 801 area
62 Is a bibliophile
63 Prefix with globin
64 Point of intersection
65 Identification

66 First place
67 Hitch, e.g.
68 Show of contempt

DOWN

1 Isn't flat
2 Go for
3 Displaced person, maybe
4 Country singer k. d. ___
5 Skydiver's start
6 Donors' group
7 Hawaiian bubbly?
8 Level
9 Saw
10 Underworld leader
11 Has an afternoon break
12 Line on a weather map showing equal temperatures
13 Clinton, e.g.: Abbr.
21 1970's Plymouth
22 ___ mode
26 Coach Parseghian
28 Friend
29 Occurs to, with "on"
30 Yalie
34 Toy holder?
36 Split
37 Avoids callers, say
38 1950 noir classic

39 Making daguerreotypes, and other things
40 Acct. earnings
41 Fr. woman
45 Synapse neighbor
46 Waterspout trajectory
48 Potpourri bag
49 Makes others wait
50 Rib
51 Quite a joke
53 Shut out
57 Harrow's rival
58 Carpenter's groove
59 Pull (in)
60 Many a 65-Across starter

by Noah Dephoure

ACROSS

1 Pilgrim's destination
6 Passing yardage, e.g.
10 Like many a cellar
14 ___ squash
15 Alice's chronicler
16 Three-ply snack
17 Mauritius, once?
19 Tackle
20 From scratch
21 Muumuu go-with
22 Point of view
23 Like black humor
25 Take the silver
28 St. Francis, e.g.?
33 First Super Bowl M.V.P.
36 Casual attire
37 Outback runner
38 Frame filler
39 Enzyme suffix
41 Mai ___
42 Prefix with night or day
43 Pose
44 French story
46 Gov't security
48 Waikiki wingding?
51 Gargle, e.g.
52 Free-for-all
56 Big brass
59 B.O. sign
61 Scrubbed mission
62 Crude bunch?
63 Passable party?
66 Part of a hat trick
67 Bellicose deity
68 Dig (into)
69 It's a starter
70 Give up
71 Over 10% of the dictionary

DOWN

1 Bawdyhouse figure
2 Low-budget prefix
3 Hacker, maybe
4 Prier's need
5 "Go on . . ."
6 What "tauto-" means
7 Gad about
8 Ryan's "Love Story" co-star
9 Whole lot
10 Duffer's challenge
11 Gazetteer datum
12 Penny-pinching
13 Left at sea
18 Auto pioneer
22 Curved sword
24 Sharon and others
26 Door frame part
27 Home to most Turks
29 High standards
30 Verne mariner
31 Strike out
32 Hardly genteel
33 Cummerbund
34 Beethoven's "Archduke ___"
35 Envelope abbr.
40 Bowl over
45 Took a shot
47 Subtle differences
49 All-seeing one
50 Roswell sightings
53 Prepares to strike
54 Source of sisal hemp
55 Cobbler's stock
56 Forum wear
57 Familiar with
58 Ready for the sack
60 Wine choice
63 Defense org. until 1992
64 Pay dirt
65 Lyrical lines

by Greg Staples

ACROSS

1 Big drawer?
6 Duck
11 Groundskeeper's purchase
14 Be of service to
15 Kind of pie
16 Forum greeting
17 Blithe fish?
19 Good time, informally
20 Suffix with block
21 From the sticks
22 Spill the beans
23 Tightly packed
25 Shake off
27 South American misfit?
33 Item on a card
36 Ingrid's "Anastasia" co-star
37 Word with sand or bottom
38 Sen. Hatch
40 Tattoo favorite
42 Cut's partner
43 More crackers
45 Start of a triple jump
47 Oodles
48 Elvis movie sequel?
51 Slave girl of opera
52 Liver is good for it
56 Act of mother hen
59 Exasperating
62 Dancer Miller
63 Bit of binary code
64 Forbidden tea?
66 Fix, in a way
67 Shingle words
68 Deductions from gross weight
69 SAS announcement
70 She played Thelma in "Thelma and Louise"
71 T, for one

DOWN

1 Colorful parrot
2 Duck
3 Had a feeling
4 Ltd., in Paris
5 Noyes or Nobel
6 With 61-Down, a Big 12 campus city
7 ___ Cong
8 Treasury Secretary Paul
9 Freezing
10 First of 50: Abbr.
11 It's a long story
12 Like an oxeye window
13 Pigeonhole's place
18 Not pale, as a complexion
22 Prevaricate
24 Was creative
26 Pen provisions
28 No-good
29 Western airline
30 To boot
31 Drudge in cyberspace
32 Son of Zeus
33 Long pass
34 Like some traditions
35 Language of Pakistan
39 Nostalgic soft drink
41 Pronoun for Miss Piggy
44 Extend, as spokes
46 Eighty-eight
49 Sing like a bird
50 They're full of bullion
53 Language from which "kiwi" comes
54 Central
55 Frequent Woody Allen theme
56 Driver's alert
57 Module
58 Nintendo rival
60 Zen riddle
61 See 6-Down
64 Telephone ___
65 "Well, ___ -di-dah!"

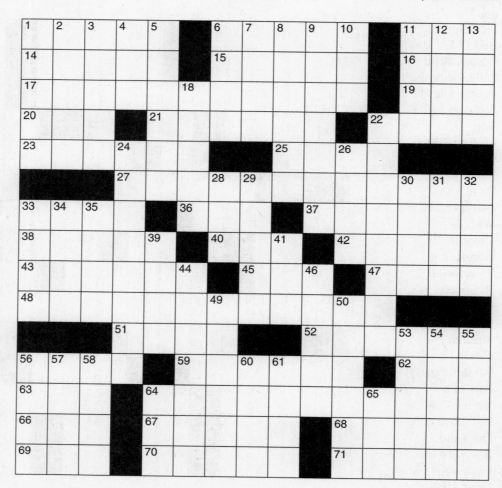

by Greg Staples

ACROSS

1 Expect
6 Bindle bearer
10 "King Kong" star
14 Sudden outburst
15 Stewpot
16 Space opener?
17 Time for a blockbuster movie, maybe
19 RR ___
20 Glaswegian's negative
21 Caravan maker
22 Guardian spirits
23 Floral arrangement
24 Favorable factors
26 Hoped-for trait in a spouse
30 Sitter's handful
31 They may be caught off base
32 Revival cry
34 Dept. of Labor agcy.
38 Israel's Eshkol
39 ___-ovo-vegetarian
40 Airport info, for short
41 They're sometimes rolled over
42 Nanjing nanny
43 Numbers for 18-Down
44 Unlikely Oscar nominee
46 "Don't go anywhere!"
48 "10" star
52 Swank
53 Verdi's "___ Miller"
54 Less friendly
56 Fast-food inits.
59 O's is 8
60 The Beatles had them
62 Short: Fr.
63 Police jacket letters

64 Relative of the beguine
65 One in bondage
66 Back talk
67 Dough raiser

DOWN

1 Part of N.B.A.: Abbr.
2 Gilda's Baba
3 On the safe side?
4 "___ got it!"
5 Big cheeses
6 Greeting from Tex, perhaps
7 Designer for Jackie
8 [expletive deleted]
9 Symbol of might

10 Shines as Robert Frost might?
11 Jockey straps
12 Links legend, informally
13 Nirvana seekers
18 Slugger Sammy
22 Bubble source
23 Devours
25 Start to type?
26 Niger neighbor
27 One who's in the hole
28 Bagel stuffer
29 Places to play b-ball
33 They have morals
35 Like some parties

36 ". . . ___ no fury . . ."
37 Mgr.'s helper
39 Couturier's fabric
43 Go for a wok?
45 Coach Parseghian
47 Huxtable son
48 Tells all
49 Beyond the fringe
50 Converted railroad car, maybe
51 Plains Indian
55 No. brains?
56 ___ Sutra
57 Whopper juniors?
58 Suffix with demo-
60 Much of an ed.'s in-box
61 Peach or tangerine

by Elizabeth C. Gorski

ACROSS

1 Pickup spot?
5 Women's group, of a sort
10 Both ways, to an electrician
14 "Fred Basset" cartoonist Graham
15 Place for a toothpick
16 Honey
17 ___ Peak, in the Sierra Nevada
18 Like windows
19 Wild
20 Hitchhiker's specialty
23 Suffix with neo-and zoo-
24 The path of virtue
25 I
28 Hwys.
32 Mass offering?
34 Brest friend
37 Stroller wear
40 Novelist Simpson
42 Like a ___ bricks
43 Part of a fantasia
44 Courting
47 Velvet finish?
48 Glacial ridge
49 Old name in oil
50 Gramm or Graham: Abbr.
51 Grammy category
54 Gymnast Comaneci
59 One-upmanship on the set
64 Fan's sound
66 Object of many knightly quests
67 With 45-Down, words after "Pssst!"
68 Good source of protein
69 Kind of suit
70 Legendary loser
71 "The flood of deadly hate": Milton
72 Get away from
73 Penny, perhaps

DOWN

1 Org. for Kweisi Mfume
2 Object of many prayers
3 Picayune
4 Precise
5 Kachina doll makers
6 Mathematician Turing
7 Best man's charge
8 Six-time U.S. Open champ
9 Press
10 Cutting tool
11 Halt
12 Blocker of "Bonanza"
13 Make a plea for sympathy, maybe
21 Angelica, for one
22 Swallow
26 One who makes dreams come true
27 Ballpark fixture
29 Comic Jacques
30 Dark, to poets
31 "The Playboy of the Western World" author
33 ___ glance
34 Oscars' org.
35 Wavy pattern
36 Pick up
38 Hair decorations
39 Govt. secrets?
41 Function
45 See 67-Across
46 Mrs. Chaplin
52 Trig figure
53 Threat
55 ___ Bowl
56 Couch
57 Like krypton
58 Say yes
60 Heart
61 "Elephant Boy" star
62 Needing overtime
63 Allure competitor
64 Gym gear: Abbr.
65 Popular

by Alan Arbesfeld

ACROSS

1 Grid great Grier
6 New issuances, for short
10 Frequently
13 Observe Yom Kippur
14 Author Zora ___ Hurston
16 Break down
17 Disoriented 1949 musical?
19 ___ pro nobis
20 "Telephone Line" grp.
21 Music store section
22 Place for brewskis
24 Hardly five-star fare
26 Grenoble's river
29 VCR button: Abbr.
30 Disoriented advice, once?
34 Soup bit
35 Really big show
36 Cork locale: Abbr.
37 Coolidge's veep
40 Not making eye contact, say
41 Delmonico alternative
43 Plug extension?
44 Where Canton is
46 Cruet filler
47 Disoriented 1979 Nick Nolte movie?
53 "Evita" role
54 Holiday numbers
55 Muted effect
56 Noble partner
58 Vigor
60 Green, in a way
61 Treasure of the Sierra Madre
62 Disoriented Steinbeck novel?
66 Platte River people
67 "The Nutcracker" girl
68 Got stage fright
69 Dreamy state?
70 Has chits out
71 Like tournament chess games

DOWN

1 Steak tartare need
2 1887 Verdi opera
3 "Already?"
4 M.D.'s specialty
5 Slangy approvals
6 One way to pay
7 Kennedy Library architect
8 Palooka
9 Divvy
10 Mario Lanza favorite
11 Tip off
12 Alpine transport
15 "The Name of the Rose" author
18 Curly-tailed dog
23 Dot follower
25 The Swiss Guards guard him
27 Mask feature
28 Classic theater name
31 Do course work?
32 "___ I can help it!"
33 Society page word
37 Female goat
38 Menu option
39 Place to come clean?
40 Rural structure
42 Totally botch
45 Harrison Ford role
46 Bone: Prefix
48 British P.M.'s house number
49 Top dogs
50 Like lotteries
51 Pluck
52 Opened wide
56 Insensitive sort
57 Emergency key
59 "All gone!"
63 Walter Reuther's org.
64 Due follower
65 "___ tu"

by Brendan Emmett Quigley

ACROSS

1 Rip (into)
5 Long suit
10 Cape Canaveral's locale: Abbr.
13 With 17-Across, NASA concern
15 Noted caravel
16 Guitar innovator Paul
17 See 13-Across
19 NASA deviation
20 Keynoted
21 Durable fabric
23 Bryn ___ College
26 Color wheel display
28 Turned on by
29 Not Astroturf
31 Where Mount Hood is
33 Country singer McDaniel
34 Spanish inquisitor, e.g.
39 NASA concern
43 20-20, e.g.
44 Reduce the fare?
46 Say "A-O.K."
49 Watershed dividing line
51 Defraud
52 Baddies
57 Rocket part
58 Occupied
60 Attack
62 Relatives of the Fox
63 NASA concern
68 Riviera season
69 Not so dotty
70 Moon follower
71 Yak in the pulpit?: Abbr.
72 Eyeball benders
73 Ore carrier

DOWN

1 Wimbledon call
2 Jungle swinger?
3 Hoops pos.
4 Bad throws, e.g.
5 Is ___ (probably will)
6 "All clear" signal
7 Like a snicker
8 LAX posting
9 Diamond : 10 :: ___ : 1
10 With 48-Down, NASA concern
11 Makeshift digs
12 Blacked out
14 Atmospheric prefix
18 Collected splinters, so to speak
22 Sacred: Prefix
23 Vegas's ___ Grand
24 Gazetteer datum
25 It's common in row houses
27 More steamed
30 Ben of Comedy Central
32 Direct elsewhere
35 The ___ beat
36 Hyde creator's monogram
37 Twitch
38 NASA concern
40 Inventory list
41 Spruce up
42 S.I. and Cosmo
45 Start of a giggle
46 Comes to mind
47 Treaty considerers
48 See 10-Down
50 All there
53 Gold Coast, today
54 Go-cart
55 Court foe of King
56 Collector's goal
59 Sinclair rival
61 ___ gratia artis
64 Fare for the toothless
65 Not the usual spelling: Abbr.
66 Clean air grp.
67 NASA vehicle

by A. J. Santora

ACROSS

1 "___," said Tom presently
5 Not chronic
10 Limey's quaff
14 N.Y.S.E. competitor
15 General denial?
16 Big partygoer?
17 "___," said Tom unremittingly
20 Hood's gun
21 Pond cover
22 Gladiator's place
23 On the main
24 Word before juris or generis
25 "___," said Tom fittingly
33 Snappish
34 Meadow denizen
35 Symbol of solidity
36 Suggestive
37 It was tested on Bikini, 1954
39 Polynesian amulet figure
40 "Little" Stowe girl
41 "Fudge!"
42 Baffler
43 "___," said Tom accordingly
47 Bettor's interest
48 Differently
49 Pretend
52 Utterly destroyed
54 State touching Can.
57 "___," said Tom patiently
60 All you can eat
61 Early settlers of Iceland
62 Top
63 Provokes splenetically
64 Emulates Babe Ruth
65 "___," said Tom haltingly

DOWN

1 Reagan cabinet member
2 Mme. Bovary
3 Let
4 Outside: Prefix
5 "Crouching Tiger, Hidden Dragon" director
6 Jackie who starred in "Tom Sawyer," 1930
7 Voice of America org.
8 It has a point
9 Work unit
10 "All in the Family" role
11 Ready for plucking
12 Saudi Arabia neighbor
13 Maja painter
18 Nice to nosh
19 Gray-brown
23 Aesthetically pretentious
24 Macedonian's neighbor
25 Spread around
26 Cry to anchor men
27 "Platoon" prize
28 Sandal strap
29 Many a skit actor
30 Complaints
31 Bilked
32 Evade
37 Dangle
38 Lifting device
39 Webster's Unabridged, e.g.
41 Sawyer of ABC
42 Linguine sauce
44 "Communist Manifesto" co-author
45 Feed
46 Gets around
49 Poodle name
50 Mideast ruler
51 Man, but not Woman
52 Be sure
53 Uttar Pradesh tourist site
54 Hankering
55 Spanish building topper
56 Quarter
58 Politicos with jobs
59 Raven's call

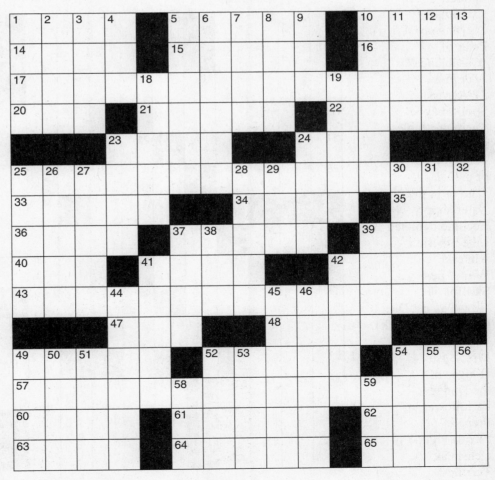

by Mel Taub and crossword class

ACROSS

1 Radio switch
5 Personality asset
10 Charles Lamb, pseudonymously
14 Vincent Lopez hit of 1922
15 Television sans picture
16 Brewski
17 Terrific place to buy lemonade?
19 Give off
20 Sharp surgical instrument
21 Mermaid's home
23 A.C. measure
24 Chicago suburb
25 Terrific leader?
28 Spotted
29 Exemplars of twinship
30 Peter of "Casablanca"
31 Spot in a 21-Across
33 Spoil, maybe
34 There are eagles in it: Abbr.
37 Terrific layer of paint?
39 Danger in the water supply
40 Become depleted
42 Like Siberian winters
44 Winter pear
45 Skillful
46 "___ Dawn I Die" (Cagney/Raft flick)
50 Terrific T-man?
52 Mrs. Bush
53 Hodges of the Dodgers
54 Fa follower
55 Prepare
56 "Yeah, right!" in teenspeak
58 Terrific sun blocker?

61 In-basket stamp: Abbr.
62 Uncredited actor
63 "Cleopatra" backdrop
64 Boris Godunov, for one
65 Honeybun
66 Turned right

DOWN

1 Some are right
2 Spirit
3 Projecting part
4 "Days of Wine and Roses" composer
5 Fracture fixer
6 Snap preceder
7 Nabokov novel
8 Hosings, maybe
9 Make's partner
10 Legal conclusion?
11 Plodded along
12 1,100-mile run
13 Teacher's joy
18 Place for a nap, maybe
22 Parcels out
25 Ooze through the cracks
26 Sentries' jobs
27 In
29 Stratagem
32 Parades
33 It has feathers and flies
34 Horn tooter?
35 They involve light lifting

36 Huston of "Prizzi's Honor"
38 Klutzes
41 ___ good deed
43 Kind of pad
45 With all the bells and whistles
47 2000 Olympics host
48 Spicy cuisine
49 Cause of some warfare
51 Nudged, dog-style
52 O.T. book
55 Like many a winter sky
57 New Deal pres.
59 School org.
60 Suffer a "brain cramp"

by Nancy Salomon and Harvey Estes

ACROSS

1 Paradoxical fellow
5 Boxing prize
9 Earns
14 Diamond family name
15 Half court game?
16 Die down
17 Central point
18 Gridiron scoreboard info
19 Seuss title creature
20 Beatings at Bloomingdale's, e.g.?
23 PETA peeve
24 Café partner
25 Ones carrying an apostle?
30 Whip but good
33 Bubbly source
34 Dallas sch.
35 Dangerous strain
37 It's got you covered
38 Madras wraps
41 McGregor of "Trainspotting"
42 1991–93 Australian Open winner
44 Disney division
45 Twist, sometimes
46 Farm female
47 Inspector at a trucking company?
51 Neanderthal's wear
52 "Groovy!"
53 Is an old French landowner?
59 "The Planets" composer
60 Seats with kneelers
61 Abdicator of 1917
63 "Wouldn't that be nice!"
64 Edison product

65 Ides rebuke
66 Winning craps roll, in Rome
67 Like some D.A.'s
68 Lip

DOWN

1 Veer suddenly
2 Crimson rivals
3 Bag of chips, say
4 Uncalled-for
5 Reputation hurter
6 Wells's oppressed race
7 Place for an egg roll
8 Excited feeling
9 Crummy feeling
10 Circa
11 Wallenda family patriarch
12 Cockpit guesses, for short
13 Census datum
21 Place for a cold one
22 Uglify
25 No longer cool
26 Crooked
27 Serviceable
28 Doc bloc
29 Like Mayberry
30 Namely
31 Santa Anna took it
32 West Coast gridder
36 Nuns, by vow

39 DOS popularizer
40 Derides
43 Encase
48 Apiece, in scores
49 Sir Thomas More novel
50 Back seat driver, e.g.
51 "Hey, buddy!"
53 British commander at Bunker Hill
54 Detrained
55 Kennedy and others
56 Is in the hole
57 Org. for 42-Across
58 Back muscles, for short
59 Hellos
62 Big chunk of Eur.

by Ethan Cooper

ACROSS

1 Grandma ___
6 Turn away
11 Like Felix and Oscar
14 Deal from the bottom
15 Ham's medium
16 Comic actor Romano
17 Eeler's musical instruments?
19 East end?
20 Crow's home
21 A colleague of Kennedy's
23 It grows on you
25 Broadway acronym
28 Pompous people
29 Motor lodge
30 Sandinista leader
32 Hit the road
33 Direct
35 Photo finish
37 Eeler's favorite singer?
42 Cream of the crop
43 Divide up
45 Bowling green
48 Pub serving
51 Afore
52 More or less
54 Carson's predecessor
55 Scored on serve
56 Schussing spots
58 Like crossword solvers, naturally
60 Down in the dumps
61 Eeler's theme song?
66 Suffix with social
67 First name in talk shows
68 Chew the scenery
69 Night of poetry
70 Horrify
71 Vixen's master

DOWN

1 Turn-of-the-century year
2 "That's your game, eh?"
3 Guard
4 All agog
5 Aerobics action
6 Fervid
7 Not standard: Abbr.
8 Part of some e-mail addresses
9 Eyeglass frames
10 Puccini opera
11 Words intended to intimidate
12 Caribbean's Gulf of ___
13 Hereditary ruler
18 Bring up
22 Also
23 Part of O.H.M.S.
24 Stud fee?
26 Painter's medium
27 Seaweed substance
30 City on the Oka
31 Took a course?
34 Balance
36 Pre-Lenin ruler
38 Lambaste verbally
39 Organ knob
40 Kind of microscope
41 Auld lang syne
44 Uncle of Caroline
45 Long-running TV series set in Calverton
46 On fire
47 Stiff
49 Decorative dangle
50 Humorist Bombeck
53 Di- doubled
55 Something from the oven
57 Haberdashery, e.g.
59 Home of Iowa State
62 Cleo's undoing
63 ___ Maria
64 Justice Dept. employee
65 Biblical word before verily

by Richard Silvestri

ACROSS

1 Quirky 70's–80's band
5 "Evita" role
8 Give confidence to
14 Mountain stat.
15 Agreement abroad
16 See 62-Across
17 Previous
19 Attacked violently
20 Bejeweled adornment
21 Bush Sr. headed it
23 "Ici on ___ français"
24 Like a street urchin
27 Jungle queen of 50's TV
30 Retaliation, in part?
31 They're affected by the ionosphere
34 Totenberg of NPR
38 True up
39 Island off India's coast
40 Theaters
41 Father of Enos
42 Spread out, timewise
44 Cup at a grease joint
45 James of "Marcus Welby, M.D."
46 Movie house popcorn choice
52 Tryon novel, with "The"
53 You might need a paddle to do this
54 Brilliance
58 Stingers?
60 Went around in circles?
62 With 16-Across, the theme of this puzzle
63 Too late for the E.R.
64 Oddball
65 Big name in swimwear
66 Pay stub abbr.
67 Frank or Francis

DOWN

1 Skilled
2 "The Time Machine" people
3 Designer Wang
4 Oppress
5 Bill's partner
6 Funny feeling
7 Children's song refrain
8 Halifax clock setting: Abbr.
9 Pull into
10 Fergie, formally
11 In ___ (unborn)
12 Empire
13 Cosmetician Lauder
18 Begin to catch up with
22 Filmmaker with total creative control
25 Spotted, to Tweety
26 "Angela's Ashes" follow-up
27 Sp. ladies
28 In good health
29 Get to work on Time?
32 Modifying word
33 Go for the gold
34 1939 Garbo role
35 Worldwide: Abbr.
36 Beverage brand
37 Org.
40 Eye bank donation
42 Scoreboard line under RHE, maybe
43 George W. deg.
44 Sun-dried, as beef
46 Ness et al.
47 Ready, as a sail
48 ___ Island red
49 Hollow rock
50 Lightheaded
51 No-brainer?
55 Nutcase
56 The King's middle name
57 Profits
59 ___-Cone
61 Pops

by Alan Arbesfeld

ACROSS

1 Top-notch
6 Capture the attention of
10 Lacking depth
14 It might be grand
15 Newman's Own competitor
16 Southernmost U.S. city
17 Press some flesh?
20 Where It.'s at
21 Call upon
22 Firth of Tay port
23 Red algae
26 Tries to reach
27 Clairvoyant's gift
28 Takes some courses?
29 Cleveland cager, for short
32 Part of IV
35 ___ jure (by law)
36 Massachusetts vacation spot, with "the"
37 Two score of low, thick lilies?
40 The works
41 Go bad
42 Alamogordo event
43 Noted casino, with "the"
44 Solder, say
45 Pizzeria output
46 Take in
48 ___ Centauri (closest star to the sun)
52 They're history
54 Fortune cover subj.
55 Left Coast baggage tag
56 Directions for a basement escort?
60 Nobelist Pavlov
61 They're found in yards
62 Spam, maybe
63 ___ a soul
64 Unnerve
65 Bits of baby talk

DOWN

1 Half-domed projections
2 Provoke
3 Hillary's successor
4 Italian article
5 "Help, quick!"
6 "Ew-w-w!"
7 General, e.g.
8 Actuary's datum
9 It's the end of the line
10 "___ God!"
11 Beaufort, for one
12 Like some shoppes
13 Teaspoonful, maybe
18 Lock holder
19 Rainbow display
24 Ricardo's landlord
25 Anthem starter
26 Maine senator Collins
28 Brush aside
30 P.D. alerts
31 ___-pocket (tiny)
32 "___ first you . . ."
33 "___ chance!"
34 Conflict provoked by Paris
35 Employee's angry cry
36 Nail polish brand
38 Pays a quick visit
39 "Charles in Charge" star
44 Big buffet
45 N.F.L., e.g., with "the"
47 Partridge Family boy
48 Calvin of the P.G.A.
49 Tale of the 34-Down
50 Santa ___
51 Jumps on the ice
52 Game point situation
53 Bagel stuffer
54 ___ Panisse (restaurant)
57 Brewer's brew
58 Proof letters
59 Thurman of "The Avengers"

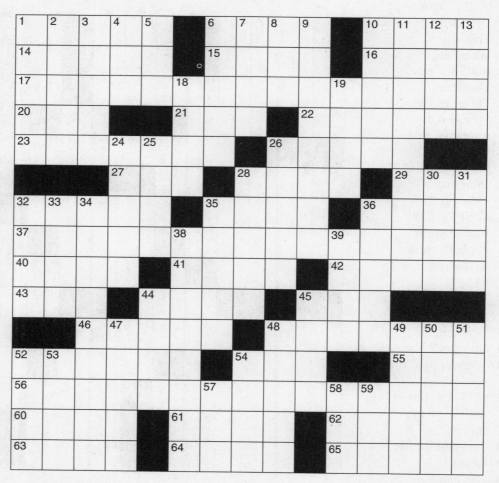

by Joe DiPietro

ACROSS

1 Open a crack
5 Shiftlessness
10 Campus area
14 "Laura" author Caspary
15 Actress Tierney
16 Old-fashioned preposition
17 The same as above
18 Sustain
19 The gamut
20 No longer mended?
22 Kind of wave
23 "Waltz for Eva and ___" (show tune)
24 Like taxis on city streets
26 London's Old ___ (criminal court)
30 In two parts
32 Sticks figures?
33 Ignored?
38 Deuce follower
39 Pitching stats
40 Air France stop
41 Uncultivated?
43 Plain writing
44 C-worthy?
45 Mollycoddle
46 40 winks
50 Droop
51 Baseball family name
52 Bald?
59 1958 #1 Elvis Presley hit
60 Cold mold
61 Like crayons
62 Summer pest
63 Lifted
64 Related
65 Hard to pin down
66 Suite spot
67 Little nosh

DOWN

1 Enthusiastic
2 Luke Skywalker, e.g.
3 Belligerent deity
4 Turnpike access
5 Anvil location
6 Tilting weapon
7 Smart comment?
8 On the mark
9 Construction crew
10 Seeming
11 No later than
12 Pay for sins
13 Nodded off
21 Top four
25 Drink at the Duck and Drake
26 Thin nail
27 Autobahn sight
28 Nile wader
29 Carnival follower
30 One who works under pressure
31 Not mint
33 "The Persistence of Memory" artist
34 "Cheers" regular
35 Steep slope
36 If not
37 Miss Clairol user
39 Haphazard
42 ". . . ___ woodchuck could chuck wood"
43 Lobby call
45 FedEx concern
46 Sponge
47 Without support
48 Scaly?
49 Ridiculous
50 Fence feature
53 Ratio words
54 Primer pet
55 Do the deck
56 "The Open Window" writer
57 Get off the road
58 Fraction of a newton

by Richard Silvestri

ACROSS

1 Poetic time of day
5 Actress Lanchester
9 Extremist
14 "Peek" follower
15 Chucklehead
16 Took on
17 Puts on
18 Jezebel's idol
19 Wordsmith's concern
20 Answer to "How are you?", Southern-style
23 Basketry twig
24 Tipplemeister
25 Take home
27 A.A.A. info.
28 Disfigure
31 Rugrats
34 Trombone feature
36 One of the Boys of Summer
37 Of exceptional quality, Southern-style
40 Paramecium propellers
42 Exemplar of leakiness
43 Parboiled
46 Kind of poodle
47 Checkout lines, briefly
50 Mack of early TV
51 Memorial designer Maya
53 Hardly laid-back
55 More than tipsy, Southern-style
60 Surveil, with "out"
61 Unit of force
62 1993 Kevin Kline movie
63 "Like a Rock" rocker
64 Hydroxyl compound
65 Just makes, with "out"
66 Italian poet Torquato
67 1140, to Flavius
68 Subtracted by

DOWN

1 Infatuated with
2 Reed player
3 Country music's Milsap
4 "Long time ___!"
5 Goes out
6 Take it easy
7 Takes off
8 Flowering
9 "Don't think so"
10 A Simpson
11 Subminimum wage earners, maybe
12 Invitation turndown
13 Cannon's end?
21 All you can carry
22 Old muscle car
26 Lao-___
29 S O S response
30 Nutritional std.
32 In on
33 Best of the Beatles
34 Potter's purchase
35 Non-P.C. suffix
37 Party wear
38 "Skedaddle!"
39 Hupmobile contemporary
40 Dallas hrs.
41 Brewed drink
44 Animal that bugles
45 Royal headwear
47 Understanding
48 Ticks off
49 Soft touch
52 "Bye Bye Bye" singers
54 Peak call?
56 Luau strings
57 Galba's predecessor
58 Dumb as ___
59 Poky part
60 Brit. Airways vehicle

by Nick Grivas

ACROSS

1 Cremona craftsman
6 Exec, slangily
10 Groucho remark
14 Where dos are done
15 "Say it ain't so!"
16 High-rise locales
17 Plot of land
18 Newsprint need
19 Midmonth day
20 Famous last words
23 Classic tattoo
24 Have an effect (on)
25 Big do
28 No visible means of support?
31 Like pine scent
35 Thai relative
36 Features of some locks
38 Bring together
39 Famous last words
42 Folded food items
43 Temple text
44 62-Across holiday
45 Back talk, slangily
47 Baseball mitt part
48 Nozzle site
49 "Zip-___ -Doo-Dah"
51 Queenside castle, in chess notation
53 Famous last words
60 C-worthy?
61 Good student's reward
62 Capital on the Red River
63 Mountain road sign abbr.
64 Aloha State bird
65 Everglades bird
66 Used to be
67 Song and dance, e.g.
68 Film units

DOWN

1 Spot of wine?
2 Sting target
3 Astronaut Bean
4 In the offing
5 Divided
6 Soaks (up)
7 "Nah!"
8 How a trucker might go up a hill
9 Worst seats in the house
10 Short snort
11 Indic language
12 Skeptic's scoff
13 Ltr. addenda
21 Boundary
22 Slop holder
25 Travels like Tinker Bell
26 Patronize, as a restaurant
27 "Vissi d'arte" opera
29 Spellbound
30 O.K.
32 Inflicted upon
33 Stock holders?
34 "Fiddler" matchmaker
36 Square dance call
37 "Without a doubt!"
40 Capable of stooping to
41 Libreville's land
46 Plane name
48 Tribute
50 Fruity-smelling compound
52 Catchall column
53 Suburban pest
54 North Sea feeder
55 Have a yen for
56 Rock groups?
57 Legalistic phrase
58 Seasonal tune
59 E's, I's and S's, in Morse code
60 Needle

by Jay Sullivan

ACROSS

1 Clinch
6 Clinched
10 Yachter's woe
14 Milo or Tessie
15 Cause of an itch
16 Girasol, e.g.
17 Corset features
18 Train locale
19 Opposite of "no no"
20 Muesli morsel
21 Replay option
23 Stradivarius's teacher
24 Snapped out of it
26 ___ a good thing
27 Attacked violently
28 "Yadda-yadda-yadda"
31 God-awful
32 Whopping
34 Deer ma'am
35 Quisling's city
36 Pronounce an "r" like a Scot
37 Drift off
38 Took the vanguard
39 Where the action is
40 Rats' hangout
41 Knocks to the floor
43 Famous last words?
45 Like some columns
46 Actress Plummer
47 They may be technical
49 Pretty
50 Crooks' methods, to cops
53 One of Chekhov's Three Sisters
54 Abbr. on some letter headings
55 Sacagawea, for one
57 Baloney
58 Calamitous
59 Wing
60 Shakespearean verb
61 Letters above 0
62 Smelling a rat

DOWN

1 Comme ci, comme ça
2 This, in Toledo
3 Start of a musical riddle
4 180° turn, slangily
5 Opener of many doors
6 Middle of the riddle
7 Surgery aid
8 Architect Saarinen
9 Pops
10 All there is
11 End of the riddle
12 Hang in there
13 Mid 11th-century date
22 Idyllic setting
23 Artist Warhol
25 ". . . ___ they say"
26 Like J.F.K. Airport: Abbr.
27 Out of port
28 Answer to the riddle
29 Moved like the Blob
30 Not e'en once
31 Veg out
33 German article
36 Walked over
37 Safe deposit box item
39 Schooner fillers
40 Dakar's land
42 Bit of media hype
44 Pillbox or porkpie
46 Other, in Bordeaux
47 Go belly up
48 Mélange
49 Little swab
51 River to the Baltic
52 Alluring
54 Ruckus
56 Maupassant novel "___ Vie"

by Michael Shteyman

ACROSS

1 Aerobic bit
5 Managing, with "out"
10 Leader in a beret
13 Stay in the closet, say
14 Written record
15 Classic detective
16 Strange-sounding city?
17 First territorial capital of Alaska
18 Posterior
19 Start of a patriotic sports trio
22 Many a storm
23 Anthropologist Fossey
24 More, in Managua
27 Warmonger
30 "Juno and the Paycock" writer
34 Actor Werner of "Ship of Fools"
36 Salt, to a chemist
38 F.D.R.'s mother
39 Middle of a patriotic sports trio
42 Mr., in Munich
43 Important wine region
44 Operatic villains, often
45 Capers
47 Number of sides on an "alto" sign
49 Word on a Ouija board
50 50.1%+
52 Singleton
54 Ironically, end of a patriotic sports trio
62 Rack's partner
63 Approves
64 "Tickle Me" boy
65 Unctuous
66 "From the Earth to the Moon" writer
67 Kind of leaves
68 Designer monogram
69 Paradises
70 Furniture wood

DOWN

1 Tool site
2 Spare item
3 Modify
4 They might cause pressure
5 Simpler
6 Make bootees, say
7 Foreword: Abbr.
8 In an embarrassing position, maybe
9 Colorful, spiky flowers
10 It may be stroked
11 "___ it all!"
12 Completes
15 Taiwan is in it
20 Butler's companion?
21 W.W. II female
24 Coffee flavor
25 Pale
26 Avoid
28 Baseball's Slaughter
29 Tended
31 Bygone teen magazine
32 Notched, as a leaf
33 Vertical graph component
35 Bitterness
37 In
40 Kitchen appliance
41 Hearty entree
46 Jailbird
48 Two halves of Congress
51 Puffed, illegally
53 Walkman button
54 Priam's home
55 French accords?
56 Brook
57 Reveal
58 Boston suburb
59 Medicinal juice
60 Gym site
61 Drunkard

by John Beck

ACROSS

1 Calculate astrologically
5 Smart player
10 Stupefy
14 Recorded proceedings
15 Easily broken
16 Rubber-stamp
17 May dance, maybe
18 Pro follower
19 ___ Horn
20 Desk item that's nothing to sneeze at?
23 Japanese honorific
24 Bartlett relatives
28 Hollow
32 Eccentric
35 Originated
36 Ballet movement
37 Stat that's good when under 3.00
38 Folk group that's nothing to sneeze at?
42 Wee hour
43 Netman Nastase
44 Chilling
45 Vinegar flavoring
48 Tricky problem
49 Krupp works city
50 Deserving a spanking
51 70's–80's show that's nothing to sneeze at?
59 Corner after "GO"
62 1976 best seller that starts in Gambia
63 Lust after, visually
64 Differential attachment
65 Slacken
66 Job opening
67 Join of arc?
68 Work with clay
69 Big buildup

DOWN

1 Comics fellow who hangs out in a pub
2 Piece of property
3 Sign on the corner
4 Pack down
5 Brawl
6 Soak
7 Alpine river
8 "La Bohème" heroine
9 Smeltery refuse
10 Person who's been given the third degree?
11 Blotter letters
12 Microwave
13 Real looker
21 Aromatic compound
22 TNT alternative
25 Sullies
26 1976 film featuring telekinesis
27 Buffy is one
28 "Breakfast at Tiffany's" author
29 Action centers
30 Electorate
31 Expert ending
32 Fagged
33 Nasty comments
34 Wedding page word
36 Ralph Lauren brand
39 Kind of iron
40 What alimony covers, minimally
41 ___ culpa
46 Staggered
47 Singer DiFranco
48 Dangler
50 Please, abroad
52 15.432 grains
53 Odd jobs doer
54 Loathsome one
55 Bag of chips, maybe
56 Unappealing
57 Lay an egg
58 It may be an honor
59 Shoot the breeze
60 Let go
61 Laid up

by Richard Silvestri

ACROSS

1 C
5 Desensitizes
10 "The Alienist" author
14 One-named supermodel
15 Rameau work
16 Similar (to)
17 Hitchcock classic
18 Old Testament collection
19 Doll's word
20 Charades, e.g.
23 Fjord
24 Cases for otologists
28 UFO passengers
29 Wood cutter
32 Shining brightly
33 Butt of jokes
36 Welcome words for a buyer
37 Studio order
40 They're taken in chess
41 Fairy
42 Improvise
44 Prefix with center
45 Bread line locale?
48 "You're on!"
51 Nozzle choice
53 DNA lab result
56 Olympic Stadium player
59 Sport in which competitors dig in their heels
60 Location
61 Big name in perfumes
62 NASA gasket
63 Name in a will
64 "The ___ stayeth for no man": William Camden
65 Income in Monopoly
66 Cellist's direction

DOWN

1 Tabloid duchess
2 Sum
3 Forces forward
4 Poet Lizette Woodworth ___
5 Words of denial
6 "___ the Roof" (Drifters hit)
7 Get together
8 "Moon Over Parador" actress
9 Much of Chad
10 Almost made it
11 Rap sheet shorthand
12 Edge
13 Genetic info carrier
21 Like California, to a Hawaiian
22 Attraction
25 Odium
26 Ezra Pound's "___ Hora"
27 Application datum
30 Semi-colon?
31 Places for petting
33 Port on the Strait of Malacca
34 Econ. figure
35 To be, at the Sorbonne
37 Pack it in
38 Pottery class projects
39 With it
40 ___-night doubleheader
43 Holy person?
45 More creative, perhaps
46 Scare ___
47 Rescuee's declaration
49 Ere
50 Brought (to)
52 Turkish bigwig
54 Copper
55 Duds
56 Summer Conn. clock setting
57 Hour on a clock
58 Bean holder

by Elizabeth C. Gorski

ACROSS

1 Turf defenders
5 Wee, in Dundee
8 What you will
14 Like many a professor
16 Ovid work
17 Start of a quote
18 Prepares for further skirmishes
19 Heathrow fig.
20 Off one's feed
21 40's agcy.
22 Quote, part 2
28 Suez sight
29 Kind of cross
30 Makes a cat's-paw of
31 To boot
32 "Va-va-va-___!"
34 Source of ad-free TV
36 Quote, part 3
40 PC key
41 Windmill blade
42 Ballantine of Ballantine Books
45 Keystone's place
48 ___ de Calais
49 Fully sufficient
51 End of the quote
55 For example
56 Just discovered
57 Go for the gold
58 Ham
60 Source of the quote
65 Keep
66 Ballerina
67 Amplifier setting
68 Aphid milker
69 Bris, e.g.

DOWN

1 Hair goop, e.g.
2 Sawbones' org.
3 Pince-___
4 Show sorrow
5 Super bargain
6 Juilliard subj.
7 Dolt
8 Countesses' husbands
9 Something in a trash heap
10 ___ man (everyone)
11 Roadway markings
12 Part of the head
13 Bacon bits
15 Minor third or flatted fifth
20 Letters of credit?
22 Rug rat
23 Carnival city
24 Heaps
25 Station
26 Russian urn
27 Bounce
33 Giant Giant
34 Warm-up spot, for short
35 Watergate and others
37 Nuclear fission discoverer Otto
38 Like the Great Plains
39 Pound's sounds
43 The Lion of God
44 Bottom line
45 Defend, as one's rights
46 Gadabout
47 Rancher's nuisance
48 Nave bench
50 Ralph of "Kiss Me Deadly"
52 Newsman Roger
53 Phileas Fogg's creator
54 ___-gardism
59 Slot filler
60 AZT approver
61 Did a 10K, e.g.
62 Him, to Henri
63 Believer
64 Alumna bio word

by Richard Hughes

ACROSS

1 Yogurt fruit
5 Outpouring
10 Kind of page
14 Leprechaun's land
15 Rhodes of Rhodesia
16 Where a puppy may be picked up
17 Not a niche audience
19 Hot times in Haiti
20 Locker room activity
21 Without a contract
23 Ogle
24 Private places
26 Get-up-and-go
29 Third-century date
30 Clobbers
33 Madrid Mrs.
34 They'll knock you out
37 "Guilty," e.g.
38 Many a Louis
39 Kettles . . . or the theme of this puzzle
41 Belushi venue, for short
42 May race, informally
44 Well-tossed pigskin
45 Lilly of pharmaceuticals
46 Bill Haley bandmate
48 In need of salting, maybe
49 Modern news source
51 More than 25% of immigrants to the U.S.
53 Spreadsheet part: Abbr.
54 Sign up
56 The U.S., to Mexicans
60 Dayan contemporary

61 It may become a queen
64 Penny-pinching
65 Plantain lily
66 Arthurian lady
67 It's under the Ponte Vecchio
68 Rubber hub
69 Grooves on

DOWN

1 Dole's 1996 running mate
2 "Dies ___"
3 Skinny one
4 Marching together
5 Map info
6 Dental plan, maybe
7 When doubled, defensive fire
8 50-50, e.g.
9 Lyrical John
10 Like some shopping
11 1968 presidential candidate
12 Fencing need
13 Progeny: Abbr.
18 Wanton destruction
22 A.T.M. maker
24 Nature films, perhaps
25 Hang in the breeze
26 "Hamlet" courtier
27 Maine town
28 Robin's sweetheart
29 "Taxi" singer
31 Potato sack wt., maybe

32 ___ law (old Frankish code)
35 Profs' help
36 Sauna site
40 Amaretto flavor
43 Kind of question
47 Up to, for short
50 Like a mansard roof
52 Greek leader
53 Untainted
54 1998 role for Uma
55 ___-do-well
56 Idaho motto starter
57 Indian princess
58 Bit of wicker
59 Winds up
62 Just fine
63 Pre-Yeltsin abbr.

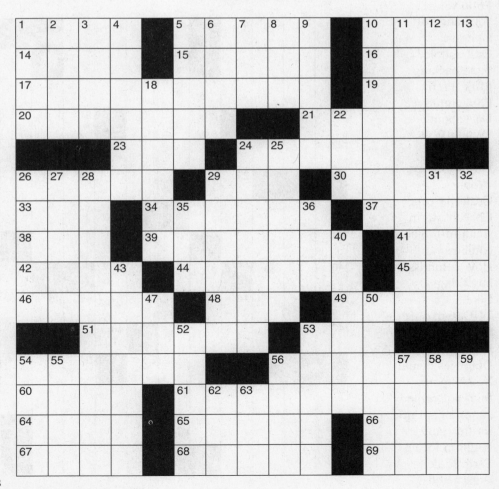

by William I. Johnston

ACROSS

1 Out of one's gourd
5 City north of Anaheim
9 Max ___ of "Barney Miller"
13 Trash bin, e.g.
14 Small islands
15 Main line
16 Eddie Murphy action comedy
19 Arctic explorer John
20 KLM announcement
21 Aleph-___
22 Bicarb and others
25 Rely on
29 Michael J. Fox romantic comedy
31 Follower of "on" and "off" in a phrase
34 Odd couple?
35 Send packing
36 Milk: Prefix
37 Pool employee
39 Dart about
40 "When Will ___ Loved"
41 Earl's inferior: Abbr.
42 Custard treats
43 Cheech Marin south-of-the-border comedy
47 How commissaries buy things
48 Like a 24-Down, once
52 Dallas, familiarly
54 Routing word
55 Dumfries denial
56 Neil Simon four-skit comedy . . . or an apt title for this puzzle
61 Leghorn locale
62 Earth force
63 Hammered obliquely
64 Pianist Brubeck
65 Rose by another name?
66 Rag doll's name

DOWN

1 Fall sign
2 Indian ___
3 Eagerly desire
4 Four quarters
5 Like Latvia or Lithuania
6 Saudi capital
7 Biblical verb ending
8 Abecedarian phrase
9 Creep
10 ___ welder
11 Name in 1995 news
12 1/4 mile, maybe
15 Sterling silver and others
17 Scout's job
18 Put to sleep
23 Shaft's end
24 Recyclable item
26 Eucalyptus muncher
27 Venom
28 "The Flowering Peach" playwright
30 Celtic sea god
31 Accused's need
32 Libreville's land
33 Biting
37 Maidenhair tree
38 Play for a sap
39 Motorist's woe
41 Malign
42 Boxer's bane
44 Marriageable
45 With 49-Down, bygone alliance
46 Sort of a disaster?
49 See 45-Down
50 Like most films
51 Indigent
53 Discontinue
56 Alfonso VI banished him
57 ___ glance
58 Short head?
59 Vane dir.
60 Actress Hagen

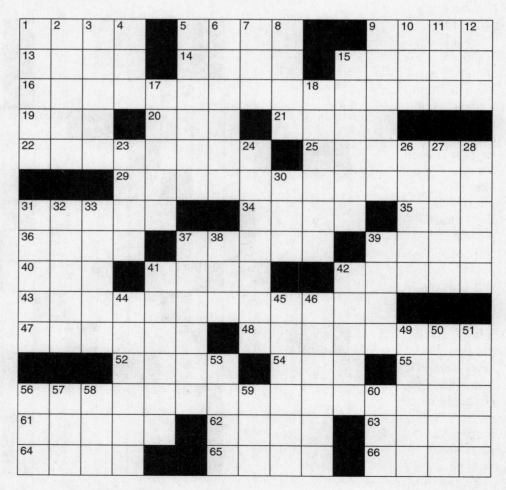

by Sam Bellotto Jr.

ACROSS

1 Skiing mecca
6 Cross of Egypt
10 Weather indicator
14 Taco topper, perhaps
15 Needy
16 Intestinal parts
17 Where ordinary folks play tennis?
20 Controversial spray
21 Tarkenton of Minnesota
22 Actor Edward James ____
23 Othello's ensign
25 "The Last Days of Pompeii" heroine
27 Enthusiastic response to a tennis shutout?
32 ____-cone
33 Glimmering
34 Household ____
37 Weapon that can cross the Atl. or Pac.
39 Expensive transport
41 First name in daredeviltry
42 Daddy Warbucks's henchman
45 Architect Saarinen
48 Where some M.D.'s work
49 What standers and waiters do in tennis?
52 Ridicule
53 Rare bills
54 Be friends (with)
57 Field opening
59 Siamese
63 Soothing words to a tennis player?
66 Crow
67 Black card
68 Legend's locale
69 Composer Alban
70 Dole (out)
71 Hardly Mr. Nice Guy

DOWN

1 Dog of detective fiction
2 Comic Mort
3 "Don't hurt me!," for one
4 Bon vivant's gift
5 Highlands negative
6 Stamps, maybe
7 Town where Augustus died
8 Chekov player on "Star Trek"
9 Many mins.
10 Reason for an "R"
11 Wound application
12 He ordered Seneca's death
13 Grub
18 Attila, the Scourge ____
19 First name in late-night TV
24 Clay, today
26 ". . . ____ quit!"
27 ____ were
28 Tiny amount of progress
29 Gambler's pass
30 Oil holder
31 White cliffs locale
35 TV's Griffin
36 Other
38 Game played in "The Joy Luck Club"
40 Place for a lab experiment
43 "____ evil"
44 Poet laureate before Southey
46 Crew member
47 Spanish bear
50 Sock type
51 Net worth
54 Singing brother of 60's–90's pop
55 French 101 verb
56 Bygone despot
58 Juillet's follower
60 Waikiki wiggle
61 Author Paton
62 Teeny
64 Cable sta. for cinema buffs
65 Grp. of relatives

by Karen Young Bonin

ACROSS

1 One of the Three Bears
5 Shouts with both hands raised, maybe
10 Cowboy, informally
14 First-rate, slangily
15 Like an old apartment
16 Ties with bows
17 With 38-Across, poem by 24-Down
20 Rossini opera
21 U.S.-Mexico border city
22 Very, musically
23 "The Woman ___" (1984 film)
25 Tanner
27 Small bone
32 Bump
35 Gift ___
37 Unpleasant guest
38 See 17-Across
42 British royal
43 Akron AA baseball team
44 Durocher, astrologically(!)
45 Ailing
48 Local political div.
49 Home to 33 mil.
51 Shampoo instruction
56 A Virgin Island
60 Not so good, as a photo
62 Poem by 24-Down
64 Squander
65 Fighting ___
66 Certificate
67 What tags may produce
68 Methods: Abbr.
69 Baseball's Slaughter

DOWN

1 Noodles, maybe
2 Serve in the capacity of
3 Hardly bigwigs
4 It may have a pet project
5 Racer Luyendyk
6 Poem by 24-Down
7 ___ Marbles, British Museum magnet
8 Colo. neighbor
9 Does salon work
10 D
11 Kin to a clarinet
12 Noted captain
13 Petrol seller
18 "Fidelio" setting
19 Bankrolls
24 Much-quoted poet
26 Amateur video subject, maybe
28 Arab name part
29 Kind of spring
30 Isolated
31 Therefore
32 Rivers of New York
33 ___ Domini
34 Bombast
36 "Yes, Scottie"
39 Wrap (up)
40 "I shall return," e.g.
41 Lively wit
46 She loved Narcissus
47 Oahu verandas
50 Roman fire
52 Silly
53 Popular camera
54 Look after
55 Sea birds
56 1944 battle site
57 G
58 Bit of banter
59 Malachite and others
61 Olympians: Abbr.
63 No longer producing

by Nancy S. Ross

ACROSS

1 With 63-Across, author of the quip starting at 17-Across
6 Chicago sights
9 Baltic country: Abbr.
13 Rest against
15 Waikiki gift
16 Cruising
17 Start of a quip
19 "___ be a cold day in hell . . ."
20 Routing word
21 Add spice to
22 Jazz trumpeter Baker
23 To be, at the Sorbonne
25 Where the U.N. is in Manhattan, with 27-Across
27 See 25-Across
28 Like Salome
31 In motion
33 Soak
34 "Yours truly" and the like
35 Middle of the quip, with 37-Across
37 See 35-Across
38 Rears
39 Name for a king or a queen?
40 About three grains of troy weight
41 Deli order
45 Columbia, e.g.: Abbr.
46 Rare string
48 Santa's reindeer, e.g.
49 Pelvic parts
51 Baltimore N.F.L.ers
54 When "77 Sunset Strip" aired: Abbr.

55 Batter's base, maybe
56 End of the quip
58 Once, once
59 Electric ___
60 Beachgoer's burden
61 Sleek fleet
62 Cunning
63 See 1-Across

DOWN

1 Major producers of oil
2 Mideast native
3 False rumor
4 Enero to enero
5 Falls apart
6 Hard to pin down
7 Name immortalized by Poe
8 Indications
9 Secular
10 "Really?"
11 Watch a monitor, say
12 They hold your horses
14 Actress Carrie
18 Hardly refined
24 Author Welty
26 Address
29 Dracula and others
30 They have a lot of pull
32 Speech sound
34 Langston Hughes's "___ Unashamed"

35 Online merchants
36 Most gutsy
37 Like caresses
38 Writers' bloc
39 With refinement
41 Commit a court infraction
42 Bar order
43 Spun, as a story
44 Solzhenitsyn, e.g.
47 They're for the birds
50 Liberal pursuits
52 212 initials
53 Put belowdecks
57 ___ polloi

by Elizabeth C. Gorski

ACROSS

1 Actor Green of "Buffy the Vampire Slayer"
5 Chicken order
10 "Bury the Dead" playwright
14 Soothing color
15 Football commentator ___ Long
16 Long green
17 Exposé of a lithographer's bad hangouts?
20 Word repeated in "___ always begets ___": Sophocles
21 "Vamoose!"
22 Supporter
23 Boils down
24 Old Clara-Clarence romance?
28 Bring up
29 "___ out?" (dealer's query)
30 Actress Hurley, for short
33 Urge
34 "Personal Injuries" author Scott
36 Pet name
37 "Shame on you!"
38 "Don't you just ___ it when . . . ?"
39 Biblical miracle-maker
40 Book subtitled "Cowgirl Evans's Favorite Desserts"?
43 Dispositions
46 Give up
47 Mafia code of silence
48 Polish sausage
52 Paradise with shortcomings?
54 Wind instrument

55 Serve
56 "Later, gator!"
57 One in custody
58 Nez ___ War of 1877
59 Title girl of a 1918 hit song

DOWN

1 Pink-slip
2 Prefix with lateral
3 Part of driving directions
4 Ready money
5 Finis
6 Played (around)
7 "As ___ saying . . ."
8 Bermuda highball ingredient

9 Common property boundary
10 Way to get to the top
11 Disorder
12 Northerner
13 Bridge positions
18 Poppycockish
19 Better Homes and Gardens concern
23 Villain at Crab Key
24 Subject of Elizabeth
25 Stable diet?
26 Part of a cigarette lighter
27 Cao da Serra de ___ (dog breed)
30 Money in the banca
31 Pagoda sight

32 Basketball defense
34 Rest
35 Western Indians
36 Prepare to pass, maybe
38 Poker Flat chronicler
39 Mix up
40 Like a boomerang
41 Like sour grapes
42 Pester
43 With zero chance
44 Life on a slide
45 "Coffee, ___ Me?"
48 Wood blemish
49 Bellini work
50 Right away
51 Call to a mate
53 Fifth, e.g.: Abbr.

by Manny Nosowsky

ACROSS

1 Is in another form?
4 Rodin sculpture at the Met
8 Best and others
13 Accident scene arrival: Abbr.
14 Hindi relative
15 Brewers' needs
17 See 32-Across
18 Morse T's
19 Parisian palace
20 Method of plant propagation
22 ___ Simbel, Egypt
23 Cartesian conclusion
24 Apiary?
26 Mr., in Mysore
27 Saved on supper, perhaps
28 Winglike appendages
29 Make doilies
30 Shaky problem
31 Court target
32 With 17-Across, Dijon's department
33 Decongestant, maybe
36 Mountain
37 Saharan sights
38 Like ___ of sunshine
39 ___ Avivian
40 Three Stooges prop
41 "The One I Love" singers
42 Golfer Ballesteros
43 Ax
46 Ninny
47 Danny's allowance?
49 "Do ___ Diddy Diddy" (1964 hit)
50 Justice Fortas
51 Fast, informally
53 Rabbitlike rodent
55 Fictional terrier
56 Prefix with athlete
57 Gist
58 Took too much, briefly
59 Cabinet dept.
60 Boxer's threat
61 "White Christmas" dancer ___-Ellen
62 Ambient music pioneer

DOWN

1 Makes one
2 It forms food vacuoles
3 It may be curbed
4 Nerve
5 Chinese parade features
6 Leigh Hunt's "Abou Ben ___"
7 Some fraternity chapters
8 Superman's revealing piercer?
9 Very fine
10 Formal refusal
11 Help with, as a project
12 Zinc ___ (ointment ingredient)
16 Arabs, e.g.
21 Time to honor Sandra?
22 Bushed
25 One out?
32 Pool ball hitter?
33 Malaysian state
34 Harbingers
35 It's blown on Yom Kippur
36 "If I Were a Rich Man" singer
37 Tab, e.g.
39 Charge for an afternoon social?
40 Cornrow creator
42 Ice lander?
44 "Roman Elegies" author
45 Like some ball games
48 ___ Island
52 Prank
54 "___ voce poco fa" (Rossini aria)
55 Mazel ___

by Robert H. Wolfe

ACROSS

1 Volvo rival
5 Nez ___
10 Longfellow bell town
14 Soup vegetable
15 Modern husband or wife
16 "The Black Camel" detective
17 63-Across film, 1931
19 Marie Antoinette lost hers
20 Place du Casino locale
21 Choose
23 Russian station
24 Bizet opera priestess
26 Dimwit
28 Egypt's Nasser
32 Some fund-raisers
34 "Billy, Don't Be ___" (1974 hit)
35 "You don't say!"
36 Where jetsam may be thrown
38 63-Across film, 1939
43 Half of a familiar Chinese duo
44 Hipster
45 Reach
46 Where a plane's engine is housed
49 Gluey plaster of Paris
50 Search for water
52 Football Hall-of-Famer Link ___
54 "Yay, team!"
55 Water of Oise
57 Like some dancers
61 "How sweet ___!"
63 Actor born 2/1/1901
66 Greek cheese
67 Freight
68 Fashionable 60's dress
69 Low part of a hand
70 One ordered to stop?
71 Leprechaun's land

DOWN

1 Chip off the old block
2 Old-time actor Tamiroff
3 Ship of myth
4 Road to Rostock
5 English tips?
6 Pertaining to primitive horses
7 Capek drama
8 Clicker
9 Zeno's home
10 Take steps
11 63-Across film, 1961
12 Connecting gears have it
13 Comatose
18 Soapmaker's need
22 Epitome of easiness
25 Without due concern
27 Party to a financial transaction
28 [That's awful!]
29 Salty shout
30 63-Across film, 1934
31 Where gladiators performed
33 O.T. book
37 Demolition supplies
39 Pilot's worry
40 Bankhead of "Lifeboat"
41 Drink that's stirred
42 Ski-___ snowmobiles
47 Average grade
48 Come forth
50 Implication
51 "Outlaws of the Range," e.g.
53 ___ the covenant
56 Billing abbr.
58 Unexciting
59 Structural beam
60 Year Marcus Aurelius became emperor
62 "By the way . . ."
64 Jackie's second
65 Die Welt article

by Frances Hansen

ACROSS

1 Lower, south of the border
5 Deck out
10 It may be made by a stargazer
14 Chug-___
15 Cook in a wok, perhaps
16 Not duped by
17 Where God is King of Kings?
20 Source of suds
21 Litigant
22 Like some auctions
23 Second baseman called "The Crab"
25 Flier
26 Fairy tale figure
28 Diversify
29 "Prince Valiant" cartoonist Foster
32 Lionesses lack them
33 One of a couple
34 Fashion
35 Tongue-twister phrase hinting at this puzzle's theme
38 So
39 Glazed unit
40 "Adam and Eve on a raft," e.g.
41 It may be tipped
42 Have too little
43 Like some salad dressings
44 Airborne unit?
45 Sea
46 Passionate
49 Plating material
50 No exemplar of grace
53 Wine-flavored espagnole
56 Quaint outburst
57 Stage presence?
58 Bit of planning
59 Ding-a-ling
60 Complaining
61 The bulk

DOWN

1 Burglar's deterrent, maybe
2 Natural balm
3 Crushing force
4 21, for one
5 Hearten
6 Hotel listing
7 Essen's region
8 Had something, so to speak
9 Emphatic affirmation
10 ___-be
11 Memo opener
12 Blow out of the water
13 Central computer
18 Burundian biter
19 Light
24 Scenes
25 Irrigate
26 Metalworker
27 Ottoman title
28 Safe place
29 Hi
30 Pitching pros
31 Guarded
33 Acadia National Park locale
34 San Rafael's county
36 Not driving while intoxicated, e.g.
37 Washington team, informally
42 25-Across's perch, perhaps
43 Stubborn as a mule
44 Buddy
45 Protected animal
46 Follow
47 Scrubbed
48 Donnybrook
49 Tubes on the dinner table
51 Tennis statistic
52 Bit of derring-do
54 Cry in Kiel
55 Cry before firing

by Manny Nosowsky

ACROSS

1 One getting a cut
6 Tout's tabulation
10 1968 folk album
14 Mother of Perseus
15 Lug
16 Animal house?
17 Producer of Eazy-E and Eminem
18 Item used in basement waterproofing
20 Sonja Henie's debut film, 1936
22 Methodical
23 Commencement dangler
24 Bully
27 Geographical connectors
29 Truth, old-style
31 Inability to speak
35 Pro ___
36 1971 James Taylor/Warren Oates cult film
41 Perfect
42 Politically incorrect coat
43 Adjust, as a brooch
45 They may have shorts
50 24-time Ryder Cup winner
51 Kind of soup
55 When tripled, an old war cry
56 1932 Bette Davis melodrama
59 "The Thin Man" producer Hunt ___
61 Hi from Ho
62 Nautical nose
63 Senate accusation
64 TV or radio station
65 Cheerleaders' practice
66 Split in the cold, perhaps
67 Marble-producing Italian city

DOWN

1 Annexes
2 Relative of cerise
3 Take to one's heart
4 Airport near Tokyo
5 New driver, maybe
6 Rembrandt, for one
7 Socialite Duke
8 Some exhaust systems
9 Subway station sight
10 Kind of flute
11 Shower apparel
12 Diminutive, in Dogpatch
13 It's fine for a refinery
19 Guitarist Lofgren
21 Harmonize
25 Sgt. Snorkel's dog
26 Larrup
28 Ogden Nash's "___ Stranger Here Myself"
30 Mork's planet
32 ThinkPad producer
33 Cutting repeatedly
34 Malacañang Palace locale
36 By way of, briefly
37 Troubles
38 Like a beat cop
39 Haole's souvenir
40 The 900's, e.g.: Abbr.
44 Benchmark
46 List ender
47 Drives (along)
48 Parts of feet
49 Most of Mauritania
52 Mediterranean ship
53 Canines
54 Cardiological concern
57 Ginsberg poem
58 Word with yes, no or thank you
59 Good looker?
60 Half of sei

by David Ainslie Macleod

ACROSS

1 XXX
5 Unnatural, in a way
10 Place for some icons
14 Up-to-the-minute
15 Opponent for Ike
16 Brown-and-white
17 What is more
18 What old enemies may do
19 Window-rattling
20 Start of a quip
22 "___ be in England . . ."
23 "Cheerio!"
24 Flop
26 A pop
27 Measures of some losses: Abbr.
28 Gymnast's place
32 Big leagues
34 When things don't go right
36 Who "is alone" in a 1987 Sondheim title
37 Middle of the quip
40 Seed coverings
41 Volleys
42 Jack and the missus
44 Go back and forth (with)
45 Kind of mask
48 Book after Philemon: Abbr.
49 Soak (up)
51 Fifth- or sixth-grader
53 Bumper ___
55 End of the quip
59 Take ___ (rest)
60 Spanish 101 verb
61 "An Essay on Criticism" writer
62 Microwave
63 "Veni"
64 Idle fellow?

65 Hearty dinner
66 Colossus
67 Go on and on

DOWN

1 Swank
2 Having a certain glow
3 Time releases
4 Alibi
5 One of Henry VIII's six
6 Old music halls
7 Sound before "Thanks, I needed that!"
8 Dog-___
9 Chinatown offering
10 Singer Guthrie
11 Diminish
12 Semisweet white wine
13 Sign on the dotted line
21 Bull sessions
25 William ___, who founded Ralston Purina
29 A lot of fluff
30 Hullabaloos
31 Half of a 60's quartet
33 Tittles
34 Kans. neighbor
35 Cry out
37 Monocled advertising figure
38 Mechanical device that operates by compression
39 Eggs
40 Waste holders
43 "Very well"
45 Woman of la casa
46 Constrain
47 Treehopper, e.g.
50 "Lethal Weapon 2," ". . . 3" and ". . . 4" actor
52 Rain check
54 Shoot
56 Sportscaster's tidbit
57 Author Janowitz
58 Songbird

by Elizabeth C. Gorski

ACROSS

1 "Goldberg Variations" composer
5 Like Beethoven
9 Crisp cookies
14 "The Intimate ___" (1990 jazz album)
15 Empire builder
16 Zipped, so to speak
17 Start of some campus graffiti
19 Extreme
20 Spode item
21 Lands, as a fish
23 TV inits.
24 Doctor's cupful, maybe
25 Teachers' org.
28 Graffiti, part 2
34 First and second
36 Wharton's Frome
37 To the ___
38 Du Pont trademark
41 Music box music
42 City whose name is derived from a Timucua Indian name
44 Rubber stamp
46 Graffiti, part 3
49 Canton ender
50 1960's revolutionary Mark
51 Snack
53 Collage, e.g.
57 Not so valuable furs
61 Experts
62 End of the graffiti
65 National competitor
66 In ___ (not piecemeal)
67 Beef ___
68 Oppose
69 Coloraturas' performances
70 Till compartment

DOWN

1 Inclination
2 "___ of the Mind" (Sam Shepard play)
3 "The Alexandria Quartet" finale
4 Deck opening
5 Kitchen sink device
6 Business letter abbr.
7 Essen interjection
8 ___ Islands, between Scotland and Iceland
9 Very narrow fit
10 Valueless
11 River isles
12 Prefix with scope
13 Cartoonist Drake
18 Maestro Mehta
22 D.C. is on it
24 It's not part of a play
25 Adverb disdained by English teachers
26 Author ___ Maria Remarque
27 Ike challenger
29 Layer
30 Manche capital
31 Relative of a leek
32 Compels to go
33 ___ nous
35 "___ never work!"
39 Employee's wrap-up: Abbr.
40 Time for le déluge?
43 Pfffsss producer
45 Gaucho's rope
47 Big ___
48 Shows honesty, in a way
52 Gallery installation
53 Thickening agent
54 Do or don't
55 Fat mouth
56 Cause for opening a window
58 Business letter abbr.
59 Ring site
60 Wraps (up)
63 ___ Canals
64 N.L. Central team inits.

by Nancy S. Ross

ACROSS

1 "One Man's San Francisco" author
5 ___ doble (Latin dance)
9 Some Olympians, nowadays
13 Stare impertinently
14 Slogan
16 Algebra topic
18 Like some rats
19 "You there?"
20 Org. that banned DDT
21 Knock over
24 Critic, at times
25 Pay the entire check
28 Fertilizer sources
31 What a cedilla indicates
33 Talk incessantly
34 Turnstile part
37 It can be found in oil
40 Game in which jacks are highest trumps
41 Inflammatory diseases
42 Radiate
43 Ripens
45 Monterrey jack?
46 Pinch-hitting great Manny ___
49 Super ___ (old video game standard)
50 Washington, to Lafayette
52 Fed
54 Chafing dish fuel
57 1947 Best Picture nominee
62 Waste away
63 Answer to the riddle "Dressed in summer, naked in winter"
64 1980's Davis Cup captain
65 Hits a fly
66 City on the Gulf of Aqaba

DOWN

1 Serving with vin
2 Río contents
3 Airline with King David Lounges
4 "Nashville" co-star
5 Outdoor dining spot
6 N.C. State plays in it
7 H. Rider Haggard novel
8 Alphabet trio
9 They talk too much
10 Angrily harangue
11 "___ Mio"
12 "Sí" man?
14 Break activity, perhaps
15 "What's that?"
17 Saw with the grain
21 Knocking noises
22 Kind of triangle
23 Louis Botha, notably
25 Recipe abbr.
26 Fleece
27 Black key
29 Guarantee
30 Blender setting
32 The Rhumba King
34 Together, in music
35 Some mail designations: Abbr.
36 San ___, Calif.
38 Something in writing?
39 An American in Paris, perhaps
43 Dugong's cousin
44 Half of quattordici
46 A Gabor sister
47 Cruel people
48 Choppers
51 Part of a baby bottle
53 Artist Gerard ___ Borch
54 Flies away
55 "Me neither"
56 1977 Scott Turow book
58 Greek letters
59 "Ker-bam!"
60 Quod ___ faciendum
61 Subway wish

by Peter Gordon

ACROSS

1 Double dates
5 Old newspaper sections
10 Something to nibble on with Beaujolais
14 "Alfred" and "Judith" composer
15 Grown
16 ___ Minor
17 Agitate
18 Lofty
19 Pipsqueak
20 "Flood cleanup wears me out!"
23 Line on an invoice
24 "Gotcha!"
25 Bridal path
26 Wilt Chamberlain was one
28 Big name in fine china
30 Strut
31 "Health club exercise is so boring!"
36 Jazzman Allison
39 Franz of operetta fame
40 Tout's concern
41 "Military service leaves me pooped!"
44 Zip-zip
45 Sweethearts
49 Lamb Chop enlivener Lewis
50 Phone menu imperative
54 ___ sense
55 One sense, figuratively
56 "Driving takes away all your energy!"
59 As one, at Orly
61 Old-style copier
62 Reformer Jacob
63 Ordered to go
64 Pretty blue
65 Memo starter
66 Irritable
67 Battery components?
68 Kind of money

DOWN

1 Of the ankle
2 Squirm
3 Out, at the library
4 One who gets what's coming
5 Actress Oakes of "CHiPs"
6 Kitchens have them
7 Like some pregnancies
8 Football Hall-of-Famer Matson
9 1930's Goldwyn star Anna
10 It now has a Union: Abbr.
11 Soak
12 Painkiller dosage phrase
13 Sleep on it
21 Long, for short
22 Louver part
27 Certain vocal part
29 Submissive type
30 It borders the state of Amazonas
32 Kind of pot
33 Still
34 Greek antepenultimate
35 Stay behind
36 She kneads people
37 Left alone
38 Campaign dirty tricks
42 Money guarantor, for short
43 Designer Schiaparelli
46 Blur remover
47 Complete
48 Got smart with
50 Cup or purse
51 Twin of myth
52 Put forth, in a way
53 They may be tapped for the stage
57 Third in a Latin recital
58 "Trinity" novelist
60 What a mess!

by Cathy Millhauser

ACROSS

1 Kellogg's brand
5 Self-styled "Original Gangster"
9 Congressional V.I.P.'s
14 "A Doll's House" heroine
15 One end of a narthex
16 Roundup
17 Alternative to a fence
18 X-file examiners
19 "All My Children" vixen
20 Cooper's tool
21 Combination punch?
23 Basketball announcer's cry
25 Parade
26 The Eagle, e.g.
27 Dirty rat
29 Many eBay users
31 Brain-teasing Rubik
32 Height for Heidi
34 Author Harper
35 Combination punch?
40 Prefix with nucleotide
41 ___ juris
42 "The Open Window" writer
44 Responsible for
48 Fizz maker
50 Big inits. in the defense industry
51 Country's Brooks
53 Supports
54 Below-the-belt combination punch?
57 Samuel's mentor
58 Turn color, maybe
59 Lush
60 "Beowulf" beverage
61 It begins "Sing, goddess, the wrath of . . ."
62 "I will sing ___ the Lord": Exodus
63 Daly of "Judging Amy"
64 Smackers
65 Drudge
66 Zig

DOWN

1 All together
2 Positive news
3 Boxing champ portrayed in the biopic "Somebody Up There Likes Me"
4 Granola bar bit
5 TV's Swenson
6 Negligee jacket
7 Six-time U.S. Open champ
8 Some Met stars
9 Has a lock on?
10 "My ___!"
11 One hanging around the house
12 Mail order company employee
13 Cramps, e.g.
21 Quite a scholar, for short
22 Heating need
24 Anteater features
28 Mexican president, 1988–94
30 Renter
33 Fujitsu products
36 Banded bandits
37 Not enter deliberately
38 Scout's skill
39 Arctic flier
43 Clique member
44 Kind of acid
45 Freely
46 Sweet spot?
47 Matured
49 Words of wonder
52 Biblical possessive
55 Laser light
56 Warner Bros. creation
60 Place for V.J.'s

by Nancy Salomon and Harvey Estes

ACROSS

1 Scotland's ___ Fyne
5 It's nothing to speak of
10 Perennial presidential campaign issue
14 Memo phrase
15 Part of a U.S. census category
16 "Did you ___ ?!"
17 Bound
18 Manly apparel
19 ___ avis
20 Half of a decoder ring
23 Former nuclear power org.
24 "Cómo ___ usted?"
25 Maserati, e.g.
29 It gives you an out
34 The Buckeyes: Abbr.
35 Heralded
38 What a rubber produces?
39 Secret message
43 Hall-of-Fame coach Mike
44 Author Wiesel
45 Clay, after transformation
46 English essayist Sir Richard
48 Unpleasant ones
51 Landers and others
54 Opus ___
55 Other half of the decoder ring
61 Thailand, once
62 More than hot
63 Gave the go-ahead
65 French 101 verb
66 Pluralizers
67 Woman of the haus
68 Its motto is L'Étoile du Nord: Abbr.
69 Thomas Jefferson, religiously
70 Inevitability

DOWN

1 Not-so-apt word for Abner
2 Suitable for service
3 Shore catch
4 One who's beat but good?
5 "Be well"
6 Catchphrase from "Clueless"
7 Poppycock
8 They may be made with Bibles
9 Present
10 Be rough with the reins
11 Flattened figure
12 Earthwork
13 Madrid Mme.
21 Big holiday mo.
22 Notched
25 Makes origami
26 Comparatively healthy
27 Deluxe accommodations
28 All-night party
30 Early auto
31 Zhou ___
32 Move like a 3-Down
33 Tournament round
36 Nothing
37 Smile
40 Classic Jaguar
41 Hit 1980's–90's NBC drama
42 Car safety feature
47 Coveted
49 Et ___ (footnote abbr.)
50 Warn
52 Hospital figure
53 Former East German secret police
55 Tubes in the kitchen
56 Tale
57 Marvel Comics heroes
58 Jeanne d'Arc et al.: Abbr.
59 Gumbo component
60 Without ice
61 Relig. training ground
64 Company in Italy?

by William I. Johnston

ACROSS

1 Race that's always a tie?
6 "West Side Story" gang
10 Purim's month
14 Baked ham spice
15 Koko Head locale
16 Sophia Loren's birthplace
17 Paraded around for a crafts class?
20 Item in Cassatt's "Woman Bathing"
21 It's spotted at a casino
22 Yonder ones
23 Was assaultive in a crafts class?
27 Wool source
30 Nathan Hale's alma mater
31 "Orphée" painter
32 Madras garment
34 Company in a 2000 merger
37 Stole from a crafts class?
41 Pre-op test
42 They cover the bases
43 Kind of joint
44 Shots, for short
46 Digestive enzyme
47 Played hoops during a crafts class?
51 Announcer Don
52 Rooter
53 Peak near the Vale of Tempe
57 Became destructive in a crafts class?
61 Hibernia
62 Feather's place
63 Are suited to
64 Foxx on the box
65 Mind
66 Prelim

DOWN

1 Peak
2 Lento
3 One if by land, two if by sea, etc.
4 Do too well
5 Bus. or res. number
6 Foster of "Sommersby"
7 Abated
8 However, briefly
9 Foot (up)
10 Jughead's pal
11 Sorrow
12 Pile up
13 Country singer Collin ___
18 Pulitzer winner Buchanan
19 Bibliog. space saver
24 Villa Borghese display
25 Persian Empire founder
26 Muskie's successor in the Cabinet
27 Yearn
28 Breakfast ___
29 Hot drink
32 Navigators Islands, today
33 Franco-Swiss collagist
34 Boy or girl lead-in
35 Is behind
36 Tales
38 Asinine
39 Except
40 Unwraps eagerly
44 Number next to a plus sign
45 Siamese "please"
46 Kind of block
47 1984 men's slalom gold medalist
48 Certain roll-on
49 Germ
50 One kind is fed fish, another chips
51 Feather: Prefix
54 Feathery
55 Commotion
56 About
58 Commotion
59 See 60-Down
60 With 59-Down, site of forensics testing

by Cathy Millhauser

ACROSS

1 New York stadium name
5 Classic toothpaste
10 Vacation spot
14 Fish for
15 Chopper blade
16 Pad sitter
17 With 27- and 47-Across, a philosophy prof's remark
20 Part of many addresses
21 Brenner Pass's region
22 Try to open a jar, say
23 Old Mideast union: Abbr.
25 With 56-Across, three-time Masters winner
27 See 17-Across
36 "___ I known!"
37 Restrain
38 Knot
39 "Where Do ___?" ("Hair" piece)
40 "The Sopranos" weapon: Var.
42 Legal scholar's deg.
43 Keep an ___ the ground
45 Mötiey ___
46 It comes at a premium
47 See 17-Across
51 Repeated cry to a vampire
52 Wasn't brave
53 Pvt.'s goal?
56 See 25-Across
60 Merry dos
64 Wiseacre's reply to the prof
67 Russian poet Akhmatova
68 Bursts (with)
69 Israel
70 Crayolalike
71 Like ___ (with equal probability)
72 Masculine side

DOWN

1 Stamp on an order
2 Bell-shaped lily
3 Caraway, e.g.
4 Barely make
5 Ruffle
6 Publicize
7 Suspect's demand: Abbr.
8 King Hussein's queen
9 Melodically
10 Leonard Bernstein's "___ Love"
11 Hotel freebie
12 Resting place
13 Drain sight
18 Quiz
19 Part of a contract
24 Singer McEntire
26 January holiday inits.
27 Swindler
28 Helmeted comics character
29 Love
30 Buster?
31 Eye site
32 Atwitter
33 City invaded by Tamerlane, 1398
34 "The Hobbit" character
35 ___ a high note
40 Order in a kids' card game
41 Sympathy evoker
44 Poet Hughes
48 Opera's Scotto
49 Slumps
50 Very stylish
53 Mouthful
54 Three-time Gold Glove winner Tony
55 Wildcat
57 When people take tours in Tours?
58 Gulf port
59 Major-___
61 Film princess
62 Soon
63 It has bars
65 Knack
66 "C'___ la vie!"

by Jim Page

ACROSS

1 It involves a lot of back-and-forth
7 Deeply connected with
14 Goes up and down
16 Subject of the Brest-Litovsk treaty, 1918
17 Tiara
18 Is uncertain to, briefly
19 Regal letters
20 "With a wink and ___"
22 Like worker bees
23 Cardinal O'Connor's successor
25 Small branch
27 What's ___ . . .
28 Shred
30 Lawn starter
31 Nervous time, maybe
32 "The Maltese Falcon" actress
34 ___ mater (brain cover)
36 Suffix with cannon
37 Camping gear
40 Bawl
42 Dot follower
43 Value system
46 With 9-Down, something to feel
47 "That's awesome!"
49 Fortune teller, maybe
51 Grammarian's bugaboo
53 Certain convertibles
55 Incompletely
56 Enjoying an activity
58 Social group
60 "Car Talk" network
61 Repair shop amenities
63 Part of a rock band
65 Glass-enclosed porches
66 Bach's "Pilgrimage," for one
67 Unwelcome handouts
68 Minneapolis's county

DOWN

1 Good watchdog
2 Bulldog's place
3 "If you play your cards right"
4 Spanish bear
5 Babushka
6 Actress Verdon and others
7 No-goodnik
8 Giving the go-ahead
9 See 46-Across
10 Old Testament figure who prophesied Nineveh's fall
11 Copied, in a way
12 Intimidate
13 Needle holder
15 Old telegram punctuation
21 Dozing
24 Bonkers
26 "Gotcha"
29 Nov. runner
33 Early touring car
35 A Warner Bros. brother
36 Sheikhs' guests, maybe
38 Switch add-on
39 Part of a long-distance company's 800 number
40 Army helicopter
41 Certain summer cottages
44 Tough guy
45 Go for the gold
46 Emergency situation
48 Canadian capital?
50 American turtle
52 Like most music
53 Take off
54 Vaughan of jazz
57 Yesterday, in Italy
59 Air
62 Trans-Atlantic carrier
64 K2 is one: Abbr.

by Manny Nosowsky

ACROSS

1 "___ tu" (aria for Renato)
4 Single dance move?
7 Increases, as production
14 Perils
16 Medical problem
17 Quite some distance (from)
18 Need after collation
19 Uncomfortable
21 Flight unit
22 Party souvenir
23 Single and double
24 Old seminar subject
25 Nobel, for one
27 Bando of baseball
30 Start to date?
33 The same, in a bibliography
36 Brake part
39 In the minority?
42 Fasten firmly, in a way
43 Water-carved gullies
44 Nursery collection
45 Blackout
46 Short
48 It hunted for Red October
52 Cole Porter's "___ Loved"
55 Actor Morales
58 Suffix with zinc
59 Stop
61 Show in which much is shown
63 Like some birthday wishes
65 Red Sea land
66 Invoice issuers
67 Rodeo activity
68 Summons
69 Fess (up)
70 Audiophile's amassment

DOWN

1 Contacts quickly, perhaps
2 Covered again, as an air route
3 Bad way to be caught
4 Carpe diem
5 "___ Go Again" (1987 #1 song)
6 To this point
7 G.R.E. takers
8 Vietnamese festivals
9 Send
10 Pontiffs, in Roma
11 Soup ingredients
12 Computerphile
13 Apiece
15 Neighbor of Scorpius
20 Start to sob?
26 Film producer De Laurentiis
28 It may be payable: Abbr.
29 "Symphonie Espagnole" composer
31 Stutz contemporary
32 Seabird
34 They may be boosted
35 Fit together
37 Sees
38 The Pointer Sisters' "___ Excited"
39 Can opener
40 Time piece?
41 Two-time U.S. Open winner
47 "You bet!"
49 Kind of acid
50 Sit in on
51 Changes prices, perhaps
53 In the least
54 Remote features
56 Letter taker
57 Hood's weapon
59 Queen Amidala's daughter
60 Forward
62 Tabulations: Abbr.
63 "I, Claudius" network
64 Brit. honor

by Robert H. Wolfe

ACROSS

1 Overthrown leader
5 Not out
10 See 61-Down
14 Actress Lamarr
15 Beau's gift
16 Till fill
17 Speaker of the quip starting at 20-Across
19 It has the spirit
20 Start of a quip
22 Slightest
23 Word of agreement
24 Sharp flavor
26 "Kate & Allie" actress Meyers
27 Young fowl
31 It could be stuffed
33 Old station identification
35 Had
36 Main city of Devon
37 Quip, part 2
40 Haunt
43 Jeff Lynne group
44 "My Uncle" star
48 Chekhov uncle
49 It should set off alarms
51 Informal footwear
52 Flutter
53 One of the Volcano Islands, for short
55 Jobs site
57 Quip, part 3
62 Subjoins
63 End of the quip
64 Saddle, e.g.
65 Tel Aviv-born person
66 French jeweler Lalique

67 "Chickery Chick" bandleader
68 Smithery employee
69 Genesis source

DOWN

1 "The Glamorous Life" singer
2 Sewing machine attachments
3 Shelley's elegy to Keats
4 Some needles
5 ___ cantabile (gentle, sad song)
6 Whistle maker?
7 China setting
8 Persisted in
9 Paper

10 Spots
11 Ticked off
12 Merry
13 "You naughty person!"
18 Start of many addresses
21 Paul V's papal predecessor
25 Part of w.p.m.
28 They can be rolled
29 Tribal language
30 Bank
32 It's just not right
34 Follow
36 TV spinoff of 1980
38 Carrier name until 1997
39 Biblical judge

40 Plant gametes
41 "I wouldn't do that"
42 Winter break, of a sort
45 Person with a loss
46 Sexton's duty
47 Summer drink
49 Platform on the back of an elephant
50 Kind of shell
54 Houdini's birth name
56 Really rains
58 Princely family name of old
59 Transient
60 Bern is on it
61 With 10-Across, skier's aid
62 "Shoot!"

by Trip Payne

ACROSS

1 Is a gamester
7 Band aid?
10 Neckline shape
13 Final words
14 Putting weight on?
16 Buy bonds, e.g.
17 Tongue-lash
18 One of the Canterbury pilgrims
19 Care
20 Be bold
21 Knuckle under
22 Smitten
24 A bit of chiding
29 Cutting remarks?
31 Matter for the gray matter
32 Box office
33 They might provide general delivery
35 Circular: Abbr.
37 Schindler of "Schindler's List"
38 Voice range
39 Poker variety
41 Blow it
42 "Yes! Yes!"
45 Singing or dancing
47 Air, to a jet engine
49 "___ that's your game!"
52 Accidentally
56 Bonnie Blue's father
57 Catch up with
58 Show scorn to
59 Flipped
60 Burning the midnight oil
61 What Leary tripped on
62 Elmore of the N.B.A.
63 High hat

DOWN

1 Macabre
2 Reason to see a hypnologist
3 Engender
4 One after another?
5 Didn't sit still?
6 Cpl.'s superior
7 Still in the game
8 "Get going now!"
9 Songs of praise
10 Life of Cicero
11 ___'acte
12 Designer von Furstenberg
15 Carried out
17 Good-natured exchange
19 Unselfish sort
21 Word on all U.S. coins
23 Fleur-de-___
25 Metric wts.
26 Assume blame
27 Destiny
28 Brynner's co-star in film's "The King and I"
29 California hometown for TV's Six Million Dollar Man
30 Join
34 Luau serving
36 Golden Hind captain
37 "You ___ it to yourself"
40 Bass, e.g.
43 Proximal's opposite
44 Like sports highlights
46 Unavailing
48 Occupied
50 Say
51 Virginia's ___ River
52 Big sports event
53 Part of Y.S.L.
54 Make whole
55 N.Y.C. subway line
56 Tow job
58 Stick (out)

by Manny Noswsky

ACROSS

1 Menus, essentially
6 Magnum and others: Abbr.
9 Trans World Dome team
13 Tee off
14 See 46-Across
15 Think out loud
17 Swedish tennis star's favorite movie?
19 Match play?
20 Capek play
21 Singer who really cuts the mustard?
23 Letters' partner
25 Works accepted as authentic
26 Madrigal accompaniment
27 Trial
29 Not sweet
31 Sábado or domingo
32 Tiny bit
34 Blew a gasket
36 Vehicle for touring Scandinavia?
40 Kind of concerto
41 Your of yore
42 "Uncle Tom's Cabin" girl
43 Time off?
46 With 14-Across, what latecomers may miss
50 Spring period
52 ___ del Sol
54 Livy's love
55 Chinese dish that casts a spell?
58 J.F.K. abbr.
59 Keep ___ out for
60 Coxcombs (and a hint to solving this puzzle)
62 Place atop
63 Prefix with annual
64 Wet spots
65 It may be ear-piercing
66 Like Nasdaq securities: Abbr.
67 Words before "Remember" and "Forget," in song titles

DOWN

1 A-mazing animal?
2 Wound
3 Sty cacophony
4 Rocky hilltop
5 Harmony, informally
6 Manner of speaking
7 Make housebound, as by bad weather
8 Hearing aides
9 Pike
10 You may get fooled when it arrives
11 Think wrongly of
12 More stuck up
16 Supreme Court, for one
18 Prolific
22 Wind dir.
24 Aid in reaching a high shelf, maybe
28 Bucolic
30 "Snow White" meanie
33 No. after a no.
35 It may have boxes and boxers
36 Change for a fin
37 "I Love Rock 'n Roll" rocker
38 Like vision in bright light
39 Italy's ___ Islands
40 "Chicago" vamp and others
44 Cologne cry
45 Approach
47 "Doesn't matter to me"
48 Reply to the impatient
49 Former Conn. governor Ella
51 "Nuts ___!"
53 Fencing, e.g.
56 Thrill
57 Cluster
61 Be discordant

by David J. Kahn

ACROSS

1 Emphatic agreement
5 Pitcher Shawn ___
10 See 48-Down
14 Circular announcement
15 Ring
16 Mine, in Montréal
17 X
20 Unusual
21 Pulls down, so to speak
22 Méditerranée, par exemple
23 You may flirt with it
26 Thun's river
27 "Farewell, My Lovely" novelist
31 Neighbor of an Afghani
34 Bohr's study
35 ___ y plata (Montana's motto)
36 X
40 Hollywood job: Abbr.
41 It means nothing to Nicolette
42 "Shake, Rattle and Roll" singer
43 Sticky situation
46 Crop
47 Sorry soul
49 Authority on diamonds?
52 "I don't buy it"
55 7,926 miles, for the earth
57 X
60 ___-eyed
61 Judging group
62 Fall preceder, perhaps
63 Throw out
64 Like God, in a fire-and-brimstone sermon
65 Some queens

DOWN

1 Land bordering Bhutan
2 Equivocal answer
3 Dramatist Rice
4 North Platte locale: Abbr.
5 No dessert for a dieter
6 Climbs, in a way
7 X X X
8 Source of lean red meat
9 Clinton, e.g.: Abbr.
10 Baseless rumor
11 Archer of myth
12 Square setting
13 Faults
18 Make a father
19 Neato
24 Less woolly, perhaps
25 Author Janowitz
26 Singer DiFranco
28 Hang out
29 Noted Folies Bergère designer
30 Like some outlooks
31 Operation Desert Storm target
32 Lipton, Inc. brand
33 Girl lead-in
34 Conflagrant
37 What cleats increase
38 Greg's sitcom wife
39 Labor org. since 1935
44 They may be sour
45 Whimper
46 How brutes behave
48 With 10-Across, ocelot and margay
49 Complete change of mind
50 Excellence
51 Gets ready
52 "Over here!"
53 Minuteman's place
54 They have participating M.D.'s
56 James of jazz
58 Grp. monitoring emissions
59 ___ Clemente

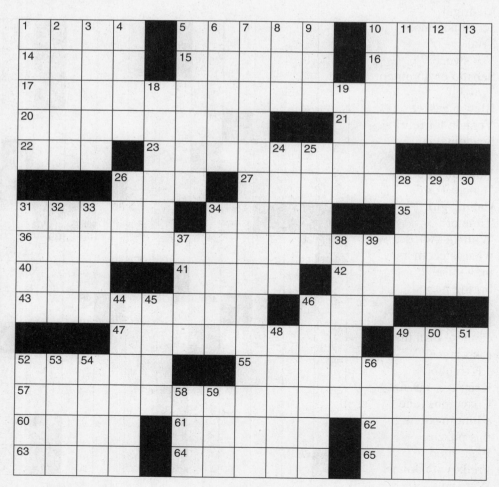

by William I. Johnston

ACROSS

1 Rich, raisiny cake
5 Knuckler alternative
10 Court helper
14 Work in the media
15 Jazz pianist Marsalis
16 Museo work
17 Fathers' robes
18 Cheery
19 Broadway luminary?
20 It rises in Lake Victoria
21 ___ X
22 Throws off
24 In-line skate part
26 Start of a simple game
27 "___ a perfumed sea . . .": Poe
28 Synchronize anew
32 Commode component
36 Flap
38 Ride in a shuttle
39 Tale of Vikings, perhaps
40 Cartoon aficionado's purchase
41 Comment after the fog clears
42 Manual consultants
44 Fish of the genus Electrophorus
45 Cold war ammunition?
46 She ranks
48 ___-Pitch
50 In addition
51 Mess up at a critical moment
56 He stopped smoking cigars in 1985
59 Hockey shutout
60 Hockey position
61 Symbol of life
62 Gives the nod to
64 One-two connector
65 In ___ (even)
66 Caribbean port
67 Footnote word
68 Tennis miss
69 Rounded end
70 Revealing work of art?

DOWN

1 Dangerous pitch
2 Unrehearsed
3 Job site?
4 One way to be lost
5 Former Windsor in-law, informally
6 "Star Trek" peoples
7 Talk on the street
8 Foil material
9 Hoosier university
10 Jailbird's burden
11 Belgian balladeer
12 Missouri's ally, once
13 Desires
23 Market corrections
25 Seoul soldier
28 Big wheel's wheels
29 Plus
30 Offed
31 Look at
32 Muddles
33 Possessive, e.g.
34 S-curve
35 Be in charge
37 River to the North Sea
43 Nostradamus, for one
45 Saturate
47 Street game
49 Relax
51 College in Crete, Neb.
52 "What Is Man?" essayist
53 Caste member
54 Through
55 It may follow the national anthem
56 "Slither" star, 1973
57 ___ meridiem
58 Little play
63 Comical lawman

by Robert H. Wolfe

ACROSS

1 Thai money
5 Theme of this puzzle
10 Greek peak
14 Sheltered, in a way
15 Johnson's partner in comedy
16 It may be fair
17 Four before 5-Across
20 ___ Wall
21 Peripheral
22 Hobby shop inventory
23 Gary's co-star in "Desire"
25 Bathysphere designer
27 College V.I.P.'s
29 Romantic interlude
30 Exactly right
31 Hypo units
34 Three before 5-Across
37 Ascap alternative
38 Field of vision?
39 ___ Thomas, the Soul Queen of New Orleans
40 Puts down
42 Oafish
43 Héloïse's correspondent
45 Gymnastics move
46 Successfully defended one's title
47 Blabs
51 Four before 5-Across
54 More
55 Look for
56 It was founded in 1440
57 Morse bits
58 Eclipses
59 Thrill

DOWN

1 Blowout
2 Resort next to Snowbird
3 Four before 5-Across
4 Not just bad
5 Gauchos' weapons
6 "Thirtysomething" co-star
7 Indiana Jones's dread
8 Pastor's field: Abbr.
9 Trial evidence, sometimes
10 Small mouthlike aperture
11 Three before 5-Across
12 It's heard on "Cops"
13 Auto pioneer Citroën
18 Refer to
19 Going (over)
23 "M*A*S*H" characters
24 Neurites
25 Lettuce variety
26 Gouda alternative
27 Basketball team, e.g.
28 Arrested
30 Con artist
32 Provide gratis
33 Weight, e.g.
35 "Friends" follower
36 They may be dull
41 Emulates Romeo and Juliet
42 Woes
43 Like rainbows
44 Beautiful, in Bologna
45 Some keys have them
47 "Jabberwocky" opener
48 Reduce a sentence, perhaps
49 The first "L" of L. L. Bean
50 Come down
52 Pinch
53 "To what do I ___ . . . ?"

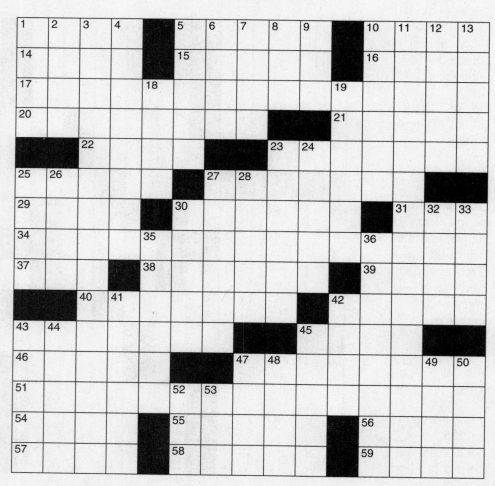

by Randolph Ross

ACROSS

1 Overexcited, slangily
6 What to call a lady
10 Not too bright
14 Jelly fruit
15 "Table Talk" essayist
16 Sen. Bayh
17 Till now
18 Swag
19 Gen. Lee's troops
20 Quaff from a gold-plated dog bowl?
23 Give the once-over
24 Unbroken
25 Holder of a number of degrees
27 Pitcher's rubber
29 Slowly
31 How-to listings
34 Latin 101 word
37 Lollobrigida of film
38 What a dog might do to pretend it's not out of breath?
41 Spreadable stick
42 Designer Cassini
43 Prime-time time
44 Oskar of "Fahrenheit 451"
46 Parade spoiler
48 Camp seat, perhaps
49 Had a hunch
52 Grp. with pull?
55 Jacket for a hunting dog?
59 Plant bristles
60 Crossing the Atlantic, maybe
61 Monopoly buy
62 Haymaker
63 Like some drinks
64 Popular watch
65 Florida ___
66 Water barrier
67 Subs

DOWN

1 Banded stone
2 Overly sentimental
3 Check casher
4 First name in derring-do
5 Facts and figures
6 Fruit salad ingredient
7 Up
8 Garlicky mayonnaise
9 Grow up
10 Pan American Highway land
11 Finding the means?
12 Daedalus creation
13 Nav. officer
21 Shooter ammo
22 Marked out
26 Kind of guard
27 Taster's aid
28 The Fighting Tigers, for short
30 Over
31 Grinch's look
32 Job's relation
33 Hospital sign
35 Ginnie ___
36 Whole bunch
39 Court motion
40 Louvre Pyramid architect
45 PC key
47 Brouhaha
50 Some Japanese-Americans
51 Not do openly
52 On the trail of
53 Don ___ de la Vega (Zorro)
54 China setting?
56 Sounds of disapproval
57 "That doesn't sound good"
58 A-E, maybe
59 Press (for)

by Mark Diehl

ACROSS

1 Union station?
6 It may help you get a grip
11 Pro with books
14 Death in Venice
15 Alternative to Italian
16 Chinese dynasty name
17 Management group for a pro team
19 N.Y.C. subway
20 Kind of dress
21 Overdue
22 Petrographer's collection
24 Salmonella's shape
26 Post-accident comment
27 "A Star Is Born" co-star
33 Capone pal
34 Sistine Chapel figure
35 No neatnik
38 Tactical station, for short
39 Smokes at a poker game
42 Sen. Roth created one
43 Kind of test
45 Home of Iowa State
46 Not so naughty
48 Gridiron ploy
51 Newscast feature
53 When the French fry?
54 Local ___
55 Like some dorms
58 Black-eyed ones
62 Dr. J's first league: Abbr.
63 Electrical device with a hint to answering 17-, 27- and 48-Across
66 Developer's investment

67 Ibid. relative
68 Certain Honda
69 Pink-slip
70 Steer shockers
71 Schussed

DOWN

1 Broadcasting bands
2 Actress Petty
3 Tramped
4 Initially
5 Official
6 Unpleasant thing to eat
7 Swimmer's assignment
8 "National Velvet" author Bagnold
9 Duke's grp.

10 Hot beginning?
11 Film popular with female audiences
12 Tundra cover-up
13 On pins and needles
18 Pother
23 Punch responses
25 Leader of a lush life in Mayberry?
26 "Woe ___"
27 Drawer part
28 Fully developed
29 #1 Carole King song
30 One of the Judds
31 Sharpened
32 Poker ploy
36 DoubleStuf treat
37 Source of some lows

40 Foreign news source
41 Huff
44 Big do
47 Chip maker
49 Sitcom set in Fort Courage
50 Adidas alternative
51 Milan's La ___
52 FedEx won't deliver to it
55 1969 Broadway musical
56 "The Wizard ___"
57 Some newts
59 Pin holder
60 One of the back 40
61 Roe source
64 Big inits. in news
65 Lived

by Peter Abide

ACROSS

1 It can be poisonous
6 Flight fleet
10 One with idyll musings?
14 "Cosmicomics" author Calvino
15 A few words in passing?
16 1952 Olympics venue
17 Whence Sir Walter Scott's Fair Maid
18 Zola novel
19 Warbler
20 Stoppard play that made money abroad?
23 Letters for Old MacDonald
24 Mimosa-family tree
25 Cukor film that made money abroad?
29 Encouragement for Escamillo
30 Three-time Masters champ
31 Part of I.R.T.
35 Biblical verb
37 Indian attire
39 Central point
40 On a 42-Across
42 Knockabout, e.g.
44 Just out
45 Rolling Stones hit that made money abroad?
48 Acid neutralizer
51 Written commentary
52 Comedienne who made money abroad?
56 Give obligingly
57 Den din
58 Much-misunderstood writing
61 S-shaped molding
62 Tilted position

63 Follow
64 Microsoft product
65 Countercurrent
66 Swedish imports

DOWN

1 Very small serving
2 Indian tongue
3 Strict sergeants, say
4 Tennis great Gibson
5 Fortune sharers, perhaps
6 Mitchell with a guitar
7 Where bidders wait online
8 "Waterworld" actress Majorino

9 P.O.W.'s place
10 Indian confederacy founder
11 Courtier in "Hamlet"
12 Nicholas Gage novel
13 Friendly Islands
21 Some horses
22 N.E.A. member: Abbr.
23 Gulf of Aqaba port
25 Qatar's capital
26 Pick on
27 Country rocker Steve
28 No exemplar of erudition
32 Spread on Lake Tahoe
33 Head sets?

34 Moist
36 Announced
38 Boating locale
41 Annual song title starter
43 State symbols of Indiana
46 Run through
47 Clavicle connectors
48 Visibly happy
49 "Hasta ___!"
50 Seven-time N.L. home run champ
53 It may be hogged
54 "We the Living" author
55 So-o-o-o SoHo
59 Gist
60 Survey choice

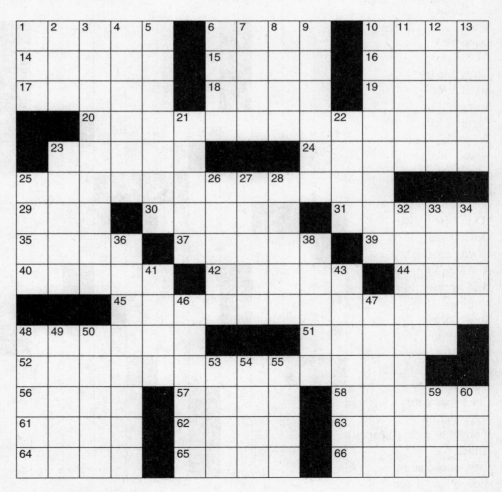

by Alan Arbesfeld

ACROSS

1 Suffix on color names
4 Shoot upward
10 1950, in copyrights
14 DVD maker
15 In
16 Role for Ingrid
17 N.Y.C. subway inits.
18 Moves suddenly
19 Eartha Kitt role
20 Summer vacation locale
22 Peter the Great, e.g.
24 Fox's prey
25 1980 Erich Segal novel
29 A little over half the world
31 Time, in Torino
32 ___ Tomé
33 Mister
35 Deep blue
36 Dict. listing
37 Percy Sledge hit of 1966
41 Star of "The Facts of Life"
42 Where E*Trade is traded: Abbr.
43 Letter abbr.
44 Howard Hughes once controlled it
45 "Don't Bring Me Down" grp.
46 Kodak founder
50 Ang Lee film, 1994 Best Foreign Film nominee
55 Sports org. since 1906
56 Unexciting
57 Eliminates
59 Place for a Christmas card
61 Aggravation
63 It might be picked apart
64 Attack
65 City whose name is Siouan for "a good place to dig potatoes"
66 End of a four-day hol., maybe
67 Mice catchers
68 Degrades
69 Draft org.

DOWN

1 Edna O'Brien or Sinéad O'Connor
2 Shrill sound
3 John Wayne film set in Africa
4 Rubella symptom
5 Place to put the feet up
6 Office building cleaner
7 Asian peninsula
8 CPR performer
9 Go out and back in an Outback, perhaps
10 Book before Nahum
11 "___ Explains It All" (cable series)
12 Phoenix setting: Abbr.
13 Song and album by the Doors
21 Meaning
23 Like a 3-4-5 triangle
26 Verboten thing
27 One who's not in the habit of wearing a habit
28 Mafia leader
30 Some fund-raisers
34 "GoodFellas" co-star
35 Cakes' partner
37 Electric guitar attachment
38 Protect from the air, in a way
39 Singer Marilyn
40 Skims
41 Map abbr.
47 Darts
48 Mother's Day baby, e.g.
49 Dugongs' kin
51 Noodleheads
52 Drummer Gene
53 Fertilizes
54 Feminine
58 Those, to José
59 Tropical fruit
60 Wrecker's job
62 Word with sister or story

by Peter Gordon

ACROSS

1 Tin lizzie
7 Concept, in Québec
11 It first aired on 8/1/81
14 Revolt leader, old-style
15 Resort island northeast of Sydney
17 Flout
18 Dickens, in his formative years
19 Like some furniture
20 Auto-stopping innovation
21 Summer slaker
22 1950's Hungarian premier Nagy
24 Tiny Archibald
25 Takes a load off
27 Instructor's charge
30 Computer bulletin board overseers
31 Sidesplitter
32 Opposite of dep.
33 Redundancies, like 20- and 50-Across and 5- and 29-Down
36 Armageddon nation
39 Parentheses, e.g.
40 Photocopier
44 Person who breaks down
46 "X-Men" creator
47 Shot fluids
48 Former blacklisting org.
49 Prince Valiant's son
50 Account access requirement, often
54 Knew the answer
56 "My stars!"
57 Spanish letter addenda?
58 Protected, in a way
59 Swallow

60 Slalom path
61 Inventors' cries
62 Simple shelter

DOWN

1 Reckless types
2 Vitamin regimen
3 People who get rid of holes
4 Cleveland Indian
5 Laptop readout
6 U.S. Constitution's first article
7 "Would you look at that!"
8 Ski-___ (snowmobiles)
9 Coastal raptors
10 Swirl
11 Flathead Indians' home
12 Speaker part
13 "View of Delft" painter
16 Egypt's Mubarak
20 13-Down's output
23 Scrooges
26 Keystone figure
27 Female in la familia
28 Mary Pickford title role of 1923
29 Cash source
31 I.C.U. personnel
34 Fall time: Abbr.
35 ___ Pedro
36 It may lead to a pilot

37 New York natives
38 Symbols of January
41 Cheer
42 Superlatively strange
43 Provides a room for, perhaps
45 Charger's weapon
46 180° from norte
48 Obeys
51 Skeleton part
52 It has its share of problems
53 Town north of Anaheim
55 Bit of ocean flora
57 Up to, informally

by William I. Johnston

ACROSS

1 Time's 1977 Man of the Year
6 Attempt
10 Festive
14 Waive one's rites?
15 Obsidian, before cooling
16 Huge-screen film format
17 Absolute
18 Firm head
19 Information unit
20 Wine shop customer?
23 Untangle
24 Andean fauna
28 Web browser entry
29 What a waste pipe provides
31 Melee memento
34 Stretch beside the water
35 Pink-slip
36 Get kicked?
40 Mentalist Geller
41 Log holder, perhaps
42 Moon, personified
43 Loses the right to
45 Cole Porter, schoolwise
47 Fried filled-tortilla dish
48 Kind of diver
52 Herring on a fishhook?
55 Flight controller?
58 Milk source
59 Arthur Ashe's "___ Road to Glory"
60 Big yard, perhaps
61 Indy 500's 200
62 Scout master?
63 Scan, say
64 Vortex
65 Keats title starter

DOWN

1 Oobleck's creator
2 Even if, briefly
3 New grandparent, often
4 Opening
5 It reigned in the 1790's
6 Wasn't up
7 Hack
8 "___ plaisir!"
9 Strong reaction
10 "The Prophet" author Kahlil ___
11 "Yentl" actress Irving
12 Global positioning fig.
13 Good hacker
21 Deborah's "The King and I" co-star
22 A-list
25 ___ Picchu, Peru
26 Time's partner
27 Medicinal plant
29 Proscriptions
30 Assign stars to
31 Things
32 "Good Christian Men, Rejoice," e.g.
33 Director Kurosawa
34 Fur or fleece
37 Marvin Gaye's "Can ___ Witness?"
38 Amorous complication
39 Careless
44 Reneged (on)
45 Dark period of poetry
46 Smooth, in scores
48 Scatterbrained
49 Classic western
50 Give ___ (heed)
51 Accessory
53 Cattle driver
54 Sgt. Friday's force
55 Dove's aversion
56 It has a chilling effect
57 Org. that fought the Brady bill

by Marjorie Richter

ACROSS

1 Refusal to buckle
6 How beef may be served
11 Brandy designation letters
14 Not engaged
15 Smidgen
16 Be distressed
17 Typical dervish?
20 Catch
21 Wager in Monte Carlo
22 Where to see Alain Delon or Geneviève Bujold
24 Like cult films, again and again
25 Get-go
29 Emerge
31 Time to get sharp?
33 Overcome
37 Market opener?
38 The Company
39 ___ Major
40 Argo, e.g.
41 Question from a confused astronaut?
44 Leaves rolling in the aisles
46 Sunday may have several of them
47 Office machine
50 Tease
52 Paper craft
54 Jones and Smith, maybe
59 What Miss Muffet believed a spider might do?
61 Great deal
62 Legal U.S. tender
63 Uses digits?
64 ___-Cat
65 Shrek and others
66 Raiser of dough

DOWN

1 Previously said
2 Work out
3 Bonding candidates
4 Twelve, maybe
5 Rubs out
6 White as a sheet
7 Tiny Tim instrument
8 It may hang by the neck
9 Bring
10 Counties overseas
11 Consider worthwhile
12 Military operation
13 Antiquated
18 Stating the obvious
19 Future bloomers
23 Least brow-wrinkling
25 Must pay
26 "Nah!"
27 TV's Hatcher
28 It brings traffic to a standstill
30 Expression of pride?
32 Sore
34 One of the primal gods in Greek myth
35 ". . . mercy on such ___": Kipling
36 Khakis
41 Becoming less 14-Across
42 Boxer Griffith
43 Hit the spot
45 Bring
47 Receipt listings
48 "What the Butler Saw" playwright
49 Soft
51 Goes down
53 "___ out?" (dealer's query)
55 Bide-___
56 Queens place
57 Fish captured in pots
58 Part of S.S.S.: Abbr.
60 Suffix with Capri

by Manny Nosowsky

ACROSS

1 Bank security devices
5 Go postal
9 Betray, in a way
14 Grp. with crude interests?
15 Zip
16 Daughter of Juan Carlos I
17 Yukon, e.g.: Abbr.
18 ___ epic scale
19 Symbol of neutrality
20 Chapeau holder, spelled out in detail?
23 With hands on hips
24 Egypt and Syria, once: Abbr.
25 Targets of some beatings, spelled out in detail?
32 Part of A.C.C.: Abbr.
35 Singer Lennon
36 Begin
37 Latched
39 Unbolt, poetically
41 With 42-Across, Somewhat
42 See 41-Across
45 Union joiner of 1896
48 Bad thing to break
49 1930's–40's tyrant, spelled out in detail?
52 European skyline sight
53 Certain electron tube
57 Illusions, spelled out in detail?
62 Oily
63 Honey, in Le Havre
64 Souvenirs with scents
65 From here
66 Men's store section
67 Pari-mutuel
68 Like some kitchens
69 Epilogs
70 Black as night

DOWN

1 Terra ___
2 Take ___ (glance)
3 Cousin of danke
4 Save's partner
5 Carnival treat
6 Half of Mork's sign-off
7 Man who was never born
8 Amount to fry
9 One may use hand signals
10 Judd's role on "Taxi"
11 Thing to have a stake in
12 Grimm beginning
13 Scottish turndown
21 Diamond stats
22 Cub scouts
26 Universal ideal
27 Suggestions
28 Bank alternative
29 Plane or square, e.g.
30 Mystique
31 Slow-cook
32 Starting
33 By way of, briefly
34 Dilly
38 Pro ___
40 Numerical suffix
43 Let up
44 Successful pitch
46 Ingenuous
47 Bickerer in the "Iliad"
50 Most recent news
51 Marketplace
54 Cineplex ___ (theater chain)
55 Mars or Mercury
56 Southend-on-Sea site
57 Typhus carrier
58 Isn't informal?
59 Year in Diocletian's reign
60 Declaration of participation
61 Wasn't honest
62 Cow or sow

by Bruce F. Adams

ACROSS

1 Church name opener
4 Vacation plan, maybe
8 Door fixture
12 Application
13 Famous squire of Spanish lit
14 Farm letters?
16 High ground
19 Emblem of the House of Lancaster
20 Made a fool of
21 Gave, as lines
22 One of the Durants
23 High ground
25 High ground
28 Love inspirer
29 Typography units
30 Amble or shamble
31 Harped (on)
32 Middle ground
35 1966 Michael Caine role
38 Big do
39 Walther ___ (007's gun)
42 Former capital of Nicaragua
43 Low ground
45 Low ground
48 Immediate occasion
49 Bearer of the Commandments
50 Discontinuity
51 Athelstane's romantic rival
53 Low ground
56 Compact stuff
57 Fluff up, as hair
58 Bud of Bud
59 Arctic sight
60 It's right on the map
61 Talent that defies sci.

DOWN

1 Get there before
2 Mark the beginning of
3 Adapts for a new audience
4 Where Kit Carson is buried
5 "Lean ___"
6 Automatic
7 Mrs. Huxtable's portrayer
8 Tinseltown gossip Hopper
9 Trouble
10 Marine bioluminescence
11 Clorox Company product
13 Speech that opens a play
15 Least explicable
17 Hunted
18 Corn serving
23 Creamy soups
24 ___-eyed (naive)
26 Substantially
27 Small carriage
31 It's poor on the moor
32 Pub order
33 Creosote source
34 Word before school or master
35 Brightest star in the Aquila constellation
36 Find out about
37 Big bite of spaghetti
39 Tiny aperture
40 Pennsylvania resort area
41 British dance party
43 Enter a nonfeeding state
44 Actress Collette of "The Sixth Sense"
46 Jibe
47 Bolted
51 Long-term finan. plans
52 Buttoned item
54 ___ ideal
55 Grassy tract

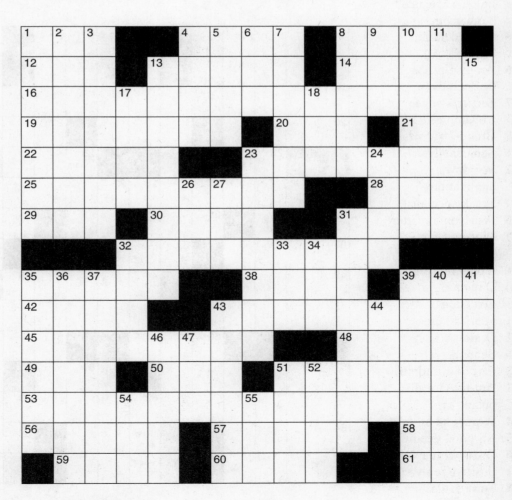

by Patrick Berry

ACROSS

1 Staff figure
6 Hull hazard
10 Cast off
14 Steamed
15 Expression
16 Rhode Island's motto
17 Be affected by electrical attraction?
20 Time or life follower
21 It may be tipped
22 Next up
23 Israel's Netanyahu, familiarly
25 Profit share
26 Bishop preparing to hold a yard sale?
34 Young 'un
35 Architectural order
36 An inspiration to Beethoven
37 Server's edge, to Sampras
39 Broods
41 Sen. Bayh
42 Windows applications?
44 Track specialist
46 Work on a platter
47 Workout for bratty kids at a mountain resort?
50 Day-care diversion
51 F.B.I. figures
52 Draft
56 Shad ___
58 Part of a Latin trio
61 Apt title for this puzzle
64 Warts and all
65 No good deed
66 Dress with a flare
67 Positive reply
68 Turn down
69 Moisten

DOWN

1 Band's schedule
2 Field goal?
3 Like most citizens
4 Like some cuisine
5 Charge
6 Pet peeve?
7 Football great Ronnie
8 Swooning sound
9 Barely make
10 Like many horses
11 Perfect
12 Big production
13 Education station
18 They're thick-skinned
19 With 55-Down, where some things come out
24 Two hearts, e.g.
25 Coop cry
26 "The Bell Jar" writer
27 Arm bones
28 Cross
29 Paramecia features
30 Word of encouragement
31 Help that's always available
32 Father of famous twins
33 Some change
38 Greatest possible
40 "The Battleship Potemkin" director Eisenstein
43 Get out of a slump?
45 It stores data permanently
48 Disposed of, with "up"
49 Snoopy, e.g.
52 Time of reckoning
53 Hillock
54 What one of the five Olympic rings stands for
55 See 19-Down
56 Picnicker's worry
57 It's near Paris
59 Rough problem to face?
60 Brood
62 Member of the first family
63 Collar

by Joe DiPietro

ACROSS

1 Novelty item in comic book ads
10 Widget
15 Rocked the boat
16 Go on ___ (rampage)
17 Previously
18 Trunks
19 Atlas abbr.
20 Shoe box marking
21 Sour
22 Provides a seat for
24 Koh-i-___ (106-carat diamond)
26 Brooder
27 Near Eastern inn
28 Egg holders: Abbr.
29 Wear a long face
30 Lies down
32 Feint
33 "The Fugitive" star of 60's TV
36 Popular, in a way
38 It may be on a roll
39 Schoolmaster, to the classroom
41 "The Birth of a Nation" group
42 A bed in the kitchen?
43 Significant others
47 Listen to one's gut?
48 Le Carré's Leamas
49 Siamese, e.g.
50 Is out, in a way
52 Moonfish
54 Place runners?: Abbr.
55 Developing solution
56 Lots
58 Calendario opener
59 Meddle
60 French Symbolist Odilon ___
61 Utmost

DOWN

1 Short holidays?
2 Faze
3 Any of the Magi
4 Itch
5 Cupcakes
6 Noodles
7 "Howards End" role
8 Sticks together
9 Venice-to-Naples dir.
10 Swamp snapper
11 Atlanta Rhythm Section's "Do ___ Die"
12 Moment of truth
13 One may work with oils
14 Word after family or object
21 Expert in bryophytes
23 He used to follow the news
25 Jittery
28 Basketball Hall-of-Famer Hawkins
29 Like some urges
31 Units of wisdom?
33 Card
34 Isolated
35 Picked up
37 "Likewise"
40 Story
44 Cry before a fall
45 Gas guzzler
46 Parlor piece
48 Welder's wear
49 In the cards
51 First name in architecture
53 Meat
56 Dynasty during which much of the Great Wall of China was built
57 Batting stat.

by Nelson Hardy

ACROSS

1 1996 best seller
16 Like some candies
17 Runners
18 Trombone attachment
19 Geezers' replies
20 Flirt
21 Key grip workplace
24 Grp. formed by the Treaty of Rome, 1957
26 Football Hall-of-Famer Hein
27 Vacation spot
30 One who prates
34 Like most sitcoms
36 Even
40 Noisy restaurant device
42 Nod
43 Modern-day part of the old Mogul empire
44 Unwrap in a hurry
46 Put away
47 Smith who wrote "Natural Blonde"
50 Make calls
51 "___ ever!"
53 Tom of "The Seven Year Itch"
56 Morse T
58 Convinced
62 Opponent of Brutus
66 Contrary to the rules
67 Force against lifting?

DOWN

1 Titan II, perhaps
2 Friend's address
3 Exactly
4 Lots of land
5 On the canvas for good
6 "Shine a Little Love" rock grp.
7 Call from home?
8 Any old time
9 Proficient
10 Post-op stop: Abbr.
11 Without hope
12 Word repeated before show
13 Not second stringers
14 Honkers
15 Debut of 8/26/57
22 C_2H_4
23 General description?
25 Under wraps
27 2000 World Series locale
28 Site of mountain route
29 Feature of 31-Down
31 Neighbor of Switz.
32 "___ Man" (1992 comedy)
33 Supporting chorus
35 Stew
37 Gyro need
38 Sci. course
39 Artist Magritte
41 Car rental freebie
45 Part of Rodney Dangerfield's trademark attire
47 The Hare
48 Cry of defiance
49 A Marx brother
52 Query in Matthew 26
54 The Earl of Kent is his courtier
55 Greek singer accompaniment
57 Blood pigment
59 Many a Norwegian
60 Oft-told tales
61 Temperance advocates
63 Time long ago
64 Triple ___
65 Honeydew eater

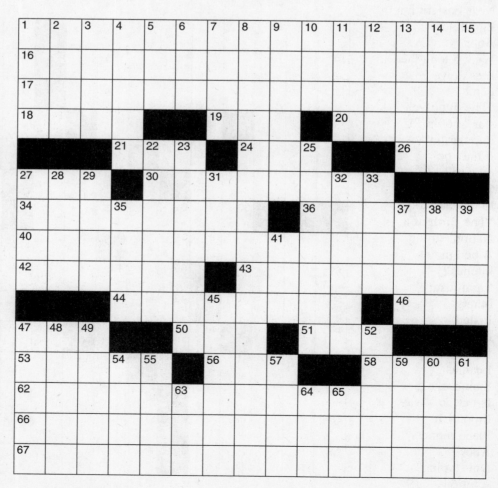

by Mark Diehl

ACROSS

1 Monarchy or parliamentary democracy
16 A little too clever
17 Oven item
18 Stray
19 Join securely
20 1984 skiing gold medalist
21 Many cottage dwellers
23 Diner orders
25 Arab League V.I.P.'s
26 Putdowns
27 Connecting points
28 Sacks
29 Piece of neckwear
32 "Let's Get ___" (1973 #1 hit)
33 Star, maybe
34 '93 Sugar Bowl champs
35 W.W. I troops: Abbr.
36 Ace of clubs?
37 Aristophanes comedy, with "The"
38 New Orleans sandwich, informally
39 Solid swats
40 Emitted steam
43 Promotes
44 Kind of warfare
45 Half of the "Wayne's World" duo
47 Author LeShan
48 Wall Street gambit
51 Camper's need
52 Comments from co-workers

DOWN

1 Former German duchy known for a breed of dog
2 Really ham it up, redundantly
3 Found out about
4 N.Y.C. subway
5 Snickers
6 " ___, she's mine . . ." (Manfred Mann lyric)
7 Columnist Herb and others
8 Farm prefix
9 Study of lakes and ponds
10 ___-Cross Championship Racing
11 Complains
12 Baseball stat
13 Church offering
14 Turn out
15 Paris parents
22 It may follow four or six, but not five
24 Silence
26 Like most cemetery plots
28 Sports org. owned by Fox
29 In which 49 is 100
30 Rash
31 What tubas play
33 Naïf
34 Place of interest?
36 Napoleon's birthplace
37 One of the brothers Grimm
38 Bill
39 Potato dishes
40 Screening device
41 Separate
42 Not in
43 Golfers' bane
46 To ___ (just so)
49 Mil. titles
50 Encouraging word

by Joe DiPietro

ACROSS

1 Escaped punishment
7 Like some stairs
15 Highest point
16 Piecemeal?
17 Put away
18 Faces facts
19 Digestion aid
20 Needing to cut down
22 Roman-fleuve
23 Well-intentioned grp.?
24 Spanish Main cargo
25 Place to play cards
26 Clean out, in a way
27 Where to spend a balboa
31 Burned up the road
32 Slight on the stump, say
34 Like some bets
36 Vacationer's hiree, perhaps
38 "Author! Author!" autobiographer
41 Choker
45 Nephew of Abel
46 Shades
48 Afflicted
49 Liberal leader?
50 A, in Aquila
51 Math figure
52 Cutting
54 Angiogram image
57 Monkey
58 Guar gum, e.g.
60 Looks
62 Ready to board the Ark
63 Word with food or group
64 License bureau procedures
65 Refuses

DOWN

1 Big talkers
2 Perfect
3 Not in time
4 Tyrant
5 Membership requirement, often
6 It has a creased crown
7 Exercise wheel locale
8 Some are pale
9 Give a 5, e.g.
10 Some clones
11 They may be ringing
12 Trample
13 Stand for trinkets
14 "China Beach" star
21 Crams
24 Sofia's portrayer in "The Color Purple"
28 Dispatch boat
29 Admeasure
30 Symbol of industry
31 Ring rampager
33 They're part of a good deal
35 Group of whizzes
37 Set-___
38 Flipped
39 Centrum competitor
40 All-out
42 Car reservoirs
43 Alabama slammer ingredient
44 Spanish Mannerist
47 Jacks
53 It may be worn after traveling
54 It opened in 1871
55 One in the sac
56 Gym set
57 Like some fireplaces
59 Cowboy's moniker
61 "Give ___ whirl"

by Joe DiPietro

ACROSS

1 Sunday dish
16 1916 Theodore Dreiser book
17 Employ gene therapy, say
18 Where Coca-Cola is KO
19 Scientific discovery of 1898
20 Oaxaca article
21 April and June
25 Scorer of 1,859 runs
26 Dash letters
29 Cartoon cat
30 Dionne Warwick's "Anyone Who ___ Heart"
33 Intricateness
39 A hydraulic motor converts it
40 It might have you both coming and going
41 Salon stock
42 Lyricist Washington
43 Son of Prince Valiant
44 Mirror
46 Derby prize
48 "Shine a Little Love" grp.
49 Kind of salad
52 Father, in the Bible
56 Slant
61 Took a firm stand
62 Reacts to breaking news, perhaps

DOWN

1 First offer?
2 "Heavens!"
3 Takes a bough?
4 "Two Women" star
5 Anka's "___ Beso"
6 Not mil.
7 Driving need
8 Driving needs
9 "Die Frau ___ Schatten" (Strauss opera)
10 Dessert, to a dieter
11 It may be medical
12 Berated, with "into"
13 Video category
14 Wheel of Fortune, e.g.
15 Focus group?
22 Sooner than soon
23 Like some enemies
24 Contacts, in a way
25 "Angel of Light" novelist
26 Bank action, briefly
27 Fall sound
28 Fictional spy ___ Helm
30 Emphatic denial
31 Astaire and others
32 Bare
34 It goes with almost anything
35 ___ chi
36 "Tutte le feste," e.g.
37 Inventor Sikorsky
38 Massachusetts city with a harbor
44 Alaskan tongue
45 ___ Novo (Benin's capital)
46 Pocahontas's husband
47 Goes across the board?
48 "The Mod Squad" co-star, 1999
49 A slew
50 Working without ___
51 Bills
53 Curricula vitae
54 Holyfield defeater, 1995
55 Miller and Lee
57 Pacifier
58 Alley of Moo
59 "___ qué?" ("Why?"): Sp.
60 Follower of Israel?

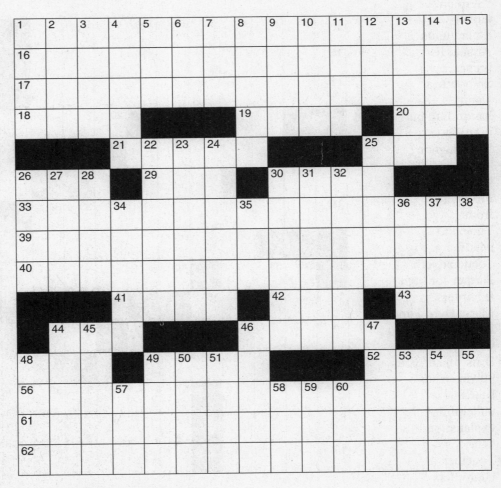

by Martin Ashwood-Smith

ACROSS

1 Kipling poem
11 Fixes
15 Shock
16 ___ above
17 Firing people?
18 Bonnie Tyler's "___ Heartache"
19 Recital hall shout
20 It may be armed
22 Part of a gym workout
26 Thing to steer clear of
27 It may be spiced
28 "Serpico" author
30 Sound units
31 Annual list preparer
35 Ship letters
36 Nanny's handful, to put it mildly
38 ___-Magnon
40 Wiltshire wonder
44 Profiteers from
46 Time and a half, e.g.
47 Poetic adverb
48 Partner for high
51 It borders Marie Byrd Land
53 Demi Moore was in it
55 Brits' thank-yous
56 90° from sur
57 Like an unhelpful explanation
62 Win
63 Together
64 High fliers
65 Who's there

DOWN

1 Fraud monitoring agcy.
2 Tail: Prefix
3 Livingstone resident
4 Conductor Mehta
5 Singer seen in the 1954 film "Secret of the Incas"
6 Peasants' Revolt leader ___ Tyler
7 Hagen of Broadway
8 Brass component
9 Strangely, Frank Beard is its only beardless member
10 Like some questions
11 Sentence structure?
12 Efforts
13 They may be pulled
14 Parts of a union
21 Shots from the foul line: Abbr.
22 Some change: Abbr.
23 "Isn't ___ bit like you and me?" (Beatles lyric)
24 Bargains
25 French toast
29 Flavor
32 Began to act
33 Kind of nerve or artery
34 Tend
37 Stephen King title
38 Salad and dessert
39 Rapper's noise
41 WKRP news director Les
42 "You don't say!"
43 Time
44 Dries out, with "up"
45 Nurse
49 Russian retreat
50 Quite a display
52 Princess in Woolf's "Orlando"
54 ___ State
58 Stock ending
59 It's worth very little in Japan
60 Tar Heels' sch.
61 He ran with R.M.N.

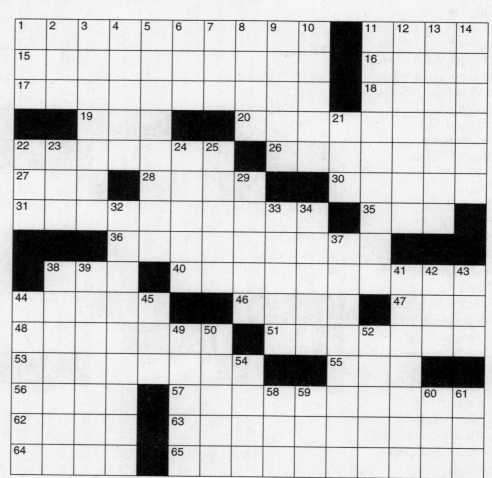

by Nelson Hardy

ACROSS

1 It's connected to a bowl
9 Course before une salade, maybe
15 A priest, not a beast
16 Kickoff
17 Trouble spot for Indiana Jones
18 Like beachgoers vis-à-vis indoor types
19 Confiscate, legally
20 Blenders
21 Busbies, boaters and billycocks
22 Roadside establishment
23 Door
25 1953 Eartha Kitt hit
29 Squalor
30 Pole star?
31 Chiller
32 It's north of New York City
33 Berkshire abode
34 Old film magazine photos
36 Alpine Museum city
37 Checkered
38 Georges who wrote "Life: A User's Manual"
39 Rudimentary
40 "Star Trek" navigator
41 Gilda Radner character
44 Like some speech sounds
47 Inuit outerwear
48 Money in a classic song title
49 Start of a #1 Beach Boys title
50 "Nature's pharmacy"
51 Smart one
52 One who doesn't take the high road

DOWN

1 False front
2 Holiday ___
3 Georgia bloomers
4 City where Alka-Seltzer was first made
5 Like a cold shower?
6 Snacks served with cerveza
7 Throw off
8 Tangle
9 Sovereign
10 Change colors, in a way
11 Curly strand
12 Daughter of James II
13 Will of Hollywood
14 Foozles
20 Foozle
22 Like opium poppy leaves
23 ___ of Nantes
24 Specialty
25 Gush
26 One who's homeward bound
27 Unconventional
28 "No Strings Attached" pop group
30 Explorer of sorts
32 Start of certain addresses
35 Inner walls of fortification ditches
36 Buy, so to speak
38 Infused with enthusiasm
40 1066 loser
41 Root words
42 Super's apartment, often
43 Hundreds of centavos
44 ___ Crane, Vera Miles's role in "Psycho"
45 Big plot
46 "The Jumblies" poet
48 Softhead

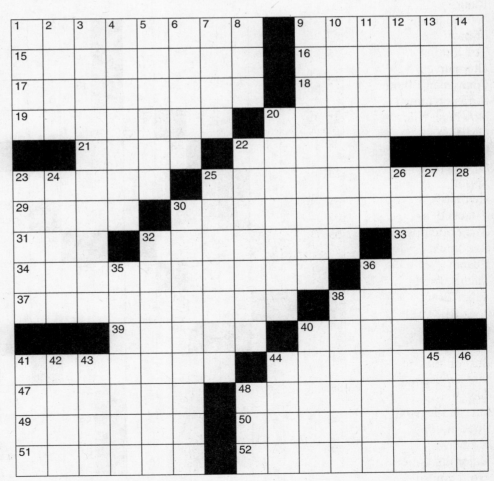

by Bob Klahn

ACROSS

1 Secret holder
8 Like some blankets
15 Like a waltz
16 The very start
17 Music
18 "1984" land
19 Toasts
20 They have bishops
22 Newspaper publisher Whitelaw ___
23 Pale yellow
24 Was on the bottom?
25 Like Bacon and Lamb: Abbr.
26 Rang
29 "How stupid of me!"
30 Toe loop alternatives
31 Funnyman Elliott
35 Strips on a map
37 Nowheresville
38 Chaff
39 Old-fashioned farm apparatus
42 Sprint alternative
43 Attacked, as a bag of chips
45 Cartoonist Keane
46 Tough wood
49 Super Bowl XXXIII M.V.P.
50 Carpenter's groove
51 Best on the balance beam, maybe
54 Like fall leaves
55 Does in, in a way
56 Major disruption
58 "Told you so!"
59 Core
60 "Mont Sainte-Victoire" painter
61 Surfaces

DOWN

1 Drag through the mud
2 To a T
3 Kind of student
4 Dig discovery
5 Electra's daughter
6 Literary contraction
7 Alter, as an image
8 Is plucky?
9 Put up
10 Stumbles
11 Figures to be maintained?
12 Purported Pentateuch penner
13 With 21-Down, Clarence Thomas's accuser
14 Kind of resistance?
21 See 13-Down
23 Long, as a garment
26 Part on the side?
27 1999 N.C.A.A. hoops champs
28 A grad may be working on it
32 Xavier Cugat's nickname
33 Frequency
34 Some vacation accommodations
36 He upset T.E.D. in 1948
37 Game, maybe
39 Babar's wife
40 "___ that again?"
41 Cornered
44 Check
46 Jellied garnish
47 Stir up
48 Pickle producer
50 Post office gizmo
52 Like many hurricanes
53 Depressed
54 York symbol
57 Follower of Lenin or Stalin

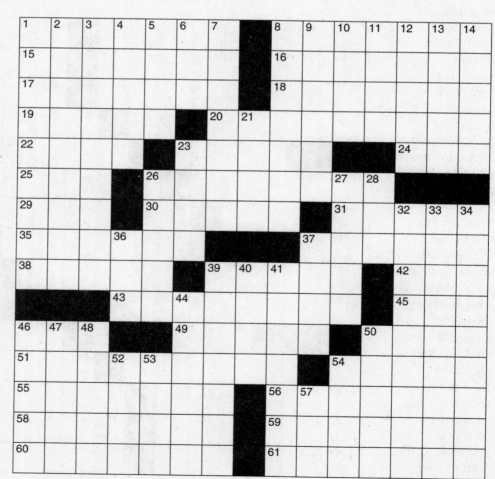

by Joe DiPietro

ACROSS

1 Be short with
7 Brunch dish
13 Servitude
14 Insincere
16 Using less than due deliberation
17 Follower
18 More frequently
19 Gathers abundantly
20 Shouldered
21 Living units: Abbr.
23 Studio sites
24 "You lose"
25 Doctor in "A Passage to India"
26 Memorial marker
27 Discussing excitedly
29 Tannery products
30 Brian who wrote "The Rise and Fall of the Soviet Empire"
32 Bantu language
36 Bond with
41 A year in Provence
42 Weizman of Israel
43 Chemical compound
44 The opponents
45 "Fools Die" author
46 Made common cause (with)
47 Certain delay
49 Bit of salt
51 Like wind and water
52 "The Ten Commandments" role
53 Resident
54 It may go up in an airplane
55 "Justine" author, 1791
56 Polite title: Abbr.

DOWN

1 Coastal birds
2 Air intake site
3 Good listener?
4 "The Liberty Tree" writer
5 Pulitzer winner James
6 Atrium flooring
7 Hard rock
8 Tragic James Fenimore Cooper character
9 Comment after an accident
10 Popular pizza
11 Provincial, so to speak
12 License
13 Cause for inaction, maybe
15 Strains
22 Flair
25 Something in the air
26 "You betcha!"
28 A train?
29 Very, in Bonn
31 Bit of fine calligraphy, maybe
32 Sang
33 Jobless
34 Flower said to have sprung from the blood of Adonis
35 Batman, to the Riddler
37 Hollywood father and son combo
38 Product enjoyer
39 Like sandals
40 First-born
42 ___ Gant, hero of "Look Homeward, Angel"
45 Easy to drive on
46 Emma of "Dynasty"
48 "___ of Lambeth" (Maugham's first novel)
50 Exceptional

by Manny Nosowsky

ACROSS

1 Arrange, as hair
5 Try to get out of something
11 Mr. Big
14 Shore soarer
15 Bad thing to be over
16 ___ bit
17 Steady
19 Quaker cereal
20 Result
21 Safari animals
23 Never outdated
26 10 square meters
27 See 18-Down
29 Type or pin follower
30 Like some early computer number systems
32 Egg holders?
33 It may be won by a knockout
38 Convince
39 Iterate
40 Imitated a siren
43 Corrupts
48 Clappers may prompt them
50 Superlatively sincere
51 Embodiments
53 Time being
54 Wobbly walker, perhaps
55 "That's a taboo topic"
58 Olsen of "Hellzapoppin"
59 Went around in circles?
60 On
61 Bushranger Kelly
62 "Alas"
63 Promulgates

DOWN

1 Put Down
2 House of William III
3 For everyone, in a way
4 Next-to-last syllable
5 Kind of ribs
6 About 3/4 of la Terre
7 Baseball's Luzinski
8 Mountain nymph
9 Items banned by Atatürk
10 It grows on ewe
11 Breaks
12 Native
13 People in the fast lane
18 With 27-Across, holiday celebrators' farewell
22 Flexible
24 Minority group
25 Hardly a celibate
28 Flew
31 Good sport, perhaps
33 Abe Lincoln, e.g., as a boy
34 Brought out
35 Designate
36 Shirt tag irritation point
37 Simon Legree
38 Enamored of
41 Like many shorelines
42 Passé
44 Honolulu Airport exchange
45 Padova's region
46 Hold in trust
47 Impregnates
49 ___ message
52 The clink
56 Solitaire, e.g.
57 Millay's "___ to Silence"

by Mitch Komro

ACROSS

1 Careless
9 Gardener's need
15 Gradually become part of
16 City near Gulfport
17 Period of the first dinosaurs
18 Shanghai
19 Panama claim
20 24-Down player
21 Leviathan
22 It may be found in a stew
23 4-0 World Series win, e.g.
26 Jerry-built
30 1930's movie bowdlerizer
31 Cartoons collected in "Cows of Our Planet"
35 You may be struck with it
36 Cheap
37 Iced, with "in"
38 Smooth-running
40 Safe harbor
41 Entered
42 A Thomas from Wales
43 Where some cabins are found
46 Magazine with dating tips
48 Congratulates oneself
50 Fictional island-dweller
54 Traveler's accessory
55 "You fool!"
56 '64 event for the Beatles
57 Acrobats' need
58 Poor housing
59 And

DOWN

1 ___ Arnold's Balsam (old patent medicine)
2 Woman with a 1960's movie theme
3 ___ were
4 Picked fruit
5 Serve, as a meal
6 Longtime Sierra Club director Adams
7 Impediment to drive-in smooching, maybe
8 Pawn
9 Way up some hills
10 Risquéness
11 Past times
12 Twisted
13 Be outstanding
14 BP purchase, maybe
23 Deposed leader
24 Baba for 20-Across
25 Views
27 Fashionable Bendel
28 Quite a bit
29 Fog
31 And so
32 Fetishist's object
33 Tosca is one
34 Elysium
36 Completely empty
39 Liking
40 Like Diogenes
42 Drop
43 Super-exceptional
44 Criticize and how!
45 Anatomical dividers
47 Bend
49 Lively
50 Tributary of the Colorado
51 Miss
52 1940's–80's actor Robert
53 ___ City, seat of a Kansas county of the same name

by Manny Nosowsky

ACROSS

1 One way to buy
9 Acela Express offerer
15 Indian royal
16 Grand ___ Island
17 Political leader who died at age 33
18 Employable
19 Quiet
20 Safari hazard
21 French auxiliary
22 Viola holders
23 Industry leaders
26 Breathes deeply?
30 Makes shine
31 One may take you in
35 Favor follower
36 Flipped (through)
37 Social service?
38 Low-priced house, informally
40 Dorm denizen
41 One may throw out a line
42 Zoltan who directed "Jungle Book"
43 Hymn
46 Like India paper
48 Books on tape, e.g.
50 Raised borders that prevent water overflow
54 Service station?
55 Part of a British Airways jet
56 It's north of Highland Park, N.J.
57 Beginning of an act
58 Student's second chance
59 The future

DOWN

1 Hebrew measure
2 Place for prayer
3 Many people now do it online
4 Old thrusters
5 Puts up
6 Defiant one
7 Stewed
8 Windows application?
9 Neighbor
10 Gift from a Catholic friend
11 Whence one wicked witch
12 They go with the flow
13 Disport
14 Some greens
23 Arrangement of locks
24 Alternative to bow ties
25 Comfort in bookstores
27 Relative of a savanna
28 "Serendipities: Language and Lunacy" author
29 Braddock took away his title
31 Have nothing to do with
32 "Believe ___ Not!"
33 Plant of the future
34 "Et voilà!"
36 Viola effects
39 Cover-up of astronomical proportions
40 Monkey puzzle tree, e.g.
42 Kyoto garment
43 Lord's Prayer
44 Soft kid
45 Allow
47 Scheherazade's milieu
49 In ecstasy
50 Play group
51 Hussein's queen
52 Italian pet form of John
53 Ocean

by Elizabeth C. Gorski

ACROSS

1 Make known
8 Newspaper report
15 Kind of assumption
16 High praise
17 Tinlike
18 Wishful one?
19 Hingis rival
20 They may come with strings attached
22 Tabloid topic
23 Sign
24 N.J. base
25 Suffer a public embarrassment, maybe
26 Good days on Wall Street
27 Distant
28 Spinning
29 Swig
31 Elegant
32 Eager joiner's comment
34 Living on plastic, e.g.
37 Inaugurates
41 Command for Queeg
42 Movie Hall of fame
43 "___ thousand times . . ."
44 Sartre's "L' ___ et le Néant"
45 Bring to ___
46 Ford offering, for short
47 Send packing
48 Many a hockey highlight
49 Barely bite
50 Tar
52 Way back when
54 Frequent Valentino co-star
55 More off-color
56 Drop
57 "Pardon me"

DOWN

1 Faint
2 Bouncy
3 Without means of support?
4 Sheets on a shelf
5 Ca++ and Cl−
6 Asian honorific
7 Podunk
8 Hypothetical
9 Bulova competitor
10 "Handsome ___ handsome does"
11 Modicum
12 Sweats out
13 Joins
14 Impressive display
21 Too-seldom-heard reply
24 Scoff at
25 ___-Alaska Pipeline
27 Home for arid climates
28 Equally
30 Tableau
31 60's TV puppet
33 Local developers, maybe
34 Chilled
35 Actress Portman who played a "Star Wars" princess
36 Fräulein's frocks
38 Poker holding
39 Food seeker
40 Major employer
42 Let up
45 "Stormy Weather" composer
46 Botch
48 Make a bundle
49 The latest
51 Military acronym
53 U.S. claim-settling dept.

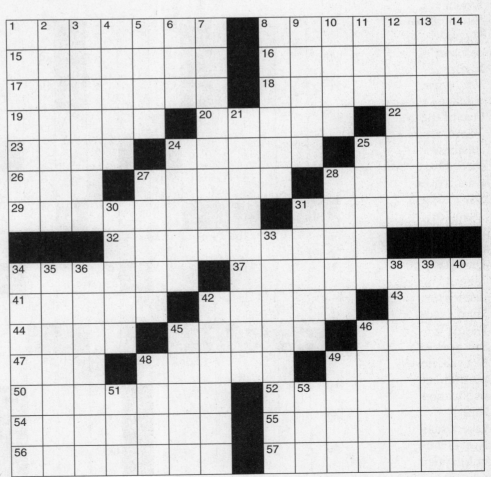

by Manny Nosowsky

ACROSS

1 Kind of scale
5 Gray, say
8 Representative
14 "Up and ___!"
15 Likewise
16 Dos, e.g.
17 When said three times, a 1970 film
18 ___ chi
19 Hankered for
20 Items useful in 35-Across
23 Exclusive
24 Hankering
25 Sources of 35-Across financing
33 Évian, e.g.
34 Eye problem
35 Upgrade, of a sort
41 Living
42 Try to win damages
43 One of the 20-Across
50 Business card abbr.
51 Concert site
52 Something 7-Down might put down
59 On a pedestal
60 Slogan ending
61 Hard ___
62 Result of a pullout?
63 Not the most prestigious publication
64 Zip
65 Like a snail
66 Nut's realm, in Egyptian religion
67 Combines

DOWN

1 Some developments
2 "My Favorite Year" star
3 Larger than life
4 Colored glass used in mosaic
5 One of four Holy Roman emperors
6 Kill time
7 Some 35-Across types
8 Rebates, basically
9 Short
10 Jazz drummer ___ Hakim
11 St. Petersburg's river
12 Angry
13 Kind of word
21 Hil on the Hill: Abbr.
22 One of L.B.J.'s beagles
26 In a crazed way
27 It may have a projection
28 Score in a univ. application
29 Fire preceder?
30 Pioneer cell phone co.
31 Oberhausen one
32 Mach 2 craft
35 Here, on a tombstone
36 ___ binge
37 Ile locale
38 Producer of a mental image, maybe
39 Common British verb ending
40 ___ Lady of . . .
44 Gymnast's goal
45 "Dr." In a 1964 film title
46 Slips
47 Kind of threat
48 Supreme Court, e.g.
49 Carlsberg and others
52 Manhattan's locale: Abbr.
53 Ricky Martin, for one
54 Stir
55 "Titanic" extras
56 Patch up
57 Patch's place
58 Bacchanal

by David J. Kahn

ACROSS

1 Enlarges
7 Purse alternatives
15 Certain fuel carrier
16 Ancient dynasty founder
17 Comes to
18 Space cadet's place
19 Sp. title
20 Good way to write
22 Chemical ending
23 Broadway opening?
24 Poet's inspiration
25 Kind of hand
26 Frock wearer
28 One looking for a hand
31 Brass
32 It may help you make up
36 Spanish ___
38 Strauss opera
39 Sting hit of 2000
43 Guinea pigs, maybe
44 1864 convention site
45 Hardly wimpy
46 Press
49 Left-hand page
51 Cartoon canine
52 Irish ___
53 Portuguese, e.g.
55 Glass of public radio
56 Unsuccessful people
58 Catch phrase?
60 Pilot's place
61 One of TV's Jeffersons
62 Don Mattingly, e.g.
63 Didn't drive well

DOWN

1 Floods and such
2 Lintel locale
3 Hackers' targets
4 Kidnappers in 1974 news: Abbr.
5 See 54-Down
6 Skater Brian
7 Separated
8 Very hot
9 Going rate?
10 It might crack after getting fired
11 Daughter of Loki
12 In-box input
13 Actress Carter
14 Went along (with)
21 Get a sudden inspiration?
25 Italian brandy
27 Maintain
29 Sweeping force
30 Mozart's "L'___ del Cairo"
32 Envelope abbr.
33 Animated series starring Jon Lovitz
34 Increasing
35 Rang
37 ". . . ___ he drove out of sight"
40 Crime motive
41 Direct
42 Loose garment
45 Golden Horde member
46 English teacher's concern
47 "Easy, boy"
48 Boastful
50 Moves effortlessly
53 Carpet place
54 With 5-Down, one seen in a cage
57 Anglo-Saxon money
59 Garçon's reply

by Joe DiPietro

ACROSS

1 Playing for meal money
8 Bottom drawer, maybe
15 Constituent of pitchblende
16 800 number, perhaps
17 "The Case of the Musical Cow" writer
18 Is rife
19 Depleted
20 "To know me ___ . . ."
22 Bridgelike game
23 Heater
25 Bow
26 Miser, abroad
27 Upend
28 It may be pitched
30 Philippe, e.g.
31 California college
34 Famed Rio hotspot, with "the"
35 252 wine gallons
36 Discrete
37 Three Gorges project
38 Flip-flop feature
40 ___ Hoek (cartoon pooch)
41 Coins displaying fleurs-de-lis
43 Part of a ballpark
44 Angular head?
45 Fumble-fingers
46 Word repeated before Marie in a 1918 song title
47 Hurtle
49 Worldcom partner
50 Skin-related
54 Conductor Markevitch
55 Snaps
57 Sting, in a way
58 Pampers

60 Like noodles, often
62 Be too precious
63 Tidy type
64 United Nations member since 1993
65 Acquiesces

DOWN

1 Dollface
2 Goddess pictured with a lyre and a crown of roses
3 Some bays and grays
4 Circuitry coil
5 Zeroed in on
6 Fret over, maybe
7 Katz of "Dallas"

8 Information Age salon
9 Cyborg enforcer
10 Mame's butler in "Auntie Mame"
11 Cooling drink
12 Sleuth from Glasgow
13 Evasive maneuver in football
14 Does some work in a tennis shop
21 Full of barbs
24 Eco-friendly feds
29 Big Easy bacchanal

31 Quaillike bird
32 Donizetti fan, e.g.
33 Baked tubes
37 Don Quixote's doña
39 Mess headgear
42 Bowl with a base and stem
43 Ground cover
48 Posture-perfect
51 Four-time baseball All-Star ___ Trillo
52 First name in jazz
53 Stew ingredients
56 Lacking
59 Ivry-___-Seine (Paris suburb)
61 Pastureland

by Chuck Deodene

ACROSS

1 Officially certify
9 Certain ticket buyers
15 Not to be trusted
16 Man of words
17 Breakfast item with coffee
19 Off-course
20 Computerized enactments, for short
21 Clock standard: Abbr.
22 Planner's woe
23 All over the place
24 Short collection?
25 King who toured the U.S. in 1977
26 Cookie flavoring
28 Riders
29 Begin, later in life
32 Outcome of some exams
33 No behind-the-back criticism
37 Physicist Ohm
38 Program listing
39 Follow-up to a ques.
41 Fashion magazine
42 "Sweet" things
43 Gift line
44 Nonexistent
45 Doofus
46 Lilongwe is its capital
48 Amoeba
51 Fine wool
52 Place for trucks and shovels
53 Lamb pieces
54 Site of Mount Olympus

DOWN

1 If you're lucky
2 Roil
3 Sildenafil ___ (Viagra's generic name)
4 Mark down, maybe
5 Neck and neck
6 Scuttlebutt
7 Belief
8 "Don't panic!"
9 "___ anything!"
10 Root beer brand
11 It may be produced by swamp gas
12 Hangs around
13 Proclaim
14 Donnybrooks
18 They can go overboard
23 Jog one's memory
24 Mrs. Gorbachev
26 Handling brilliantly
27 Sans ice
28 Floats like a butterfly
30 Really like
31 Noted Renaissance patron
33 Lions and tigers (oh my)
34 Some are high
35 Darling
36 One with omniscience
37 Modern map subject
40 Cutesy drawing
42 Some shirts
43 Decides by chance
45 Just say no
46 Place for a comb
47 Added details
49 The Company
50 Morse T

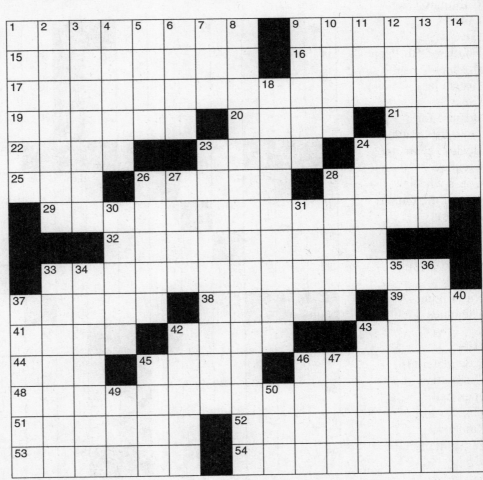

by Mark Diehl

ACROSS

1 Buck
8 Lemonlike
14 "Pines of Rome" composer
16 Iroquoian language
17 Stretched out
18 Toyota model
19 Grocery store workers
20 Regret
21 Food sticker
22 Hungers (for)
23 Eccentric
26 Graduate record?
30 "Hold it, buster!"
31 Easy-to-please companions
35 Chilling Chaney
36 Cuts
37 Give it ___
38 Emulated Bo-Peep
40 In shape
41 British tars
42 Clear
43 Prepare for a long trip, maybe
46 Beckett character
48 Creature
50 Cop's wheels
54 One of the Gilbert Islands
55 Louvre lady
56 Chi ___ (some college women)
57 Peppy
58 Night flight
59 The blues

DOWN

1 Raw materials
2 Shout at an open call
3 This, to Jorge
4 Rainbows
5 Part of a digital display
6 City near Brigham City
7 "Everything is going to be okay . . ."
8 Scuttle's contents
9 Some shut-ins
10 Group wearing red, white and blue uniforms
11 Gets to
12 Words before care or mind
13 Tilts
15 Some may have photos
23 Rice University nickname
24 Worrisome remark by a surgeon
25 Muscle condition
27 Intoxicating
28 Is nosy
29 Zipped
31 Mr. Miniver in "Mrs. Miniver"
32 "___ Road" (1999 Maeve Binchy best seller)
33 Authority: Var.
34 A few
36 Remove gradually, with "at"
39 Peacock's pride
40 "With All Disrespect" humorist
42 The prince in "The Prince and the Pauper"
43 Big snapper
44 "What's in ___?"
45 Fathered
47 Asia Minor region
49 Work like a certain medical device
50 Blair and Thatcher: Abbr.
51 Specify
52 "___ Death" (Grieg work)
53 Dangerous dosage units

by Elizabeth C. Gorski

ACROSS

1 Presidential appointments
16 It's secured before hitching
17 Objects to
18 Lao-___
19 Former Hawaii senator Hiram
20 Producer of some dishes
23 Outdated atlas abbr.
24 Back of the thigh
28 Unwinding
32 Guitar attachment
33 Father's office
35 Furry folivore
36 Gate-crashed, e.g.
37 The way things go?
39 Hardly prolix
40 One-eighty
42 Pick
43 Cold
44 ___ prayer
45 Physical responses?
47 Parts of forks: Abbr.
48 It's given to a newborn
50 Plan for patients, briefly
53 Powers at sea
61 Unlock Pandora's box
62 Minor obsession

DOWN

1 Hearing aid?
2 K follower
3 Josip ___ Tito
4 Former Met maestro
5 Prussian pronoun
6 Carrier to Copenhagen
7 Income sharer: Abbr.
8 Goethe's "Die Leiden ___ jungen Werthers"
9 Several Norwegian kings
10 Asperity
11 Read at the supermarket?
12 Rage
13 Room offerer
14 Letter addenda
15 It may follow a wash
21 Secret
22 Leeds's river
23 Base leader?: Abbr.
25 Co-designee as Time's 1993 Man of the Year
26 Venom
27 Out of touch, with "out"
28 Treats with 26-Down
29 Diplomat Harriman
30 Diving fisher
31 Zilch
32 Didn't directly deal with, with "over"
34 School near Slough
38 Remscheid's region
41 Tend tables
45 Florentine friend
46 Samson
49 ___ all-time high
51 Even's opposite
52 "Lay it ___!"
53 Syndicate
54 Copier
55 Riddle-me-___
56 Vane dir.
57 Discouraging words
58 Edwards, for one: Abbr.
59 Double standard?
60 Unrealized 60's Boeing project

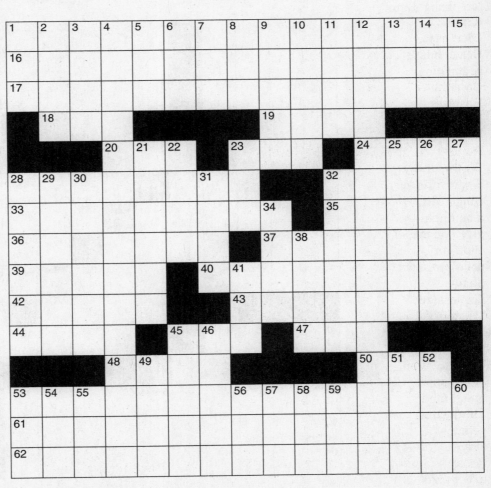

by Martin Ashwood-Smith

152 FRIDAY

ACROSS
1 Baltic native
5 Man famous for his dogs
15 Neural appendage
16 Panic buttons?
17 Mao, for one
18 Crumble
19 Cartoonist Browne
20 Unwelcome rooter
21 Hair color, e.g.
22 Hair color
23 Little ___ (Brighton Beach nickname)
26 Some extensions
27 Greet and seat
29 Expressed one's disapproval
31 Not straight up
33 Kitties
34 Alert asea
37 Beach bum's acquisition
39 Contribute
41 Business card abbr.
42 Wind in a pit
44 Dome
45 Washes away
47 Smart follower
48 Bingo call
51 You might give one the slip
53 Wolf or devil preceder
54 Shows displeasure
56 "History of Rome" author
57 South Korea's Roh ___ Woo
58 When appropriate
61 Small mount
62 Third game, perhaps
63 Drive
64 It may be used to get parts
65 Flower fanciers

DOWN
1 Saved
2 Whiskey Rebellion impetus
3 Cheered up
4 W.W.F. airer
5 Money motto starter
6 End of a rainbow?
7 Deserves a hand?
8 Prefix with orthodox
9 Music genre
10 Have ___ to pick
11 Zigged or zagged
12 It's slow going
13 First black major-league baseball coach Buck ___
14 Watch-pocket places
20 Watch closely
24 Don't go on
25 Where the last flight ends?
28 Class
30 Río de la Plata, e.g.
32 Río de la Plata explorer
34 It may stock pumps
35 Simple garage job
36 Cast of two
38 Orbital point
40 U.S. Army E-4
43 Long and sinuous
45 Garb
46 Attacks à la "Ghostbusters"
48 Elizabeth's subjects
49 Bartender's supply
50 Itchy
52 Upset
55 Upset
59 Home in the hills
60 Wield a shuttle
61 Where to find porters

by Joe DiPietro

ACROSS

1 Comment after a compliment
9 Dr. Seuss character
15 Try to get off easier, perhaps
16 Exaggerate
17 Rosencrantz or Guildenstern
18 Monthly
19 Einstein's birthplace
20 Theoretically
22 Org. with an influential journal
23 Not hidden
25 Old lampshade material
26 Used-up checkbook, perhaps
28 Result
30 Originally
31 There are 12 in a year
32 Big name in diamonds
35 Daily riser
36 Mr. High-and-Mighty
39 Corsair crew
41 Opera opener
42 Get to the point of?
44 Kite part
45 Jargon suffix
46 Cholesterol, e.g.
50 Deep cavity
52 Part of Nascar: Abbr.
54 With 5-Down, approached
55 They may be real or imaginary: Abbr.
56 "Cato" playwright
59 Brother
60 Smoke out
62 Conscience
64 Deli order
65 Took unwanted steps

66 Relatives of sunflowers
67 A little night music

DOWN

1 Charge
2 Like some caps
3 Spewed forth
4 Bit of feigned laughter
5 See 54-Across
6 Singer Black
7 Not panic
8 Cake maker
9 A smattering of
10 Swears
11 Door sign
12 Dodger's comeuppance?
13 Eliot novel
14 Slow flower
21 A teen may succumb to it
24 Bores
27 Mammoth
29 Dallas City Hall designer
33 Shot from an air rifle
34 Nurse
36 "Carmen" highlight
37 Slammer isolation cells
38 Sits tight
40 Sem. study
43 Hockey stat
47 "Dallas" role

48 Painted a mental picture of
49 Make sense of
51 Electromagnetic wave amplifier
53 Without face value
57 Some holes in the ground
58 "Scream" star Campbell
61 Eng. Award
63 Cartoon dog

by Bob Peoples

ACROSS

1 Becomes nonproductive
8 Pioneer item
14 Song title that means "Farewell to Thee"
15 Like some computer searches
16 Roald Dahl title character
17 Cut off
18 Mythomaniac
19 Landed
20 Lille lily
21 Pamper, with "on"
22 Product package abbr.
24 Angel
26 Thwart
28 Relaxing bath
30 Silent film star Nielsen
31 Gave guff
33 Upwardly mobile one?
35 Triumvirates
37 Articles
41 "Fuggedaboutit!"
46 Kind of teeth
47 Old comic strip family name
49 China Clipper carrier
50 Troop encampment
52 "Does This Make Me Look Fat?" author Feldon
54 "King Lear" bowdlerizer
55 Berlin bombers of W.W. II
56 M.'s counterpart
58 Libelant
60 Like some semirural towns
62 Parents, e.g.
63 Kind of store

64 Automaker Maserati
65 Schindler and others
66 University named for a hatmaker

DOWN

1 Some hotels
2 Kirov Ballet debutant of 1928
3 Puts on the staff?
4 Sock souvenirs?
5 "The Burning Giraffe" painter
6 Giant film pterodactyl
7 Sugar fermenters
8 Unremarkable
9 Honey
10 Conduit corner
11 No dreamer
12 Chip away at
13 Like a brigadier general
15 Hot air
23 Hammy cry
25 Towers, at times: Abbr.
27 Québécois head
29 Shakespearean actor Edmund
32 Knock out, in a way
34 Brandy bottle abbr.
36 Sumptuous
37 Cabby's query
38 Charges with another duty
39 Depressed
40 Medicine label abbr.
42 Collection of records for computer processing
43 Topsy-turvy
44 Humor
45 "The Over-Soul" essayist
48 Losers to the Yankees in the 1998 Series
51 Leftover bit
53 Breast beater
57 Staffs
59 Like some print
61 Indianapolis's ___ Dome

by Brendan Emmett Quigley

ACROSS

1 Flu prevention program
6 No-win situations?
10 So
14 "Exodus" actor
15 Veterans
17 It may require a fee
18 Tar Heel rival, in the A.C.C.
19 Unborn person?
20 Trifle
21 Source of current events?
22 Tear up
25 Just so
26 Minuteman's housing
29 Set straight
32 Jeanne ___
35 Confucian ideal
36 Has the last laugh
38 Bungle
40 It has potential for development
41 Penetrate slowly
43 Not seeing eye to eye
44 Put one's foot down
46 Desk drawer item
48 Tear up
54 Rub down
56 Range components: Abbr.
57 Lie low
58 A lion, but not a giraffe
60 Honkers
61 "Theme From 'Summer of '42'" pianist
62 Relatively light
63 Risked getting ticketed
64 Guff
65 Mix up

DOWN

1 Mirror marrer
2 Language of 366 million
3 Like draft
4 They may come out of the woodwork
5 Kind of flour
6 As well
7 Mistreated
8 E-address ending
9 Stockholder's responsibility?
10 Corrects
11 Saw more of
12 Friendly look
13 First Olympic venue for giant slalom
16 Not engaged
20 David, for one
23 Things to avoid
24 Close up, perhaps
27 Panegyrize
28 Error message?
29 Good mousers
30 Scream
31 Blend
33 Sunday dinners
34 Dish
37 Crawl (with)
39 Poor loser
42 Base coats
45 Ran on
47 Enron Field team
49 Frankfurt an der ___
50 Helps off a dependency
51 Furnish
52 50's fiasco
53 Tractor handle?
54 Band gear
55 Caller's prompt
59 Leaves in a bag
60 2.5, e.g.

by Harvey Estes and Nancy Salomon

ACROSS

1 Hereditary prince
5 One of two, e.g.
9 Pull on
14 Helps for a time
16 Places in the heart
17 Start of a famous motto from literature
18 Farley Granger's role in "Hans Christian Andersen"
19 Tables
20 Tallboy, e.g.
21 Indian ___
22 Japanese sandals
24 Juan Carlos, to his people
27 Electronic trial
30 Fictional Edwin
31 Sourpuss
32 Where the NEAR space probe landed
33 Line up
34 Darkness
35 Ridicule
37 Is at the end of one's rope?
38 Advance portion of a book or magazine
39 Perfume
40 Pan, e.g.
41 Florida football team, on a 44-Across
42 Early automaker Harry C. ___
44 Record keeper
50 Dark orange-yellow
51 1983 America's Cup winner
52 Good snorkeling site
53 Gives a false alarm

54 Like a game overtime
55 The constellation Carina
56 Pudding ingredient

DOWN

1 Substitute for unmentioned text
2 Uris's "___ 18"
3 One way to stand by
4 Judges
5 Rocker, in kiddie-talk
6 Bypass
7 Allow to use
8 Complete exclusion

9 Seven-piece Chinese puzzle
10 Flexible baseball player
11 Lubricators
12 "What ___ you?" (doc's query)
13 Putin quoter
15 Zoomed
23 Some Sooners
24 Wrongdoing
25 Regarded
26 Composition of a proverbial soft bed
27 Vocal complaint
28 Computer hazard
29 They're intended to instill shame

30 "Ed Wood" title role player
31 Big bag
33 Bail out
36 Form into small, crisp curls
37 Good spellers?
39 Trustbuster's concern
41 Actress Bissett
42 Temperature regulator, informally
43 Convey
45 Pickle
46 Avian sounds
47 Jesus, for one
48 Get to
49 Crackers

by Manny Nosowsky

ACROSS

1 Ability to rotate polarized light
16 Hold off
17 Novel featuring Adela Quested
18 Fashion initials
19 Big name in music compilations
20 Way for the wind to blow: Abbr.
21 "For sure, Fernando!"
23 17-Across topic
25 1944 E.T.O. battleground
29 They're hired to spin
32 Markers
35 A hand
36 Leave things unresolved, perhaps
41 Disregard
42 Desert danger
43 Ripple producer
44 Alone, in Arles
45 Syllable in oldies
46 Like a punished G.I., perhaps
48 Fighter with horns
50 For whom Sherman was veep
54 Concert stage sight
57 Synthesizer pioneer
60 What some players turn
61 What a poor diet may need
66 #1 Tommy Edwards hit of 1958
67 Inferentially

DOWN

1 Signs off on
2 Kind of challenge
3 Some dabblers
4 Tape recorder speed meas.
5 Cooper's creation
6 Rat tail?
7 It may be found in a schooner
8 "Guys and Dolls" tune
9 Summons: Abbr.
10 General ___ chicken
11 Exclamation of confirmation
12 Windmill parts
13 Swing voter, perhaps: Abbr.
14 Cable company that merged with AT&T
15 Indeed
22 Words of explanation
24 Floorboard supporter
26 Anklebones
27 Hoodwink, in a way
28 Ancient Greek theater
30 General transportation?
31 Buyer be where?
33 Teetotalers' opposites
34 Doctor's order
36 Word said explosively
37 Collect slowly
38 "The Fountainhead" character
39 "___ Own" (1994–95 sitcom)
40 Insinuate
47 Custard apple
49 Billing period
51 Hive-related
52 Wharton protagonist
53 Chromatic nuances
55 Abbr. on a French envelope
56 One-named sports star
58 Prince's "Sign ___ Times"
59 Many a plaid wearer
61 Family member
62 Chief Ouray, e.g.
63 What most L.A. Lakers games are played on
64 Div. of a degree
65 ___ Friday's (restaurant)

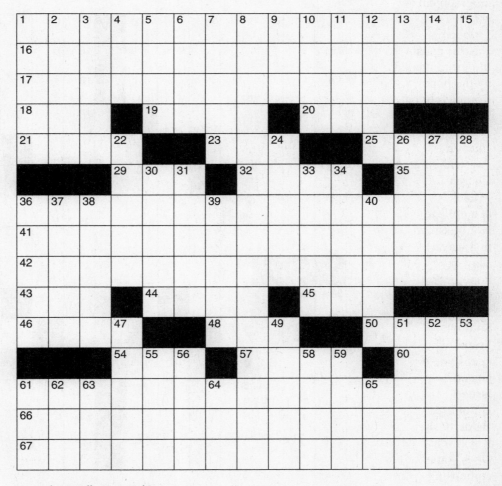

by William I. Johnston

ACROSS
1 Change places
8 First state?
15 Covers up
16 Red rash cause
17 Polish remover
18 College that pioneered in coeducation
19 Use experimentally
20 Crown
21 Cartoon cry
22 Soul mate?
23 Wine vat waste
24 Newton fraction
25 Marc Antony request
26 Gore Vidal biographical novel
27 Clobber
28 Nasdaq cousin
29 It's promulgated by the pope
31 Completely out
36 Veto
37 A mean Amin
38 Cherish
41 Political columnist Charen
42 "Teach" at a college
43 Not missing, in a way
44 May day honorees?
45 Hosiery material
46 Rumpus
47 Sold out
48 Friend who keeps you posted?
49 Issued
51 Umpire
52 Balderdash
53 Royal issue
54 Does some composing
55 Yearns

DOWN
1 Nitwit
2 Swell
3 It's open to interpretation
4 Chopper parts
5 Moving around
6 Netting site
7 Suffix with computer
8 Uncommon things in language
9 Country cousins
10 Wild goat
11 Étoile de ___ (starfish, to Cousteau)
12 Roads less traveled
13 With 26-Down, regular customers
14 Bluecoat
20 Landing field
23 Periods of revolution?
24 It begins as a crack
26 See 13-Down
27 Downsize
29 Kind of art
30 Notorious mistress Montez
32 Not be alert
33 Flying zone
34 Violator of the second Commandment
35 Lacking zip
38 Things to go through
39 It departs late at night
40 Completely smooth, now
42 Echo's activity
44 Squeaker
45 Shown to one's seat
47 Begin enthusiastically
48 Where the Ucayali begins
50 "The things we do to make you happy" sloganeer
51 Dash abbr.

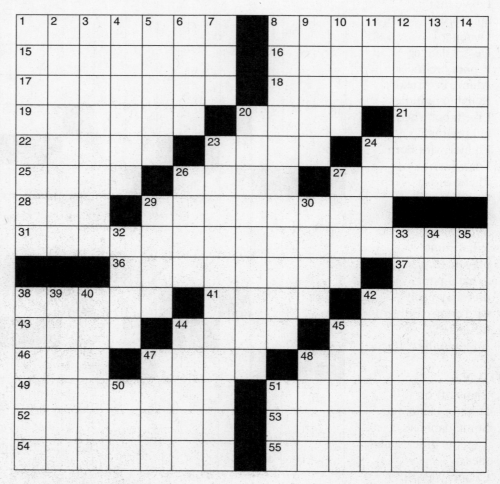

by Holden Baker

ACROSS

1 No Apple product
8 Progress
15 Circular file?
16 Accept blame without beefing
17 Past
18 Daughter of Ferdinand III
19 Kind of strand
20 Plan foilers, perhaps
22 Passenger's concern, in brief
23 Tintinnabulation
25 Mark of excellence
26 Start of a guess
27 Places for pins
29 Area of responsibility
30 Bell heather, e.g.
31 Dressing-down
33 Russian democracy champion Bonner
34 It may be a trap
35 Particular, for short
36 Bracing doses
38 Band-aid
42 Thick
43 Kennel club reject
44 "Careless Hands" singer
45 Put away
46 Puts together
48 Guy ___ (Garrison Keillor character)
49 Spanish direction
50 Figures to be analyzed
52 Classic muscle car
53 Chic
55 "Chocolat" studio
57 Went beyond
58 Magnify
59 1936 Gary Cooper title role
60 Like some glass

DOWN

1 One tending to steer out of control?
2 Intimate
3 Make a huge profit
4 One's fortune
5 Cosmos creator, in myth
6 Temple of Zeus locale
7 Archetype
8 Escorts to a penthouse, e.g.
9 Grimm collection
10 Direction givers' suggestions: Abbr.
11 Violinist Haendel
12 Has a traditional meal
13 Anaïs Nin output
14 Layers
21 It serves Jerusalem
24 Encompassed
26 Opinion opener
28 Like Santa on Christmas morning?
30 Make an officer, maybe
32 Columnist Marilyn ___ Savant
33 Dermal opening?
35 They're not given
36 Not serious
37 Divisor, e.g.
38 Mouthful of tobacco
39 Underwater salvager, e.g.
40 Copy
41 Copied
42 Deprive of heat?
43 Is obviously afraid
46 Blasé
47 Circus sight
50 Cover ground?
51 Acreage
54 First name in slapstick
56 Prefix with fauna

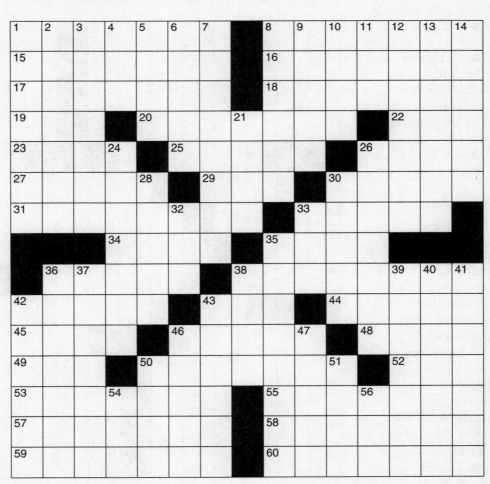

by Brendan Emmett Quigley

ACROSS

1 Blue ribbon
9 Follows, as advice
15 Funny bit
16 Least open
17 "Way to go!"
18 Snapper
19 In direct opposition
20 Wanes
21 Talk of the Gaelic
22 Haughty response
23 Specks
26 Western fight site
30 Grand
31 Destiny determiners
35 Tom Clancy subj.
36 Island whose chief port is Mahón
37 In the capacity of
38 Stew
40 Skater's jump
41 One with encumbered property
42 Do not continue
43 ___-American
46 2000 World Series venue
48 Shrine figure
50 Gossip fodder
54 Nodding
55 Bucolic
56 "___ playing our song"
57 Perfect substitute
58 Most of the kids in a certain kids' game
59 Crusades locale

DOWN

1 Just right
2 Enlightened about
3 "Our Gang" dog
4 Level off
5 Hard times
6 J.F.K., e.g.
7 Pinpoints
8 "House of Dracula" director ___ C. Kenton
9 Movie dog
10 Spritzer ingredient
11 Cause for revolution
12 Row
13 Knighted Canadian physician William
14 1998 headline event in India
23 Problem with hives
24 Ulysses Grant's birthplace
25 Hopper
27 Battery pole
28 Massive
29 As soon as
31 "Egad!"
32 Plane starter?
33 "Phooey!"
34 See stars, maybe
36 German address
39 Come-hither look
40 Galena
42 Snapper in a bowl
43 Take ___ (lose big)
44 Side order with udon
45 Lollygagged
47 "___ luego!"
49 Monkeys' uncles?
50 Cross
51 Surveyor's subject
52 Isn't caught up
53 Position to fill

by Manny Nosowsky

ACROSS

1 Far from ruddy
7 "Though banish'd, yet a ___ Englishman": "Richard II"
15 Play an ace?
16 Pull-off
17 "Woman" writer
18 Classic caller
19 Early 60's TV listing
20 Switch
22 Cockpit data: Abbr.
23 Effects
25 OT filler
28 "And ___ bed"
30 "Go Down, Moses" and others
33 One of two Roberts
34 Football Hall-of-Famer Ford
35 ___ the finish
36 Org. that provides many instructions
37 Globetrotter's catchphrase
42 Time before
43 Bird whose name is the same as its call
44 Mancinelli opera "___ e Leandro"
45 It's a scream
46 Private cabins
50 Spy's spot
52 Singer of the multimillion-selling album "Watermark"
53 Frank ___, Best Director of 1928–29
55 Actress Hatcher
57 Upper half?
59 "Pay ___ mind"
60 Fujitsu competitor
63 Multitude
65 Thimbleweeds
66 Newspaper starting in 1912
67 Reef wriggler
68 Most together

DOWN

1 Symbols of victory
2 Dodges
3 Means of identification
4 Refuse use
5 Witt rink rival
6 Headway
7 Famous landing site
8 White-collar worker, for short?
9 Tour organizer: Abbr.
10 Catania threatener
11 Muddles, with "up"
12 Choir piece
13 St. John's team
14 Word in Parliament
21 Given (to)
24 Some circus performers
26 Eastern royal
27 Gatorade, e.g.
29 Chantilly's department
31 Stir
32 Fatty tissue compound
37 Craving
38 Extra meaning
39 Sri Lanka export
40 Actor McGregor
41 Tough
47 Teacup handle
48 Murder mystery necessity
49 High councils
51 Some senior moments?
54 Filmdom's Mr. Chips
56 Pistol, slangily
58 Where Davos is
60 Household heads
61 ___ whim
62 Albanian coin
64 Big time?

by Jim Page

ACROSS

1 Kind of atty.
5 Funny producer
15 Prefix with dermal
16 Frozen treat
17 "Did you forget about me?"
18 Given to forcefully
19 They may be fawning
20 Two-time U.S. Open winner Fraser
21 Loam component
22 Debut of Oct. 11, 1975
23 Savior
24 Philosopher Diderot
25 Member of the First Triumvirate
27 Mount ___ (Minnesota ski resort)
30 Pleiades pursuer
31 Stay on top of trends
35 Where the going rate is charged?
37 She followed Lou as first lady
39 No posh hotels
41 Mentor of Eminem
42 1999 air strike authorizer
43 Deep sleeps
44 Michael Bolton's "How ___ Be Lovers"
48 Doing business
50 Hoops competition, briefly
51 Specialty
52 Pluto's purview
54 Castor and Pollux's mother
55 Program interruption
57 Scene of heavy W.W. I fighting
58 Tom, say

59 Catalog
60 Millionaire's address?
61 Grub

DOWN

1 Place of poor radio reception
2 Recognizing
3 Heavy metal producer?
4 Some cats
5 Passenger vehicle
6 Choice word?
7 Literally, empty orchestra
8 End of the year, for some
9 Smart-alecky
10 Backstabber
11 Loo message
12 It may be made on the rebound
13 Potentially pathogenic strain
14 Checks for letters?
23 Plant of the nightshade family
24 Gave extra attention
26 End of the world?
28 Wows
29 No later than, informally
31 No angel
32 Heavenly sight
33 Land of 13,500+ islands
34 Most scorching
36 Case studier's org.
38 They may follow computer crashes
40 "Ha, that was funny"
43 Certain stanza
44 Camp craft
45 Rock tour venue
46 Semiaquatic swimmers
47 Somewhat irresolute?
49 Nez ___
52 Weight
53 Parrot
54 1988 Masters winner
56 Court matter

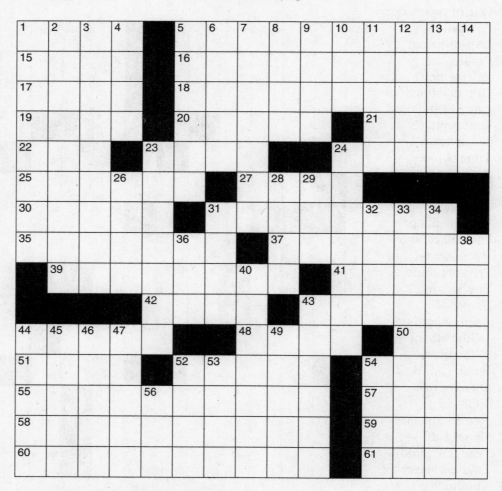

by Brendan Emmett Quigley

ACROSS

1 Off-topic remark?
9 Elbow
15 "Eleni" star
16 Person of great interest?
17 Combined
18 Time piece?
19 It's not clean
20 Unforested tract
22 Enumeration follower
23 Some bridge players
25 Program problem
26 Court ruling?
27 Anglers' burdens
29 Strauss's "___ Heldenleben"
30 Word with bed or saddle
31 Critics, often
33 Dissolve
34 Family name of 50's–60's TV
37 Shake alternatives
39 Entertainers
40 Clothing category
42 Broadway opener
43 Small hearing aid?
44 Draws out
48 Long-jawed swimmer
49 It may be in the closet
51 Lover of lean cuisine
52 Loss leader?
53 Restless
55 Damaged by drought
56 Newspaper ads figure
58 Equestrian exhibition
60 Big feller?
61 Start of a letter accompanying a manuscript
62 Golf legend's family
63 Skedaddles

DOWN

1 Shortly
2 San Diego suburb
3 Maltreat
4 Beautiful people
5 Sen division
6 They're inflatable
7 Henri's health
8 Snidely Whiplash, often
9 Reprimand
10 Purple willow, e.g.
11 Juliet, to Romeo
12 Juliet, to Romeo
13 Educated
14 Construction crew
21 Periscope parts
24 People along the old Iron Curtain
28 ___ Anne de Bellevue, Que.
30 Begins a business
32 Fine coat
33 Winter toy-store stock
34 "Morning Mystery" and "Bouquet de Fleurs," e.g.
35 A film may be shot on it
36 Keep at a distance
38 Polymer follower
41 No mere cold snaps
43 Workers with headlights?
45 Laugh line, e.g.
46 Bread maker
47 Positions
49 Raced down a chute, perhaps
50 "Bye Bye Bye" band
54 Sir George Williams's org.
57 Ottoman officer
59 Initials at J.F.K.

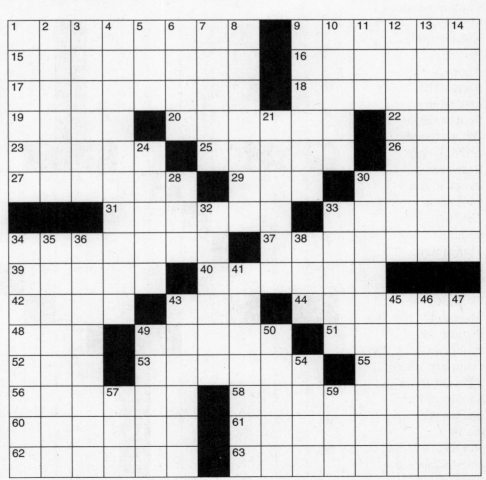

by Elizabeth C. Gorski

ACROSS

1 Ins and outs of finance?
9 Red in the face
15 Isolated
16 Where a candlestick parks?
17 Caulks
18 Vehicle in no-parking zone, maybe
19 It lets the sun shine in
20 "Count me in!"
21 Apart from this
22 Old "Hits the spot" sloganeer
23 Remains for the day
26 Refrain syllables
30 Meccas
31 Needed things
35 Part of NATO: Abbr.
36 Arrival that may annoy
37 Perfect figure
38 Where Laval University is
40 Between a rock and a hard place
41 Gets dark, perhaps
42 Thingamajig
43 Picker-upper
46 "Hey, wait ___"
48 Combat zones
50 Tries to hit
54 Prepare the way (to)
55 Helm cry after "Ready about"
56 Victim of the green-eyed monster
57 Not easily denied
58 Unbending
59 Far-ranging adventures

DOWN

1 1848 presidential candidate after whom eight U.S. counties are named
2 Fashion model Wek
3 Have rolling in the aisles
4 Whose comet?
5 Gives a thrashing
6 Pant sizes
7 Undecided
8 9 o'clock, to some
9 Spot of wine?
10 Certain vitamins
11 It's good for climbing hills
12 Take the lid off
13 Cons
14 Words after "Ready or not"
23 N.B.A. all-star
24 Dancing outfit
25 In a position to help
27 Welcome, say
28 Gives help
29 Diurnally
31 Way in or out
32 Full range
33 Insurance policy specification
34 Part of A.D.
36 "The Plains of Passage" author
39 Daisy's mistress
40 Alternative to Certs
42 Some sparklers
43 Scheherazade's stock-in-trade
44 "___ I a woman?": Sojourner Truth
45 Turn green
47 Popular board game
49 Moving well
50 Drive off
51 Hedge plant with white flowers
52 Unsubstantial
53 Spreads for drying

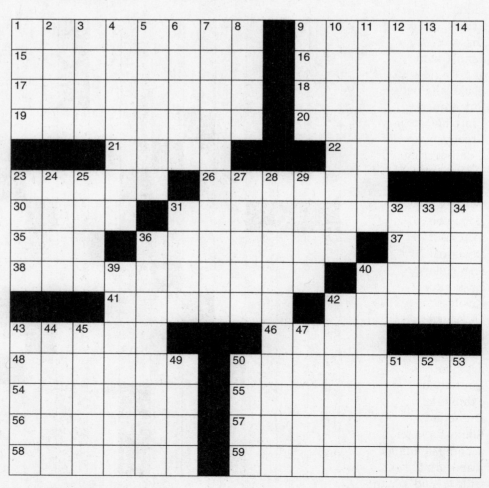

by Manny Nosowsky

ACROSS

1 Flash light?
7 Duchess of ____ (Goya model)
11 Queen ____
14 Head cases?
15 Runs over
17 Peak performances?
18 Prime-time times
19 Notorious courtroom strategy of 1979
21 Pilot's accessory
22 Pilot's problem
23 Effective leveler
25 Wright wing
26 Sandbank site
28 Kill, in a way
29 Cut corners?
31 Too
33 Nile crosser
36 Break dancing accompaniment
38 They may carry burdens
39 Lays out
41 Bait
43 See 3-Down
44 It originally included 51 states
46 Physics Nobelist Landau
49 A camel may be executed on it
50 With 61-Across, bigwig: Var.
51 Like a gymnast
54 Best seat in the house?
57 Sloth
58 Borneo creatures
59 Firearm, after firing
60 More than look up to
61 See 50-Across
62 Banks on the runway
63 Not optional

DOWN

1 Swath producer
2 It may turn up some dirt
3 With 43-Across, Michelin product
4 Successively
5 Chisels
6 Like the path of least resistance
7 Like some ports
8 Words accompanying a smack
9 Fusion cuisine?
10 Good ____ (fixed)
11 Scream elicitors
12 Rough
13 British cars
16 Artist Maya
20 Preoperative delivery of old
24 Playpen pile
27 Spout rhetoric
28 It may be under a jacket
29 Locks in a barn?
30 Kind of candidate: Abbr.
32 Moving option
33 Sparkling wine, familiarly
34 Indian refreshment
35 Cry after a lucky strike?
37 King of Greece, 1947–64
40 Without expression
42 Figure in some mysterious 15th-century tapestries
45 Unhappy audience member, maybe
46 Advanced
47 New citizen, perhaps
48 Up on, with "in"
50 Take as a given
52 Rocky debris
53 Make smooth, in a way
55 Schmaltz
56 Dame Hess
57 Moon, e.g.

by Elizabeth C. Gorski

ACROSS

1 "___ seems"
5 Tries to cover up
15 About
16 Opening pair?
17 Seismologist's field: Abbr.
18 Bristly
19 Kind of thinking
21 Like "Miró, Miró on the wall"
22 Rainbow maker
23 "___ Central Park" (1945 Broadway hit)
25 One who can't bear family life?
26 Like some securities, for short
27 Bread in 43-Across
30 River past Armentières
31 Convincing debater
33 For the full orchestra
35 Swords made with finely tempered steel
37 Barely get the words out
41 Actor Green and others
43 Place to use 27-Across
44 "___ magic!"
47 Ones drawn to scale?
49 Dude
50 Literally, "I am unwilling"
52 Political suffix
53 Lacquer ingredient
55 Sheriff Lobo portrayer Claude
57 Commemorating
59 Ratline
61 Adriatic port
62 State university locale
63 To ___

64 No place for a draft dodger
65 Médoc and Chianti

DOWN

1 Pointer
2 Hardly any
3 Not straightforward
4 Doesn't conceal
5 Castle protector, maybe
6 Words to go with
7 Low wall
8 Professor ___
9 Word often heard in triplicate
10 Go bonkers
11 Disrepute and then some

12 Springy?
13 In a monotone
14 Colors over
20 Handicapped
24 Yackety-yak
28 Aphrodisiac
29 1948 presidential contender
32 "O.K."
34 Rascal
36 Victor at Five Forks, 1865
38 Cause disintegration
39 Under the spell (of)
40 Approves
42 Sub
44 Aligned
45 Site of film bridges

46 Sandal type
48 Flammable gas
51 Upright
54 Kind of pneumonia
56 Token taker
58 City south of Moscow
60 ___ Darya (river to the Aral Sea)

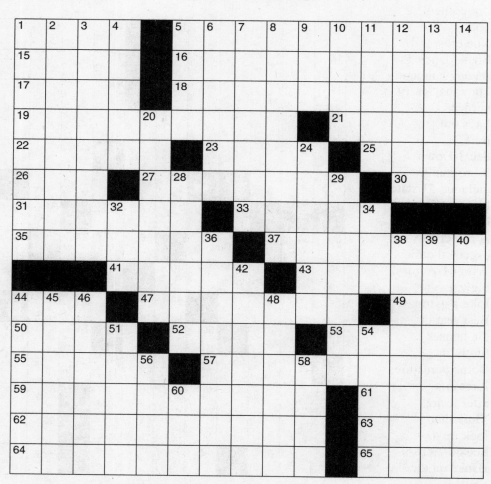

by Manny Nosowsky

ACROSS

1 Semiterrestrial hopper
10 Bob Marley, for one
15 Fish on a dish
16 Big shows
17 Like virgin land
18 Netanyahu's predecessor
19 Note
20 Baby ___
21 Touch upon, with "to"
22 Lagerlöf's "The Wonderful Adventures of ___"
24 Religious residence
26 Let go
27 Legend
29 Kind of fair: Abbr.
30 Small price to pay
31 Hot stuff
35 Went around
38 Taken wrong?
39 Breakfast treat
41 One into the bar scene?: Abbr.
42 Spleen
43 1998 Australian Open winner
47 Morse T
48 Without reciprocity
51 "___ seems"
52 Issue
54 Hedgerow nester
56 Fr. address
57 Racehorse of a sort
58 1989 Nobel Peace Prize winner
60 Sans sense
61 They may be religious
62 Tops
63 No place for skirts

DOWN

1 Model builder's activity
2 "The Two Sisters" painter
3 A nurse may draw from it
4 La lead-in
5 Kind of appeal
6 Shooter's setting
7 Turbine turner
8 The Rebels
9 Dropout's doc.
10 It's much requested
11 Skating pioneer Paulsen
12 Groom
13 Emulate an étoile
14 Gave in
21 Like a melody
23 Smooth
25 Strike, with "to"
28 "Look what I did!"
30 Argentine leader Menem
32 Hearty sentiment?
33 Like a load
34 Display of displeasure
35 Scholar's milieu
36 Cold fighter
37 Hiding out
40 Tradition-breaking
44 It's made of ewe's milk
45 Light switcher?
46 Relaxing words
48 Mythical maneaters
49 "Get Happy" songwriter
50 Sentence units
53 Québécois Lévesque
55 Immature parasites
58 Monk's title
59 You may build on it

by Joe DiPietro

ACROSS

1 Cons
9 Italian paper once edited by Mussolini
15 Redeemed
16 Mark
17 Facing
18 Suspended
19 Much
20 Features of some camps
22 "___ Need" (1985 hit)
23 Boxer's problem
25 Smell ___
26 Lenient
27 Affectionate address
30 $200 purchases: Abbr.
32 Educ. test
33 Sword handle
34 More mawkish
36 Associate
39 They may be cut or slashed
40 "The Sibylline ___" (ancient religious collection)
42 1997 Jackie Robinson commemoration site
43 Network based in D.C.
44 Letters that please an angel
45 Lamented
48 Get friendlier
50 Uto-Aztecan language
52 NASA pressure unit
54 Epidemic
55 La Scala debut of 1887
58 Incandescent, in product names
59 Undisturbed
61 Prelude to an explosion, perhaps
63 Be poised (on)
64 Be false
65 Rangers and Citations
66 Is sure not to miss

DOWN

1 "That's nothing!," for example
2 An incendiary
3 Ocean diver
4 "___ says?!"
5 Taunt
6 Comics dog
7 Cameo
8 Mean mien
9 Entr'acte part
10 ___ rouge
11 Ottoman potentates
12 Linguistically groundbreaking
13 One way to call
14 Poets
21 Receiver accessory, slangily
24 Literally, "for this"
28 Court figures
29 Late
31 Bacchanal
35 Kind of roll or bar
36 Repentant
37 No longer sponsored
38 Bugs
41 Pipe sullier
42 Omelet site
46 Deluge
47 Texas border city
49 Justice replaced by Ginsburg
51 Buttinskies
53 Lost cause
56 "Come Back, Little Sheba" wife
57 Big-eyed
60 ___ Hay, Israeli memorial
62 Coll. conferrals

by Rich Norris

ACROSS

1 Treasuries
7 Stolen, in London
13 Heavyweight event?
14 Got one's fill of?
16 70's–80's Chrysler
17 Pellet
18 Burial receptacle
19 Someone who watches his head?
21 Companion of "Stay!"
22 Tend a turkey, e.g.
24 Bit of Braille
25 Automatic selection?
27 Others, to Ovid
28 They're nuts for drinks
30 Continuously
31 1964 Hudson/Day comedy
34 Beg
35 Absolutely clobber
41 Harmonia's father
42 Macy's competitor
43 Boughpot
44 ___-car
46 Application info: Abbr.
47 Perfume, in a way
48 Anti body?
49 Not so nice
52 Hero
53 Villain of Spider-Man
55 Bitterly cold
57 Camp necessity
58 Building with many layers
59 Starts of some melees
60 Wee

DOWN

1 "A Mighty Fortress Is Our God," e.g.
2 Is obtrusive
3 LAX listing
4 One of a multitude in a devil's-snuffbox
5 Big blow for a band?
6 Try to get a better view, maybe
7 Continually
8 Anent
9 Garden green
10 Where the Cimarron flows: Abbr.
11 Slippery
12 Emancipate
13 Heavy breathers?
15 Checks
20 What NBC's peacock once signified
23 Like the perfect homemaker's home
26 Fix, as a rug
28 Visored caps
29 In Britain they're called thieves' kitchens
32 "Delicious!"
33 Four quarters
35 Artist Duchamp
36 Biological interstices
37 Scottish name meaning "handsome"
38 Flowers with yellow, buttonlike blooms
39 Burial receptacle
40 Without much power
45 When Antony dies in "Antony and Cleopatra"
47 Davit
50 "Rise, Glory, Rise" composer
51 Part of a C.S.A. signature
54 ___-Magnon
56 Letters for a King?

by Martin Ashwood-Smith

ACROSS

1 Blues or folk group
8 Shoot over
14 It's about 55 and up
15 Where Austerlitz is
16 Exerciser's wear
17 Like a pageant winner
18 Hot ___
19 Ending
21 Prefix with genetic
22 Earth, in Essen
23 Got hooked quickly
26 Sugar
27 Audition
28 Independent
30 Three-time Cotton Bowl champs: Abbr.
31 Classic Morris Motors cars
32 Ore used for old radio crystals
33 Maneuvering room
35 "Love ___"
36 More than a favorite
39 Bud
40 Not get off easily?
43 Battle assignment, once
45 Shooters may need them
47 Park, e.g.: Abbr.
48 Kind of rug
50 Gym site
51 "Common sense" philosopher Thomas
53 High-performance Camaro ___-Z
54 Head out on the ocean?
55 Will part
58 Stews
60 Charms
61 Property recipient, at law
62 Changes hands?
63 Experts

DOWN

1 Quartz variety
2 They make a lot of calls
3 Certain Pontiac
4 Felt certain of
5 Stick in
6 Cressida, to Pandarus
7 Hymn of praise
8 Romain de ___ (typeface)
9 Procter & Gamble brand
10 Diet
11 Sir Arthur Sullivan opera
12 Rest
13 "Crazy for You" singer
15 Philippines' highest peak: Abbr.
20 Gets into
24 TV actress Georgia
25 Not working
29 School cafeteria dishes
31 Exodus miracle
34 Celebrity
35 Culinary herb
36 Not so common
37 "Try it!"
38 Five Nations members
39 Kind of orchard
41 Fresh horse
42 Boatsman
44 Iniquities
46 Descendant of Japanese immigrants
49 Florida county seat
52 F.D.R. locale
56 Simple resting place
57 Grp. that's true to form?
59 "O, ___ me the lass . . .": Burns

by Rich Norris

ACROSS

1 Farrah Fawcett played her in "The Great American Beauty Contest"
10 It's hot stuff
15 Album
16 Cantonese caregivers
17 Unfairly burdened
18 They're hot stuff
19 "___ you one!"
20 Truckload
21 Opposite of plus
22 Place on an angle
23 They go overboard
25 Wounded helper?
27 Opera conductor Daniel ___
28 Patsy Cline's "___ Got You"
29 Refrain syllable
31 Won't shut up
33 "___ pales in Heaven the morning star": Lowell
34 Fresheners
38 "Harmony in Red" artist
40 Siouan
41 "Jabberwocky" opener
43 Sonny boy
44 Modern mall features
49 Pacific ___ College
48 Commodity in a bear market?
52 Holy roller?
55 Indigenous Canadian
56 Used no inflection, maybe
57 Org. involved in seizures
58 Filly
59 Indigenous Canadian
60 Keeps at it
62 Polite title
63 Aida or Carmen
64 Dynamic start?
65 Followers

DOWN

1 Red Guard ideology
2 Pray for
3 Like some prunes
4 Termagant
5 New walker
6 Make merry
7 Love letters?
8 Go-between's business
9 Pink Floyd's Barrett
10 House of Seven Gables site
11 Valuable violas
12 Showers
13 Goes to pieces?
14 One who is charged
21 Receiver of exotic stamps, perhaps
24 Printer's unit
26 Hardy Boys' pal
30 "Lady Oracle" novelist
32 Doctor's order
34 Bar keeper?
35 Any one of 25 U.S. presidents
36 Like some sentences
37 Car since 1949
39 "Well!"
42 Helmet, in cyclist's slang
45 Higher-ranking
47 One may follow a lead
49 Tap
50 Make drinkable, in a way
51 Enthusiastic approval
53 Kind of area
54 It's on a quarter's back
60 Class-conscious grp.
61 Church talk: Abbr.

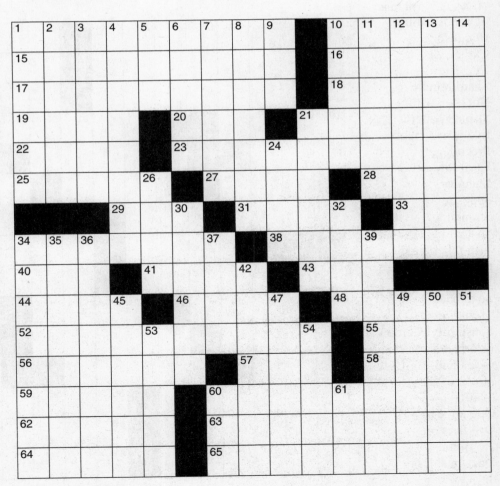

by Elizabeth C. Gorski

ACROSS

1 Hardly a favorite
9 Aspect
15 1953 Frankie Laine hit
16 Plane, in a way
17 Like most Norwegians
18 Fur
19 Confirmation, for one
20 Part of a step
22 Hot air
23 Purdue Univ. major
24 Turned
25 Partner of letters
26 Realize
28 River People of the Southwest
29 "It's ___!" (phrase of confirmation)
30 Berates
32 Cat's ___
34 Curse
35 Sharp rebuke
36 Not too swift
39 Striped patterns
43 Like some chairs
44 Precollege
46 Farm fare
47 Mañana's opposite
48 Strange
49 "Is that ___?"
50 Trip-taker's aid, perhaps
51 Moisten
52 Send back
53 "Sense and Sensibility" heroine
55 Contracted
58 Cisco Kid player of the 1940's
59 One up, e.g.
60 Dwellers on the Baltic
61 Does business on, as a holiday

DOWN

1 Study
2 Bond recipient, in law
3 Uninvolved
4 Jollity
5 You, abroad
6 "Hold it!"
7 Due a refund, in a way
8 Monotony
9 Repair a perfboard, e.g.
10 At all
11 Set
12 Twist of phrase, perhaps
13 Annual Henley-on-Thames event
14 Prepares for cooking
21 Plays a kids' game involving centrifugal force
24 Rows
25 Converts
27 Farmer, at times
29 "When it's ___" (old riddle answer)
31 Came out with
33 Novelist ___-René Lesage
36 Mountaineers, in a way
37 Knocks down
38 Old calling fee
40 Words before time, money or respect
41 Unlikely protagonist
42 Cleric famous for bloopers
45 Misinforms
48 Houston hockey team of the 70's
51 Gun stat
52 Env. contents
54 "20,000 Leagues" mate ___ Land
56 Dakota Indian
57 J.F.K. was in it

by Rich Norris

ACROSS

1 Fight
10 Plans
15 Family troublemakers, perhaps
16 Saturday Night Massacre figure
17 Game in which losers have a blast?
19 Actress Kruger and others
20 Canterbury's home
21 Department head?
22 South Korea's Roh ___ Woo
23 Cooling-off periods
26 "Frasier" producer
27 Boiardo's patron
29 "Das Rheingold" goddess
30 Pasta choice
32 They work with many schedules
34 Leaf apertures
36 Deep sleeps
39 It's spotted in South America
40 Hunter's companion
42 Tan too long
43 Deep pink
44 Harem chambers
46 Vacationer in a camper, informally
50 She gave Odysseus a magic veil
51 Skippers
54 Suffix with urban
55 Rank leaders?: Abbr.
57 16-Across, to some
58 Flowed to and fro
60 Unstitched?
63 Missouri feeder
64 Ill-fated mission of 1967

65 Porter's "Ev'ry Time ___ Goodbye"
66 Sentimental do-gooder

DOWN

1 Place less value on
2 Anatomical hangers
3 Lot
4 Opera lass who broke a vow
5 Formal phrase of identification
6 Letters on some liners
7 Hogs
8 Like junk mail, usually
9 1992 presidential contender
10 Chevy vehicle, briefly
11 Artist Mondrian
12 Like some modems
13 Start liking
14 Disdain
18 Peyotism practicer
24 Cut out
25 "Baby and Child Care" author
28 Commercial prefix with "car"
31 High guy in Dubai
33 Run off
35 One who's a goner
36 Wrecked ship of sitcomdom
37 Unsolved crime
38 Oafs
41 Mrs. John Quincy Adams and others
42 Withdrawal carrying a steep penalty?
45 From the top, musically
47 Boob tube addict
48 Ageless, once
49 Comparatively undercooked
52 F.D.A. guideline
53 Pens
56 Nintendo rival
59 Native Nigerians
61 "L.A. Law" actress
62 Hirschfeld et al.

by Robert Bridges

ACROSS

1 Door opener
9 Massachusetts town with an Algonquian name
15 Dinky
16 Lunar phenomenon
17 They may get fired at factories
18 Game similar to Black Lady
19 Assent
20 Baby
22 It may come with instructions
23 Flower of Lille
24 Dispute
25 Power problem
27 Beer order
30 Genesis man
32 Inept
33 Jessica of "Dark Angel"
35 Trick
37 Bribe
40 Buried
41 Magazine designer's aid
42 Race
43 ___ world
44 Data source
46 Punkie
49 "Them" novelist
51 Stalk
53 Part of cheesecake, maybe
55 First Burmese prime minister
56 Pitched perfectly
58 1971 Pan American Games site
59 Lie in pleasing surroundings
61 Trade subjects?
63 Ajax and others
64 Reserved
65 Trials
66 Sham

DOWN

1 The slow way to go
2 Weak
3 1942 Oscar winner Wright
4 Detective of note
5 Prefix meaning "same"
6 Austrian conductor Josef
7 Prison warden's concern
8 One going along
9 Discomfort
10 Habitués
11 Scorpius neighbor
12 Where things get done
13 Sophocles tragedy
14 Subjugated
21 Where money is made
26 Good news on Wall Street
28 Try
29 Parmenides' home
31 Reasoned
34 Harp toter of yore
36 Chase in the field
37 Gather with difficulty
38 Loser's destination
39 Breaks
45 Losing general at Spotsylvania Courthouse
47 They're used in classified ads
48 Scout's quest
50 Smooth
52 Bombay-born maestro
54 Johnny Mathis classic
57 Stack part
58 Gospel singer Winans
60 It may be served in spots
62 Year in Nero's reign

by Rich Norris

ACROSS

1 Picnic dish
10 Rook
14 A pocket radio might have one
15 Onetime White House resident
16 Whip up
17 Jim Croce's "I Got ___"
18 Presidential inits.
19 It might need to be picked up
20 One shooting from the mouth?
21 Sieve, essentially
22 Takeout option
23 Husbandry
26 Kofi Annan's home
27 Thrilling
28 One of a pair by Debussy
32 Jejune
33 Shrovetide dish
34 "I'm happy" in Siamese?
35 Health
37 True
38 Moved very carefully
39 Goldfish, at carnivals
40 Get set?
43 Rifle part
44 ". . . heaven hath pleas'd it so, / To punish me . . ." speaker
45 Go bad, in a way
46 Ancient symbol of sovereignty
49 Open
50 Torment
52 Fearful
53 727 and others
54 They have shells
55 Commando target

DOWN

1 Blowout
2 Chow
3 Some
4 Vet's memory, maybe
5 Floor
6 Exultant cry
7 Percolate
8 Museo offering
9 Turn green, maybe
10 Dessert not for the calorie-conscious
11 Something to uphold
12 Park Avenue sights
13 City on the Ashuelot
15 Not terrestrial, perhaps
20 Abu ___
21 Like most of suburbia
22 Common name in Taipei
23 Detente
24 Accounted for, in a way
25 Marsh resident
26 Rat race
28 Not terrestrial, perhaps
29 Kind of kid
30 Egg
31 Shore scavengers
33 Surrounded (by)
36 Napoleon locale
37 Paul Poiret style
39 Radio wave producer
40 Stethoscope sound
41 4-Down locale
42 Charge, as with feeling
43 Orchardist's woe
45 A ___ technicality
46 Quattro maker
47 Some Fr. nuns
48 43-Down, e.g.
50 Like some answers
51 Heart, in prescriptions

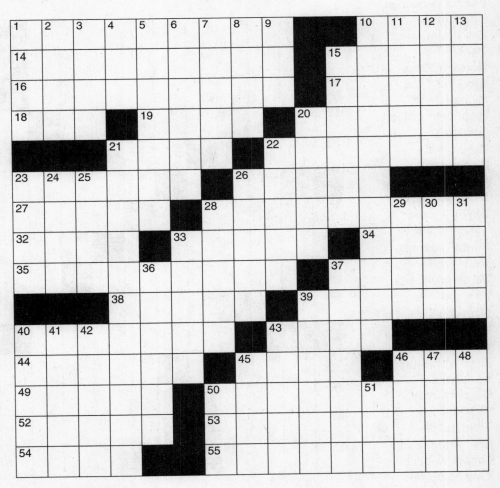

by Fraser Simpson

ACROSS

1 Emulate a "Beat Street" performer
11 Lake of Emerson, Lake & Palmer
15 Latitude
16 Student's need, often
17 Brings together
18 Role for Ingrid
19 Head, slangily
20 Flop-___
21 Sound
22 Circle
24 Sound
26 You may wrestle with it
28 Art of jazz
29 Buttonhole, maybe
32 Painter surnamed Vecellio
35 Early admission?
37 1972 White House biography subtitled "The Years Alone"
39 Prelude to peace, perhaps
40 Bush pilot's destination
42 Fresh
43 Judge's object
44 Blows a gasket
46 "The Perfect Storm" setting, with "the"
47 Terhune classic
49 Law grp.
52 Denver university
55 Bullish start?
57 Place to pasture
58 Shake ___
59 Quizzee, maybe
61 "Two by Two" role
62 Like some drinks
63 Tabloid fodder
64 Vera Miles, in 1948

DOWN

1 African master
2 Inexorability
3 They may give you a good whipping
4 Cabinet dept.
5 Bauhaus School member
6 "The Millinery Shop" painter
7 Sight after a flood
8 Reporter's need
9 Having two heads, in a way
10 See 36-Down
11 Inkling
12 Coin collection
13 Let up
14 Black ___ (fishing fly)
21 They may have flight plans
23 Many famous ones are from Italy
25 Noted student of Bernoulli
27 "Rig-Veda" selections
29 List recipient
30 "Symphony in Black" artist
31 It's often rooted out
32 Fly
33 First name in 70's tennis
34 Satellite-tracking program
36 With 10-Down, region of Lower Saxony
38 Trattoria offering
41 Know-it-alls
45 Goes to a warmer place, perhaps
47 Smoker's request
48 Like pi
50 Holder of an annual Colloquium
51 Cocktail party preparations
52 Big name in mapmaking
53 H. G. Wells race
54 Ropes, pads, etc.
56 Division of Labor: Abbr.
59 Dot follower
60 Raft

by Charles E. Gersch

ACROSS

1 Monitors' requests
11 Cracked
15 Eloquent
16 Relief
17 Expresses condolences, perhaps
18 De bene ___
19 Writing shortcut
20 Followers of tax cheats
21 Home of Lafayette College
23 Foreign leader exiled in Hawaii, 1960
25 Breaks Down
27 Doña ___, New Mexico's second-largest county
28 Colorful garments
30 Bar
31 Attack word
32 Extinguished
34 Most vicious
36 Behind in the regatta
39 Pitches, in a way
40 Aromatic herb used in soups and salads
42 Chart with many lines
43 Gore follower?
44 "Enchanted April" setting
46 Facetious
50 Conversation, for some
51 Ice skater's spin
52 Chaser, in a way
53 Emblem of victory
55 Make or break
58 Reunion Arena player, briefly
59 Another, abroad
60 Express a thought

63 Brushoffs
64 Awesome
65 Breaks off
66 Writer's request

DOWN

1 Swindlers, slangily
2 1968 album subtitled "Lady Soul"
3 Halberdier's opponent
4 Ford's Crown Victoria, e.g.
5 Appointment
6 "Eugene ___" (1832 Bulwer-Lytton novel)
7 Strengthened
8 Quick breads
9 Have
10 Teen party, maybe
11 Super-duper
12 "Hold on"
13 Incendiary
14 Plays over
22 Aimed
24 Quilt filler
26 When Nancy bakes?
29 Army, for one
33 "A Girl Like I" autobiographer
35 Looks askance
36 Eschew assistance
37 Like some English furniture
38 Not smooth

41 Beat . . . or beat it
42 Product in a 1982 recall
45 Funny business
47 Resistance figure
48 Not fancy at all
49 "The Road to Ensenada" singer
54 Lord in Shakespeare's "Richard II"
56 Teeming
57 Chief
61 Wager
62 U.S. Library of Medicine maintainer

by Rich Norris

ACROSS

1 Nursery rhyme starter
11 Band over a bathing suit, maybe
15 Rambo
16 Start of some cloud names
17 Gen. Hooker fought in it
18 Slight remark
19 Not a veteran
20 "Can ___?"
21 Strauss opera
23 Kiri Te Kanawa and others
25 Traditional
27 Have fun on a white bed?
28 "Quién ___?"
29 It has two doors
30 Al Capp creation
33 Northern flier
34 "___ never believe it!"
37 Track records
39 Part of ASCAP: Abbr.
40 Pasture item
44 Gulf rival
46 Opera character with a dream
47 Gym set
51 Modernizes, maybe
53 Country or folk
54 "Cymbeline" heroine
55 Campaign worker
57 Go out
58 Somebody
59 "Eeew!"
62 Situation favoring the server
63 It may be taken before swinging
64 Zealots, for one
65 Al Capone portrayer of 1959

DOWN

1 They're made in hospitals
2 Free, in a way
3 Look good on
4 Cannes confidant
5 17-Across figure
6 Mile, e.g.
7 Panamanian mintage
8 "Young" TV physician
9 Mia's portrayer in "Pulp Fiction"
10 1960's folk rockers, with "The"
11 Plato's "tenth Muse"
12 No place for a draft dodger?
13 It's useful for dictators
14 Lost
22 Swallow
24 Vortex
26 F.D.R., e.g.
28 One may be raised on a farm
31 Garden bower, e.g.
32 Dog star
34 Catherine and others
35 Like some meals
36 Like some forecasts
38 Australia's largest lake
41 In need of a change, perhaps
42 Like punch?
43 Appoints
45 Forceful
48 Bad thing to give away
49 King's issue
50 "Turn! Turn! Turn!" songwriter
52 Slashed words?
53 Chanson de ___
56 Sneeze inducer
60 Dotcom's dream, maybe
61 Red ___ (sushi fish)

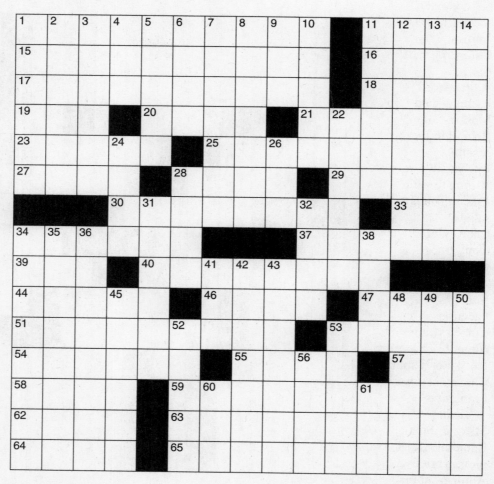

by Mark Diehl

ACROSS

1 Copy
9 Prepare for dinner, say
15 Tenderfoot
16 Fight
17 Comprehensive
18 Big name in retail
19 1995 and '97 A.L. champs, in scoreboards
20 Racer
22 Realizes
23 Fly (around)
25 Squeezed
26 Kenyan president Daniel arap ___
27 Oil source
30 Compound with two carbon atoms
32 Flap
33 Haitian monetary unit
35 Actor Quinn
37 Word after "I do"
40 Hospital supplies
42 The other woman in "The Age of Innocence"
43 Try not to have an accident, say
45 Boise's county
46 Genesis son
48 Ran out
52 Handle overseas?
53 Ravel's "Gaspard de la ___"
55 A runner may break it
56 Some low-budget hotels, for short
58 Not hide
61 Kisser?
62 "Invisible Man" setting
64 Make excuses, maybe
66 Brainstorm
67 Without dissent
68 Yahoo, for one
69 Flipped

DOWN

1 Gifts
2 "South Pacific" heroine
3 Ones involved in barn raisings?
4 Year in the papacy of St. Zephyrinus
5 King ___
6 Literary sequel of 1847
7 Hardly an authorized dealer
8 Lost one's cool
9 Is inadequate
10 Go ___
11 English
12 Domestic
13 It may be found in a box on the street
14 Fixed payments
21 Go back
24 Boston College athlete
28 Complaints
29 English, e.g.: Abbr.
31 Grub
34 Get renewed
36 Clueless
37 Academic domain
38 1967 John Wayne film
39 Dissatisfied type
41 www destination
44 Subject to simultaneous opposing forces
47 Crown covering
49 Antipasto morsel
50 Long and impressive
51 Ride (on)
54 Needle
57 Strip
59 River through Wiltshire
60 Let
63 Sorority letter
65 ". . . let thy words be ___": Eccl.

by Rich Norris

ACROSS

1 Country singer Ketchum
4 Home of the Tate Gallery
15 What gives a pose poise?
16 Musical work with a duel
17 Darling of the baseball world
18 Frank
19 Trekkers
21 Geom. shape
22 Appealing, perhaps
23 Variety show showing
26 Like a clear-cut area
27 The Sneetches' creator
28 Leader of France
29 Bit of fancy footwork
30 60's grp.
31 Stewart's replacement on the bench
33 Year Dacia was captured by Trajan
36 Put on
37 "The Good Earth" heroine
38 Kip spender
40 Comes to the point?
42 Waltzlike dances
43 Term of endearment
44 Blast, for instance
45 Like Jupiter's four largest moons
46 Maximizes efficiency
50 Point toward the top
51 PBS personality
52 O.R. amounts
53 Steely Dan hit, 1980
54 "But then again . . ."

DOWN

1 Angels, in many images
2 Chosen
3 Some Matisse creations
4 Sponge
5 Queen's name
6 Move forward, or jump back
7 Speaker from Cleveland
8 When "The Lucy Show" aired: Abbr.
9 Some drippers, for short
10 Day break
11 Lay away
12 Underground purchases
13 Puts up
14 Lets out
20 Seward Peninsula city
23 Everybody's doing it
24 In the matter of
25 "Laughable Lyrics" writer
27 "Funny Face" director Stanley
29 Worn sheets
31 Chemistry Nobelist Hahn
32 Noted exile
33 Mercy
34 Case for a planning board
35 Most touched
36 Voice of the car in "My Mother, the Car"
37 Virgin Valley valuable
38 Execrate
39 Lead ___
40 "Unto the Sons" author
41 Up and about
42 "Mocking of Christ" painter
43 Woodskin
45 Hemmed in
47 1996 Olympic torch lighter
48 60 ticks: Abbr.
49 Bruce or Brenda

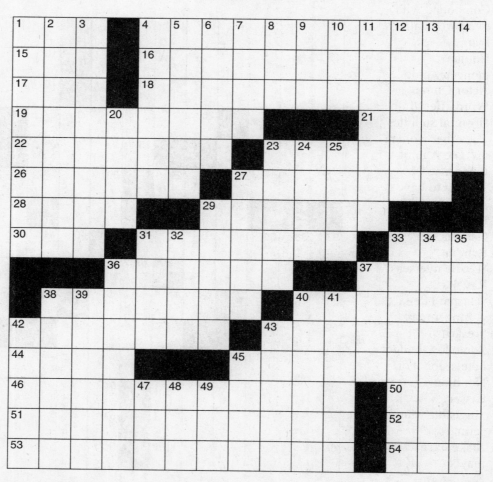

by Trip Payne

ACROSS

1 Outdoes
8 Crowned
15 Opening in wastewater management?
16 Malign
17 Like a club, maybe
18 French pioneer in planetary orbital theory
19 Dietary ideal, briefly
20 Toughish
22 Not-so-subtle no
23 Zaragoza's river
25 Bien-___ (well-being): Fr.
26 Lotion abbr.
27 Not tacit
28 19th-century novelist with an appropriate name
30 Certain draft
31 Heads off
33 Happen without a struggle
35 Chips, etc.
38 Confined, in dialect
41 Witch's brew ingredient
44 Actress Sofer
45 Fed. bill
48 "Hold it!"
50 License giver: Abbr.
51 Lohengrin, the Knight of the ___
52 Smooth
53 Burns up
55 Bracers
57 Apply
58 Review
60 In order
62 Put out of order
63 Vigilant
64 Hot
65 Plunderings

DOWN

1 Marshmallow treats
2 Compact carrier
3 California 500 race site
4 The Four Seasons' "___ Loves You"
5 In order (to)
6 Woodstock, N.Y., county
7 Bantam
8 Discussed
9 "Well, well!"
10 Computer program, informally
11 Blood grp.?
12 Noted lake with more than 10% salinity
13 Some are narrow
14 Make tempura, e.g.
21 Police news
24 Texas city with an annual Shakespeare Festival
29 Comic Philips
30 Moistens, in a way
32 ___-Cat
34 Quite a while
36 Hill dweller
37 Cleaned up
38 Spinners?
39 Signee, maybe
40 Altar offering
42 "City Without Walls" poet
43 Ritual shaving of the head
46 Make fit
47 Live oak
49 Pros
54 Soft spot
55 Modern prefix with banking
56 Instantaneous
59 Dash
61 Samuel's teacher

by Rich Norris

ACROSS

1 Pioneering film in stop-motion animation
9 Synthetic polyamide used in fiber-making
15 Soft drink bottle size
16 Expedition
17 Heir, often
18 Is part of, as a committee
19 Actress Kedrova
20 To come
22 H.S. requirement
23 Have ___ to pick
24 North Sea feeder
25 Maroon
26 Recreation for two
29 Discommode, with "at"
30 Pedestal part
31 Ginsberg and others
33 John H. ___, Jackson's first Secretary of War
34 Threw a change-up, in baseball lingo
39 Words starting a response to "What?"
40 Kind of system
41 Title courtesan in an 1880 novel
42 Super-duper success
43 College official
48 Ensured: Abbr.
49 "Hard Road to Glory" author
51 View from Catania
52 "Eldorado" poet
53 Design
55 Univ. worker
56 Adjective for a "Ripley's Believe it or Not!" feature
58 Saint of Hollywood

60 Classic work of existentialism
61 Mountain curve requirement
62 Shortchanged
63 Like some voices

DOWN

1 Cuddly-looking critters
2 Obeying
3 Emile's love on Broadway
4 Crows, maybe
5 Young ferret
6 Baseballers Ed and Mel
7 "Valley of the Dolls" woman

8 Make it easier to go
9 Hold
10 Bust
11 Stern view?
12 Quattroporte maker
13 Applied, in a way
14 Announcement of a visitor
21 Promo
27 Lying, maybe
28 "___ rather go naked than wear fur" (slogan)
30 ___ es Salaam
32 Not more than
33 Brute leader?
34 Olympic game since 1988
35 Paper in four sections

36 Finally reached, with "in"
37 ___ Fail, Ireland's coronation stone
38 Family member
42 It may show an opening
44 Goes further ahead of, in a race
45 Typed intro?
46 ___ régime
47 For everyone
50 Ballade stanza
53 "Oh, that's what you mean"
54 Arise
57 Psych. research topic
59 E-mail, e.g.: Abbr.

by David J. Kahn

ACROSS

1 Hikes
8 Trick
15 Not working
16 V.I.P. in a rush?
17 Posers
18 Unstable
19 Depresses, with "out"
20 French birthplace of England's Henry II
22 Garden store offering
23 Movement word
24 It has six sides
25 Wanderer
26 Lift handle?
28 Trouble
30 Slang expert Partridge
31 Comedian Ed and others
33 Jersey feature
35 Tops
38 Appeared
41 Debut of 1/14/1900
45 River to the North Sea
46 Impact sound
49 Best Actress of 1963
50 Fingered
51 Achromous
52 Wall St. figure
53 Suffix with Nu- and Agri- in garden product names
54 Trust
56 Fit
57 Like Lake Mead
59 More robust
61 Periodically
62 Eager
63 It may be under a coat
64 Stinker

DOWN

1 Unremarkable sort
2 Portfolio item
3 Board
4 Bud holders?
5 Wal-Mart founder Walton
6 Heat flow measure in insulation
7 It carries the words "Rey de España"
8 1932 Greta Garbo role
9 "God ___ our side"
10 Fast fleet
11 High school subj.
12 Run-down building, maybe
13 Kind of dancing
14 Repair site
21 Ryder Cup scoring method
25 Entertainer Jim
27 Deceived
29 X
32 Petition
34 Humid
36 Giant sixes?: Abbr.
37 Least rigid
38 Bad marks
39 H_2SO_4, e.g.
40 City on the Susquehanna
42 Albatross, e.g.
43 Without wheels?
44 Fujimori of Peru
47 Greetings
48 Held to its full time, in music
54 One of nine Siamese kings
55 Fall place
56 Like
58 Cool number?
60 Doo-wop syllable

by Rich Norris

ACROSS

1 Documentation
7 "GoodFellas" co-star
13 They may be tickled
15 Major handgun manufacturer
16 Hardly everything
18 Pool stroke
19 Bars on wheels
20 Early man prefix
21 Suffix with super
22 Garden blight
23 Football referee's need
24 Plays with masks
25 BP purchase
26 Trunks
27 Picture receivers
29 Enjoy
30 Noted centenarian of August 4, 2000
32 Gulf of ___ (arm of the Mediterranean)
33 D.C. Rep. ___ Holmes Norton
35 Radiance
36 Year Fra Filippo Lippi was born
37 Coming after: Abbr.
39 Discounted
40 Let
41 Prefix with sexual
42 Published
43 Chub
44 Know like ___
45 Part of a professional's home/office
48 They don't care about you
49 "The moon was a ghostly ___": Noyes
50 Subject of Article I, Section 3, of the Constitution
51 Coral creatures

DOWN

1 Miners
2 Ace
3 Makes an important proposal
4 Jagged
5 Filled
6 Firm
7 Makes more powerful?
8 Guadeloupe and Martinique
9 Tout's hangout: Abbr.
10 1986 Martin Scorsese film
11 Boston ___
12 Some lasers used in laser shows
14 Devil, to Muslims
15 ___ Coyote
17 Atypical example
22 Goes for the gold?
23 Group of 13
25 ___ wait
26 Faith that teaches the unity of all races
28 Whistle blowers' concerns
29 Allen or Martin
31 "The 12 Days of Christmas," e.g.
32 A strong impulse
34 Movie lawman
35 Trigonometric figures
36 Measures
38 Compares
40 Morning waker-upper
41 What the Staten Island Yankees play, informally
43 Securely
44 Author/poet ___ Bates
46 Itinerary part
47 Water source

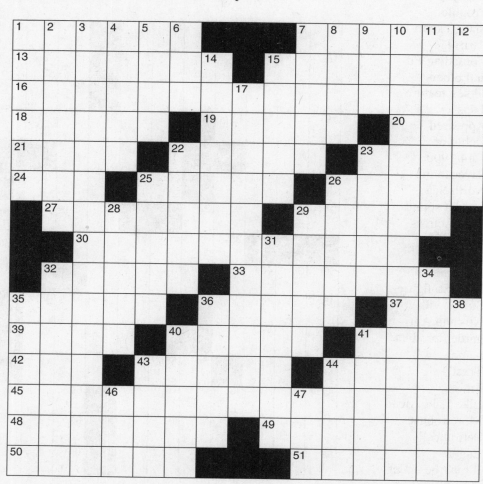

by Randolph Ross

ACROSS

1 Conscious now
6 Head of a pub?
10 Some duplicates: Abbr.
13 Lack of vitality
15 Peak in the mythical war of the Giants
16 Calls one's own
17 Head-turning attire
20 Thanks monetarily
21 Muchacho
22 N.C.A.A. tournament division
23 High rollers?
24 Telephone line?
26 They're painted on some frat houses
28 It may help you see an error
30 Big automotive parts company
32 Crack, so to speak
33 Noted Reagan speechwriter
35 Not-to-do list
37 You may draw on it
40 Serving need
41 1930's–40's villain
42 Latin series starter
43 Prevent
45 Pioneer in Surrealism
48 "Tasty!"
50 Passed on by oral tradition
52 One-time bridge
53 It has a blunt end
55 "Melrose Place" actor
56 Not orig.
57 Fellow, perhaps
60 Olympic swimmer Thorpe
61 Person kicking himself, maybe
62 Happily accepting
63 No place for a neatnik
64 They may be beaten
65 False

DOWN

1 Doesn't use
2 "Long Day's Journey Into Night" writer
3 Stays with a friend, say
4 Life-saving team
5 U.S. research org.
6 Washington and Madison, for two
7 Popular Sunday TV host
8 Tough wood
9 Earned
10 Mating ritual?
11 Like some stomachs
12 Lottery letters
14 Florence is on it
18 One whose success is well-earned?
19 It may be beaten
24 Addicted
25 "Of course"
27 Part of 12-Down: Abbr.
29 Faux
31 Untouchable
34 Compound in fireworks
36 Anglo-___ War
37 Pack
38 Repeatedly attack
39 Containing gold
44 Surpassed
46 Jobs
47 Kind of artist
49 Kind of school
51 Mother of Apollo
54 Mark alternative
56 Prefix with logical
57 W.W. II group
58 I.R.S. employee: Abbr.
59 Fox competitor

by Michael Shteyman

ACROSS

1 ___ President
6 Cries of aversion
10 Capital of Valle del Cauca department
14 Accord
15 Governessy
16 Benefit package providers
17 Almond or walnut
18 It's set in a ring
20 Raw ___
22 Pumpkin pigment
23 Pathetic play
25 Mountains
27 Like Serling stories: Var.
28 Bamboozled
32 New Mexico's Dona ___ county
33 De Gaulle's predecessor
34 Fuss
35 Film flaw
37 One might use a life line
38 Residue left after alcohol has been distilled
39 Two or three, but not one
40 Never, in Neuss
41 Bergen spoke for him
42 Debussy's "Beau ___"
43 Some punches
44 Slip
47 They bite
50 It may require you to use your head
53 Capital
55 Must, informally
56 Blowout result
57 Kadett maker
58 Scrimshaw medium
59 Some archery bows

60 1980's–90's actress Copley
61 Demeter, to Romans

DOWN

1 Fellows
2 Mine, in Marseille
3 No expert
4 Makes up
5 William's "The Thin Man" co-star
6 Prosperous periods
7 Place to take a list
8 Sainted fifth-century pope
9 Exhibit smugness, in a way

10 Modern hangout
11 Sedan sweetie
12 Desolate
13 Psychiatrist's reply
19 Slight support
21 Iris ring
24 Leap in a tutu
25 Arctic dwellers
26 Frank option
29 Public relations pro
30 Jack's beloved in "The Yeomen of the Guard"
31 They're set for marriage
33 Least emotional
34 "I'm OK - You're Okay" author

36 Angels, fancifully
37 Nice word to see on a bill
39 It may be loopy
42 Predicament
43 Low-traffic spot
45 "La Danse des Nymphes" artist
46 It makes sense
47 Up in the air
48 Sight in Memphis
49 Sticking point
51 Arles auxiliary
52 They're caught on beaches
54 Philip Roth's "___, the Fanatic"

by Dana Motley

ACROSS

1 Study
9 Go this way and that
15 Instantly
16 Hypothyroidism preventer
17 Accept recognition
18 Like some flaps
19 Alphabetical run
20 Easy
22 Course often taught by volunteers: Abbr.
23 Work (out)
25 A bit, colloquially
26 Crown
27 Early Iroquois foes
29 Lab service: Abbr.
30 Singer Anita
31 Casual wear
33 Dilettantes
35 They're hard to get out of
37 Essence
38 Insurer's concern
42 Adult
46 His, in old Rome
47 Be off
48 Scotland coronation site until 1651
49 They may be overhead
50 Get ready to drive
53 German reunifier
54 Bambi's aunt
55 Daughter of Tethys, in myth
57 ___ cross
58 Ark site after the conquest of Canaan
60 Crown
62 Charge

63 Bearing
64 Known to be in working order
65 Squirters

DOWN

1 Not on the level?
2 Impetuously, maybe
3 Amasses
4 Season at a café
5 Kind of tradition
6 Aura, slangily
7 Lodge opening?
8 Made some new connections
9 Railway tower, in England
10 Yahoo
11 Fleet runner: Abbr.
12 Tangy drink
13 Like an undistinguished hotel
14 Sets of numbers
21 Old science lab equipment
24 Patricia Hearst, e.g.
26 "Out of Africa" director
28 Censor's concern
32 Like some truths
34 Stickers
36 One-piece garment: Var.
38 Accepts responsibility
39 Friend of Richard I, in fiction
40 Detritus
41 Radio components
43 Street noise
44 Build up
45 Torrents
51 Like certain math operations
52 Closefisted type
55 Go very slowly
56 First name in 50's TV
59 Plastered
61 Scope

by Rich Norris

ACROSS

1 City north of Breslau
6 Penn, for one: Abbr.
9 Actor/singer Wooley
13 Place for a match
14 Make ___ (get paid well)
15 Means
16 Rain check?
19 Aircraft's altitude limit
20 Bank
21 Special insight
22 "Crusade in Europe" auth.
23 Bug someone, e.g.
25 "The Way of Perfection" writer
30 Word on the way out?
33 Designer Wang
34 Slugger's swing
35 Crime lab staff
39 Former ring leader
40 Language from which "Nebraska" comes
41 Come after
42 Lay atop
45 It has a wet floor
46 Suffix with form
47 Turn black, maybe
49 Prefix with star or bucks
53 Point producer
58 Étoile's area
59 Don Juan's kiss
60 Zebra feature
61 Break off
62 Some camera work
63 Flight board listing: Abbr.
64 Strains

DOWN

1 Manhandle
2 Antelope with spikelike horns
3 Meaning
4 Check beneficiary
5 Pelé's org.
6 It's in the same position every minute
7 Magnesium silicate
8 A grand total may include it
9 Luck or fate, at times
10 They have their reservations
11 Fall venue
12 "Lulu" composer
14 Islets
17 Army helicopter
18 Like some loads
24 "Let us spray," e.g.
26 One may undergo surgery
27 Slips
28 Ex ___ (not in its original habitat)
29 Stained-glass window site
30 Way off
31 Charity distribution
32 Freesia's relative
33 Marlon's Oscar-winning role
36 Carbon dioxide absorber
37 Second of April?
38 Pottery worker, sometimes
43 Copper Bowl locale
44 48-Down team
45 Vojvodina resident
48 See 44-Down
50 Zhou ___
51 Fools
52 Cádiz crafts
53 Highly toxic pollutants
54 Juice: Abbr.
55 Magellan's org.
56 "Begone!"
57 A handshake may seal it

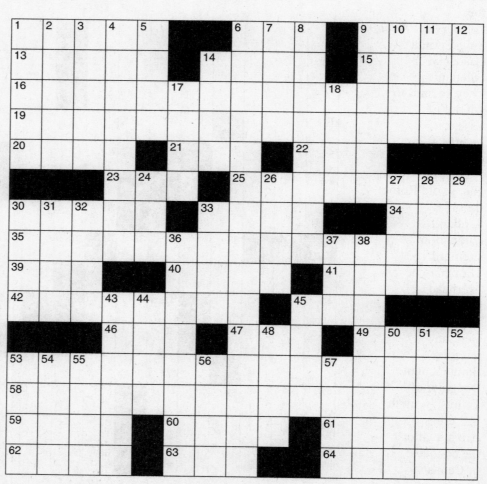

by Jim Page

ACROSS

1 Manage
8 "If it were now to die, / 'Twere now to be most happy" speaker
15 "It's Too Late Now" autobiographer
16 Lately developed
17 Epitome of logic
18 Binds
19 Ace
20 Humdingers
22 One-quarter of an H, in Morse code
23 1968 Chemistry Nobelist Onsager
25 Southeastern Conference player
26 Whitewash
27 Register
29 Bank site: Abbr.
30 Railroad car
31 They're just getting started
33 Works on moving pictures?
35 Protective garden structure
37 Kind of concert
39 Amateur on a board
42 "___ Heartbeat" (Amy Grant hit)
43 Foreign agreements
45 Language family that includes Ute, Shoshone and Comanche
47 Forswear
48 Drained
50 Word of contempt
51 Ashes site
52 Acted humble
54 Holy title: Abbr.
55 Noise
57 Marlowe title character
59 Glazed fabrics
60 Museum display
61 Marley's ghost, for one
62 TV director's order

DOWN

1 Polling need
2 Justify
3 1960 #1 Brenda Lee hit
4 Tang
5 Radiation sign
6 Disguised, briefly
7 William Shatner sci-fi novel
8 Glance
9 Start of a statement about divinity
10 Bustles
11 Chronological threshold
12 Imparting
13 Tribune Co. subsidiary
14 Corporate move
21 Like some Chinese dishes
24 Inquisition target
26 Arranged for
28 Nuts
30 Steadfast friend of Greek legend
32 Patty Hearst kidnap grp.
34 "Yeah, right!"
36 Scatter
37 Shared part
38 Book cover?
40 1997 Spielberg epic
41 Trouble
42 Inferences
44 Sounds of contempt
46 Not flat
48 Direct
49 Property
52 Buckling down
53 Yellowfin, e.g.
56 HBO alternative
58 One with an office on Constitution Ave.

by Rich1 Norris

ACROSS

1 Hard to understand
7 Maneuver
11 Passé platters
14 They fill some cavities
15 Hokkaido native
16 Dig into
17 One way to love someone
19 Masseur's workplace, maybe
20 Way to go?
21 Let up
22 Words starting a supposition
24 Dorothy Parker deliveries
27 Masseur's stock
28 Succotash ingredients
31 Figures of speech?
33 The Maldives, e.g.
35 Calculated-risk takers
38 Makeshift cookie cutters
40 Not deep-sea
41 Relative of Finnish
43 ___ Club
44 Crop-raising sites
46 Lock
47 Stew
49 Bay State symbol
51 Charles de Gaulle's birthplace
53 Admirer
54 Cuba libre ingredient
58 Clay, eventually
59 Amaryllis family member
62 Word before "I don't know"
63 Asian tongue
64 It has a canopy
65 Mt. Hermon locale: Abbr.

66 Swillbellies
67 Where Marion Jones won three golds

DOWN

1 Look accompanying a line
2 Grand ___
3 1983 Hawaiian Open winner
4 Feathered Serpent
5 Hagen with three Tonys
6 It's near Gelsenkirchen
7 Highway speedsters
8 Book review types
9 Start for step or stop
10 Cosmonaut Gagarin
11 Mies van der Rohe's motto
12 Like some bulls
13 Is a good dog, perhaps
18 Verdi villain
23 Just so you know
25 Part of many a chain
26 Floors
28 Fall-blooming, say
29 Illness's end?
30 Winooski River city
32 Kind of training
34 Malicious
36 Transgresses
37 Civil rights activist Ralph
39 It's wind-driven
42 Wellington, to Napoleon
45 1 out of 3, e.g.
47 Post office needs
48 "Little Orphant Annie" poet
50 Trumps when unable to follow suit
52 Terrestrial newts
55 "___ Wingrave" (Britten opera)
56 ___-majesté
57 Dilettantish
60 Christogram component
61 Powell's detective film co-star

by Dana Motley

ACROSS

1 Block houses?
7 Good-for-nothings
14 Oregon Indian
15 Took liberties (with)
16 They're in
17 Sloth's order
18 Word after coal or dust
19 Unaltered
21 Powerful ad word
22 "The Dream of Gerontius" composer
25 Like some club members
29 Hackneyed work based on an old idea
31 Decorative jacket insert
32 Lose it
35 What some commentators do
36 Saw backstage
46 Where baby Moses was found
47 It's direct
48 Like pen pals
51 Flat sign
52 KLM announcement
53 With 4-Down, upbraid in no uncertain terms
55 Retail store opening?
56 Split
60 Historic city badly damaged in the Spanish Civil War
63 Trill relatives
64 Imposing residences
65 Trying one
66 Field and others

DOWN

1 Big chunk of the Atlantic?
2 Early sunspot studier
3 Deceiving
4 See 53-Across
5 Carbohydrate ending
6 Gen. Assembly event
7 Former German state
8 Suffix with grape
9 Entertainment center site
10 Young newt
11 Unyielding
12 Settle the score
13 Ocean oxygen source
15 It may start with "re"
20 "You said it!"
23 Pet shop sound
24 Webster's or Bartlett's
26 Antipathetic
27 Hook shape
28 Rx amt.
30 Not marked up
33 Barrel hoop composition
34 They may be reasonable
36 Miramare Castle locale
37 Nimrods
38 Bolts
39 "___ nuff!"
40 She-lobster
41 Event in a lunar calendar
42 Day-___
43 Drilling result
44 Dosage frequency, often
45 Red ink amount
49 Stage presence?
50 49-Down's aids
54 King and queen: Abbr.
57 Grp. of G.P.'s
58 Tony winner Dotrice
59 Bitter ___
61 By the agency of
62 Down with something

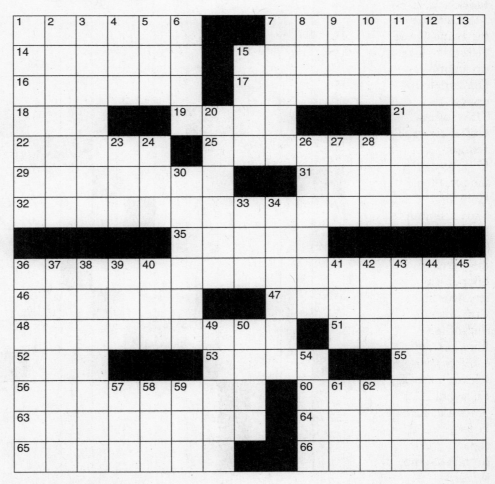

by David J. Kahn

ACROSS

1 It may be driven
12 It may be driven
15 Like
16 Kin of -ian
17 1989 #1 hit for Mike + The Mechanics, with "The"
18 Touch
19 When températures rise
20 Unsmooth
21 Barrie's Newfoundland
22 Extreme group
25 ___ alcohol (cosmetics emollient)
26 Flock's area
27 "The Silence of the Lambs" role
29 California lake or county
32 Unrestricted opportunity
33 Tries to beat
35 Out of the can?
36 Extorts
37 You may keep tabs on them
38 Units of 100 ergs/gram
39 Blotto
40 They can't take the pressure
44 Supper, say
45 It yawns
47 17th chapter
48 Star of the film version of "Abie's Irish Rose"
49 Crown material
52 Financial ___
53 "Merci beaucoup": France :: ___ : Japan
54 Initials of a noted Wizard
55 Game shows?

DOWN

1 Relatively robust
2 Santa ___
3 Went wild
4 Year in Vigilius's papacy
5 ___ vivant
6 It's not making things better
7 Kir ___ (champagne apéritif)
8 Shot
9 Rush order?
10 Response to a compliment
11 They may be whole: Abbr.
12 Leadfoots' comeuppances
13 By hook or by crook
14 Signals to scramble
21 Square to the max
23 To the max
24 Like some receptions
25 False rumors
27 Expert in ledger-domain?
28 Workout wear
29 Derided
30 Some of a speaker's income
31 An attenuator decreases it
32 Full of: Suffix
34 N.Y.C. sights beginning in the 1870's
38 Charge
40 Half of an Asian capital?
41 "Aunt ___ Cope Book"
42 Butler of fiction
43 Is helpless?
45 Place for pigeons
46 Primate genus
49 Bowl highlights, briefly
50 Actor Cage, to friends
51 Khan's title

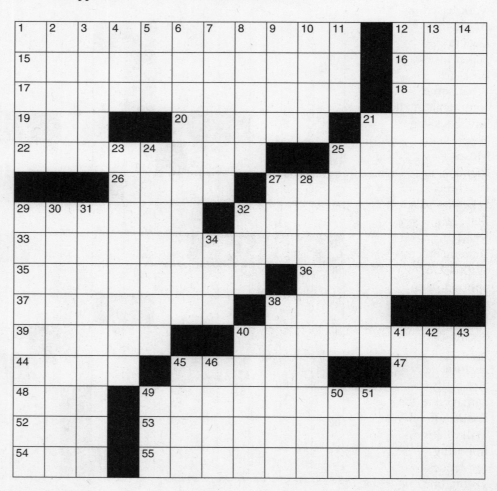

by Frank Longo

ACROSS
1 With 5-Across,
blow a fuse
5 See 1-Across
15 Instant,
or a 1988 Whitney
Houston hit
17 Don't hold back
18 ___-American
19 Papuan port
in W.W. II
fighting
20 Dark times,
to poets
21 John ___
22 Category
24 Letter in the
Daily Mirror
27 Spain joined it
in 1986: Abbr.
28 Flattens
31 One-act Strauss
opera
34 Waste
37 They're used
to stress
39 Chinese dish
40 Rap productions?
42 Children's author
Greenfield
43 Self-employed
people?
44 Play conclusion?
45 Cartoon dog
46 Extended
opera
solo
48 With 46-Down,
famous provider
of hospitality
51 Jesus on
the field
53 Ref. work
55 Horatian work
57 Unalaska and
others
60 Ticking
somebody off
61 Uncommitted
62 Manx tongue

DOWN
1 Anouk Aimée
title role
2 With no break
3 "Ready, ___!"
4 "The Experimental
Novel" novelist
5 Medical suffix
6 Paramour of
England's Charles II
7 Ties up
8 It's active in
Washington
9 Córdoba kinswoman
10 Politically incorrect
endings
11 Homeowners take
them out: Abbr.
12 Nuclear binder
13 Outback residents
14 Abbr. after a name
16 They lived
along the Missouri
23 Relatively sharp
25 Issue
26 Time piece?
28 Boutros's
successor
29 Sharer's word
30 Ophthalmology case
31 Lord, old-style
32 Not much
33 Some muscles,
informally
35 It may be used
on a nail
36 Very important
38 Early time
41 Airport near Limerick
46 See 48-Across
47 Doll
49 You may be
bound by it
50 Norse epics
51 Chrysler Building
architect William
Van ___
52 Baryshnikov, by birth
54 George
W. Bush, now: Abbr.
55 Loop loopers
56 90° from norte
57 Back
58 Gershwin's
"Concerto ___"
59 Religious office

by Robert H. Wolfe

ACROSS

1 It helps you get a ride
8 Time and temperature, e.g.
15 Like some zoning in the suburbs
16 Style
17 Be a "Survivor" contestant
18 Public hangings?
19 Precise
20 Babka need
21 Privately
23 E-mail address ending
24 Native: Suffix
25 Where zippers may get caught
29 Role in many teen flicks
31 Normally
32 They were named after Henry's son
34 Assets aplenty
38 Indulge
42 Give birth to
43 Really interrogates
46 Dundee disavowal
47 Be in another form
48 They may appear before ramps
52 Part of a pound
56 College head
57 Prerecorded
58 Cornmeal mush
59 Noted Big Apple bistro
60 Muscle that rotates a part outward
61 Turn over again
62 Bases

DOWN

1 Puzo family name
2 Made sacred, in a way
3 Iterates
4 Product made with yeast
5 Pale yellow
6 Sect follower
7 Schedule C figure
8 Not so dense
9 Actress Williams of "The Defiant Ones"
10 Start to freeze?
11 Miss
12 Having a worse case of the flu
13 Title girl of a 1965 hit song
14 Clinches
22 ___ notch
26 Prefix with bond
27 Year in Justinian I's reign
28 Texas ___
30 Pack of sharks?
31 About
33 Parts of some choruses
35 Keep
36 Home of Kendall College
37 React to a sidewinder
39 Challenge for Hillary
40 Presiding masquer in a Mardi Gras festival
41 Fall initiator, perhaps
43 Onetime TV judge
44 Firebird
45 They ring some necks
49 Valuable find
50 Old Roman sandal
51 "The Strange Love of Martha ___" (1946 film)
53 Cat's eye, sometimes
54 Playwright Howe
55 Of all time

by David J. Kahn

ACROSS

1 Hardly a Rambo movie
11 Guests may do it
15 Biohazard protection
16 Arthur's onetime court rival
17 Member of a legendary outlaw band
18 Holds (down)
19 It has many keys: Abbr.
20 Quarrel settler, maybe
21 Racine tragedy
23 See 53-Across
25 Beet, for one
27 Playbook play
29 Controversial spray
30 Its area is about 3.7 million sq. mi.
31 Roll back, say
32 A lot of talk show talk
34 Scaloppine, usually
36 Abandon
37 Compartmentalized cuisine?
41 Bad-mouth
45 Liquide vital
46 An Indian may be in it
47 Not even
48 Auto supply inventory
51 "Love and Basketball" co-star
52 Like a mean dog
53 With 23-Across, where campers eat
55 One might be on a crib sheet
56 First to be counted?
57 Capitol
60 Alphabet bit
61 Winner of three Grammys in 1984
62 Bit of instruction
63 61-Across, e.g.

DOWN

1 Artisan
2 Greek
3 Montreal and others
4 Balancing pro
5 Like some souls or words
6 Women of the haus
7 Put on board
8 Like "scaloppine"
9 Newspaper div.
10 Jewish ravioli
11 More fully developed
12 Removed with little effort
13 Marsannay or California Grenache
14 Spanish bread
22 Rounding up figures?
24 Fountain near the Spanish Steps
26 Beatify
28 Piece of silver, perhaps
32 Like Argus
33 "Swan Lake" siren
35 Bear Stearns employees
37 Flirts
38 Most conceited
39 "All Star Revue" host of 50's TV
40 German mathematician for whom a branch of geometry is named
42 Radio offering
43 Is against
44 Birds
47 Wealth
49 Cook quickly, colloquially
50 Change prices, say
54 Barricade
58 Castilian kinsman
59 Ice legend

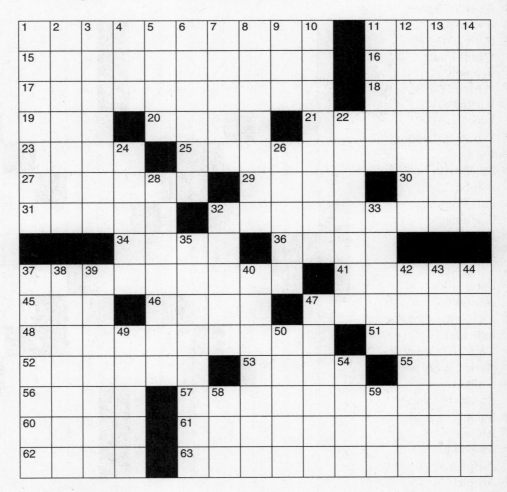

by Mark Diehl

ACROSS

1 Expression of bafflement
8 Progress
15 [Yawn]
16 Least inspiring
17 Riot squad item
18 Dictator once exiled on Madeira
19 "Cantar de ___ Cid" (Spanish epic poem)
20 "That's ___"
22 Stock figure
23 ___ Romana (chef's phrase)
25 Rap
26 Where some Picassos hang
27 Novelist Shute
29 Successful
30 Spring sign
31 Exterminate, in a way
33 "Drive" pop group
35 Kicked
37 Row
39 Where Zeus took Europa
42 Spice with rice, maybe
43 Part of a dog's name
45 Deep, as a color
47 Rustic
48 "Man in the Shower" cartoonist
49 Law firm employee, informally
50 "Wo! ___ was!" (German cry)
51 Fathers
54 Annuaire listing
55 Stick on a trail
57 Alert
59 Carpenter, at times
60 Article afterthought

61 Some "Star Trek" personnel
62 Good and mad

DOWN

1 Cheese
2 Sent on an impulse?
3 Clear
4 Smothers with humor?
5 Span. titles
6 Coordinate
7 Noted TV judge
8 Rest periods
9 Attribute
10 Ostentatious display
11 Dictator who idolized Adolf
12 Film noir feature

13 Big spreads
14 They're usually fixed
21 Highway divider
24 Landing place for private planes
26 Get a bigger car, say
28 Jolson portrayer Parks
30 Sharp
32 Dartmoor topographical feature
34 Short space saver?
36 Some toys
37 Race
38 Whelps
40 Window not in a wall

41 Coming or going
42 Not loose
44 Chips and such
46 Forced down
48 "We're Off to See the Wizard" composer
51 Simple game
52 It may be pitched
53 One-named jazzy singer
56 Islands dish
58 Genealogical info

by Rich Norris

ACROSS

1 Professional org. with the magazine Playback
6 Collectible caps
10 Part of many a discount store's name
13 It may be blank
14 Prefix in some alloy names
15 Cain raiser
16 Kingdom south of Samoa
17 1994 Peace Prize winner
18 Boulogne-sur-___
19 Working cooperatively
21 Sammy Kaye's "___ Big Girl Now"
22 Downtown display
23 Blue-green
24 Hints
25 Host of 1950's TV's "Twenty-One"
26 Rubylike gems
28 Earn and earn and earn
29 Maya Lin or I. M. Pei
31 In the best shape
32 What ".00" may mean
33 Modern Greek name for Greece
34 Calculator job
35 Star quality
36 O.K.
40 Dress
41 Principle involving the temperature and density of gases
42 Cow, maybe
43 "___ Cock-Horse" (nursery rhyme)
44 Michael of R.E.M.
45 "___ Alibi" (1989 film)
46 Cover
47 Not merely ready
48 Yearbook sect.
49 Glitz
50 Directors Ferrara and Gance

DOWN

1 Actor MacKenzie ___
2 Many a sculpture
3 Poem part
4 Sabatini or Vilas
5 Tooth quality
6 Beautifully clear
7 Rounds
8 Shows satisfaction
9 Lay
10 Like early hominid posture
11 Some prayers
12 "Auf Wiederseh'n Sweetheart" singer, 1952
14 "___ Rock" (Muppet show)
20 N.Y.P.D. description
23 Trying
25 It's north of Norway
26 Preferable for new swimmers
27 Huns, e.g.
28 Formula
29 Fast ones
30 1920's Duesenbergs
34 ___ National Park (Mount Desert Island's locale)
36 ___ of beans
37 Music's Mary J. ___
38 Place for a pin
39 Still-life subjects
41 What a climber may clutch

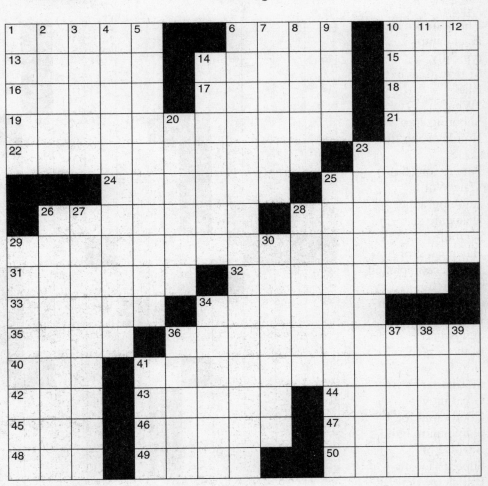

by Randolph Ross

ACROSS

1 Football play-stopper
10 Threads, for clothing
15 Unhastily
16 Its point is blunt
17 Approach
18 Medical pronouncement
19 Rikki-Tikki-___
20 "No way that's gonna happen!"
22 "Later"
23 Blood type, briefly
24 Thorny issues?
26 Have ___ for
27 Single word
28 Paleontological topic
29 Check information
30 Boot camp, typically
32 M.B.A., maybe
33 Buck
35 "What ___!"
37 Shooting star?
40 Holiday song title starter
42 Put ___ on (limit)
46 "The Words" autobiographer
48 Delaware state symbol
49 Hawaiian crop
50 It's unaccompanied in church
52 Caesarean section?
53 Different
54 Sedgwick of the screen
55 Holiday song title starter
56 Great moves
58 Good thing for a politician to build
61 Basilica of Superga locale
62 British manicurist, at times

63 Memo taker
64 #1 hit for McCartney and Jackson

DOWN

1 Bit of trivia
2 Where Home Depot is headquartered
3 "Fabulous!"
4 Given up
5 Fr. business letters
6 Do-do link
7 Deli offering
8 Passed over
9 "Iceland" star
10 Duluth-to-St. Paul dir.
11 Elder of Confucius
12 Uncle of Lot
13 You may use it after retiring
14 Young tough
21 "The X-Files" figure
24 Sunbathing locale
25 1995 N.C.A.A. hoops champs
31 Eroded
34 Knock down, so to speak
36 In an excessively fulfilling way
37 Parts
38 Yell
39 Kind of mark
41 "My ___" (#1 hit for the Knack)
43 Jeans and T-shirt, e.g.
44 Fast-shrinking body
45 Like some snow
47 Man's accessory
51 Pumps up
57 ___-Cat
59 Millennium ends?
60 "Danny Boy" star

by David J. Kahn

ACROSS

1 Click
9 Inferior
15 1964 Lennon/McCartney song
16 Developed
17 Lightener
18 One taking the stage?
19 To a tee
20 Essences
22 Bridge bid, informally
25 ___-cochere (carriage entrance)
26 Domingo, e.g.
28 Hint
30 "Uh-uh"
31 Shed
32 Baits
34 Kosher
35 Like some port authorities
38 Scuttlebutt
40 Roaring Fork River city
41 Beat
43 First U.S. vice president not to become president
44 Literary monogram
45 Rather inclined
48 Mil. address
49 Monopoly decision
51 Opening
53 Become affected
56 "In Dreams" actor, 1999
57 Declining state
58 They can be produced by shifting
61 Shark
62 Blown away by
63 Satisfies
64 Breaking items?

DOWN

1 Congo basin denizen
2 Clarifying words
3 More sharp
4 Workers' grp.
5 Medical examiner's subj.
6 Narc linkup?
7 Disgusted
8 San Francisco Bay city
9 Polished
10 Fancy
11 "___ way!"
12 Stubborn types
13 Capital since 1960
14 Fine-grained wood
21 Lowbrow
23 Go on
24 Swell area
27 Mason, e.g.: Abbr.
29 One may be seen after a crash: Abbr.
31 Hybrids of the 24-Down
33 Darius I's land
34 "Hideaway" actress
35 Yeast cake
36 Hemmer's comment
37 Appear overnight
39 They can cover a lot of space
42 Corkscrew
44 Signal receivers
46 Place for impulse buying?
47 Like some undergrad studies
49 Military pilot's concern
50 Plays
52 Brewery equipment
54 Historic Irish village
55 Row
57 Written in a major key, in music
59 Brutal ending?
60 Mark of perfection

by Rich Norris

ACROSS

1 P.C. program
4 Graceless group
8 Slow strolls
14 Is overwhelmed by
16 Go by
17 Causing to expand
18 King of pop
19 King of Pop
21 Artist August ___ of the Blaue Reiter school
22 Knight's noise
23 Suffix with brom-
24 Burst
26 Mezzo Borodina
30 Relatively wretched
32 Attractive fingers?
35 Helpless?
36 Wrinkly-skinned dog
37 Some antiterrorists
38 Carmine-orange hue
39 St. Louis's ___ Bridge
40 Part of the leg
42 Suffix with butyl
43 Dome-shaped Buddhist shrine
45 Grumps
47 Other half of another country?
52 Cause of some droughts
53 Como and Columbo
55 Strive to achieve
56 Travel agency info
57 Maneuvers
58 Small price to pay
59 Bernadette, e.g.: Abbr.

DOWN

1 Recipe word
2 Tantrum thrower
3 Bust
4 Separately
5 Java is in it
6 Calls may be made in it
7 Fishing lines
8 Texas's state tree
9 "Wellaway!"
10 One of the Channel Islands
11 "Iliad" or "Odyssey"
12 Edvard Munch Museum locale
13 Beheld
15 Very bad, slangily
20 Baronet who wrote of a pirate
21 Manhandle
25 One may exert pressure
26 Regatta participants
27 Silent types
28 Military specialist
29 They might be in parentheses
31 Home run swings
33 Spiced Indian tea
34 "Tomb Raider" adventuress
41 Emetic root
43 Echo finder
44 Moves quickly
46 Femme fatale in "The Carpetbaggers"
47 Kitty chorus
48 Truckloads
49 Subject preceder
50 Go for
51 Delivered
54 Birmingham-to-Montgomery dir.

by Frank Longo

1

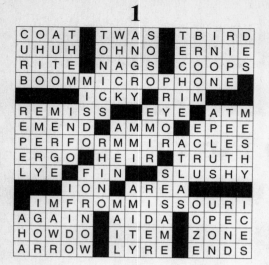

```
COAT  TWAS  TBIRD
UHUH  OHNO  ERNIE
RITE  NAGS  COOPS
BOOMMICROPHONE
     ICKY  RIM
REMISS   EYE  ATM
EMEND  AMMO  EPEE
PERFORMMIRACLES
ERGO  HEIR  TRUTH
LYE  FIN   SLUSHY
    ION   AREA
IMFROMMISSOURI
AGAIN  AIDA  OPEC
HOWDO  ITEM  ZONE
ARROW  LYRE  ENDS
```

2

```
MUGS  CHAP  BRADS
ISIT  LOBO  REBUT
LEGO  APES  OCEAN
DRIVEUPTHEWALL
      ELSE   ASP
CAP  TERMITE  DAM
ALAMO   ERE   PAGE
GETONONESNERVES
ERIC  PAT   LOINS
ROO  CRYSTAL  STY
    TOA   IDEA
RUBTHEWRONGWAY
PINOT  CHAR  LIMO
AMINO  HIDE  ONOR
SEVEN  OPED  WORK
```

3

```
SLAG  RIOS  SCALE
HALO  ARCH  COMET
AUTO  PACE  OVENS
FRENCHQUARTER
TAR  HAIR  ATTIRE
   WOE   SPY  CAM
NEWORLEANS  EAVE
OVINE  CPU  OWNER
HANK  THEBIGEASY
ODD  TAO   RLS
WESSEX  FLOE  MAO
  DIXIELANDJAZZ
LEONA  RARA  INTO
ASWAN  RIGG  LIEN
DENIS  SLOE  LACE
```

4

```
ASST  NOLAN  AQUA
MUCH  APACE  TURN
ESAU  DEVIL  SENT
BALDFACEDLIE
ANDSO    INAJAM
    BOBSLED  OLA
AMID  RITA  IONIC
BAWLEDLIKEABABY
CROIX  GEEK  ISIS
DIN  TRESSES
ENTIRE    OGRES
   BALLEDUPFIST
BUSS  IOTAS  LATE
INRE  SCALE  ATOM
ZION  HOLES  TAPS
```

5

```
GRAPH  RATE  NITS
AERIE  AGEE  AROW
SOCCERBALL  BANE
    ALIBI  TOTAL
ABA  DINNERBELL
PALACE  IRIS
ARENA  CONES  CAB
COUNTERFEITBILL
ENT  ABUTS  AORTA
   SLAM  BRACED
COTTONBOLL  ARE
SPRIG  RAISE
PEEL  RAGINGBULL
ARAL  ETAT  TRAIT
NATS  PONY  SOWED
```

6

```
TOIL  ILSA  MOGUL
ANNE  BOON  ABASE
BAHHUMBUG  RIGHT
ATEAT  SPITS  RET
SORROW  YEAHSURE
COE  PAT  JAILER
OTS  INAWE  ZEDS
   FATCHANCE
BEAU  KOREA  ASH
IQTEST  PAR  SPA
PUHLEASE  PESTER
LIL  CRETE  STAND
ANEAR  THATSRICH
NOTRE  TASK  AREA
EXERT  ONTO  PERT
```

7

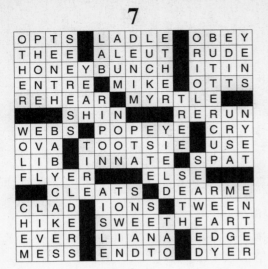

```
OPTS  LADLE  OBEY
THEE  ALEUT  RUDE
HONEYBUNCH   ITIN
ENTRE  MIKE   OTTS
REHEAR  MYRTLE
      SHIN    RERUN
WEBS   POPEYE  CRY
OVA   TOOTSIE  USE
LIB   INNATE  SPAT
FLYER      ELSE
      CLEATS  DEARME
CLAD  IONS   TWEEN
HIKE  SWEETHEART
EVER  LIANA   EDGE
MESS  ENDTO   DYER
```

8

```
PASTED   DRJ   BASS
EUNICE   ROE   LINT
PROMULGATE    OREO
SAW   POWERMOWER
      PATHOS   AMAZE
DELTOID   CAR   YES
VROOM   FOOLER
DAWN   ROAMS   OSLO
      EEYORE   BLEED
WSW   MED   HOLLAND
ATARI      TOPTEN
SIGHTRHYME    BAA
ARNO   EISENSTEIN
BIEN   ADO   UTHANT
INRE   DEN   PUENTE
```

9

```
GAGA   FICHE   ALPS
ALEX   ALLOY   MARY
FLOE   COUPE   OMEN
FAR   WAVESBYEBYE
ENGARDE      ROB
      ERIE   STOWAWAY
BESET  SCOWL   ELI
ALAS   CHADS   STOP
BAN   BRAND   LOBES
ANDROIDS     COIL
      ATT   PRELATE
SUNSHINELAW   NIL
EPIC   CONAN   SKAT
ETNA   ATONE   AERO
POOL   LOSES   STAN
```

10

```
GLOW   STOMP   ASPS
NOVA   CEDAR   NOAH
ALEX   ACEVENTURA
WARPATHS    SAILED
      ACH    MENS
STEPHENKING    SLY
PUREE   EAST   TEE
ODOR   WATTS   LAVA
ROD   ERIE   AOLER
ERE   ELLERYQUEEN
      DALY    AUG
ABSURD   INWARDLY
JACKLONDON   ARIA
ALOE   NOOSE   NARY
RETD   ELLER   TWAS
```

11

```
BBC   AHEART   HIDE
ALA   CALLAS   ONER
RUT   CLIFFHANGER
NEHRU   ASTIR   ORO
      EARS   RIOTER
SIDESPLITTER
NOR   TOOLE   SAWED
ONAN   TRINI   LADE
WALES   EVERS   LIE
      SPINETINGLER
STATUS       SEEP
AUF   NAMES   EMAIL
BLOCKBUSTER   POE
LIRE   ESTATE   ETS
EPEE   LEANER   RAT
```

12

```
ASSES   ASHE   OFFS
AMINO   LION   CROP
HINDU   ALPO   TORA
ETA   TIMEISMONEY
DEIGHTON      APT
      UPS   CIRCUITS
PASTA   DELI   SEAL
ONT   WOEISME   RCA
NERF   URSA   MUSKY
DWARFING      PBS
      WEB   ONIONDIP
LOVEISBLIND    ERE
AVOW   CEDE   INCAS
META   ALEC   ERATO
PREY   MANE   SAFES
```

13

```
S T E A L █ A C D C █ E R A T
P A D R E █ C O R A █ T A L E
E R E C T O R S E T █ C Z A R
W O N █ T U E █ A N A H E I M
█ █ L E T █ E D I N A █ █ █
S T A I R W A Y █ P A S T E S
H O R N █ I T E M █ S K I L L
O P E C █ T I L E R █ E A S E
P I N O T █ P E T E █ T R E E
S C A L E D █ T E L E C A S T
█ N A I L S █ A S H █ █ █
A R A L S E A █ O T C █ L S U
H A L O █ T I N K E R T O Y S
A G O G █ E T U I █ O V I N E
B E T S █ R Y N E █ W A N E D
```

14

```
S O N A R █ I C E █ U P S E T
I D A H O █ M R T █ S U A V E
R E P A Y █ E O N █ U N F E D
█ B A L L C A R R I E R S
A G O █ L E D █ H E C K █
F O U L W E A T H E R █ E R G
T U T E E █ R O T █ G E A R
E G O S █ G S U I T █ U P T O
R E F S █ O R E █ T R I E S
S R A █ F A I R G R O U N D S
█ F L A P █ O B S █ G R E
S T R I K E I T R I C H █
P A I N E █ S O D █ A O R T A
U L C E R █ P R O █ L O U I S
D E A N S █ Y E N █ E D G E S
```

15

```
E L L E N █ R I P █ S T E I N
L I E T O █ E M U █ H O R D E
B A N C S █ D I L L I N G E R
O N T H E P O D I U M █ O A F
W E S █ E E E █ C O O N █
█ P A W S █ W I N S O M E
S N A I L █ O A T █ I M A X
W I N N I N G T H E P R I Z E
A C A D █ A P T █ R I C E S
B E L A R U S █ F E E S █
█ G R O G █ M R S █ R C A
E Y E █ T H R E E C H E E R S
L A S S I T U D E █ I T S O K
A L I E N █ N O S █ D O O N E
L U C C I █ A C T █ E N D E D
```

16

```
C O L A █ E M I R █ G A P E S
O P A L █ M I C E █ E L I Z A
P U B L I C (C D E F) E N D E R S
E S S █ N E S S █ R I A T A S
█ S T E T █ H O E S █
B A I T E D █ H I T S █ O D E
O R D E R █ S A R I █ A V I S
F I L (M N O) I R A C T R E S S
F E E S █ I T E M █ S I N C E
O L D █ S L U M █ S E A S O N
█ S E E P █ H O T S █
A N S W E R █ P O L S █ T O E
P E T E R (S T U) Y V E S A N T
E R O D E █ E R L E █ E X E C
S O W E D █ N E E D █ W I S H
```

17

```
A T O M █ T A T A R █ A B C S
S A V E █ U H U R U █ S L I T
O X E N █ M O T E T █ C U R E
F I R S T B L U S H █ O N C E
█ O L D █ L A T T E R
A B L A R E █ A R E A █
L O U S Y █ P L U S H P I L E
M I L K █ A L O E S █ R O O T
S L U S H F U N D █ R O T O R
█ A T M E █ S E D A T E
E S T A T E █ D E E █
S T A B █ R O Y A L F L U S H
S I L L █ A B O V E █ A C H E
A L I E █ L O G I C █ S L U E
Y E A R █ L E A S T █ H A N D
```

18

```
O A F █ B A T █ C A L I F
H M O █ A M O S █ E L E V E N
M A C A R E N A █ S O N A T A
S T I C K S A N D S T O N E S
█ T A I L F I N █ A S H
P R E S T O █ O R A T E █
A I R █ W I R E █ A L O H A
S T A R S A N D S T R I P E S
S E T U P █ H A T H █ A R K
█ M A Y A N █ O O D L E S
A R C █ A N D O R R A █
S O U P A N D S A N D W I C H
A T R I S K █ O R I E N T E D
P O I N T E █ N E E R █ E D T
█ R O S I E █ D R S █ R E V
```

19

```
PLOTZ HAY CHASM
COBRA ADE AORTA
BOSUN IDA STEER
EYEFORDETAIL
ITAL VANNA USNA
DOTIME LOB
EARFORMUSIC GAP
ADIEU ASP HORNE
SSA NOSEFORNEWS
OTB PETCAT
GEAR OVINE HORS
ITMAKESSENSE
RHINE ISR UMPED
LEGGY GUT MAGOO
SLOES NES SPANS
```

20

```
BATS ASCII OMAR
AROO MAINS RARE
GAFF MUTTS EGAD
BUTTONYOURLIP
WUSA EIS
SNEAD SAM PEACE
PENROD EAR CAN
ORDERINTHECOURT
IVE PAN FACTOR
LEDGE GAS SCENE
USS ESTA
QUIETONTHESET
CURL EVITA IDOL
HINT PANEL OGRE
ITSY SLEET NYET
```

21

```
TIMED TREE CAST
ARISE HELM ONTO
CATSCRADLE UTES
ONE LENS RENEWS
CASK PANT
SPORT WILDROSE
WHITE BAND YAWL
AINT MULES CRAM
INTO ODDS GLENS
LEONARDO LAUDS
CLOY BARB
MOSAIC BALD LAD
OWEN CARBONCOPY
VEND AREA ERASE
EDDY NETS RYDER
```

22

```
SIMP BRED BESET
TOIL EURO RATSO
ETNA ASIN ORATE
PAINTTHETOWNRED
SOLE PSS
BAD REROUTE APE
AMISS SKI OMEN
CALLONTHECARPET
ONLY ONE SALVE
NAY ANTARES EER
BEE ELEE
SILENTTREATMENT
INANE HIFI BLAB
ATSEA AMEN ELSA
MOTTS WERE REAR
```

23

```
CEOS FEWER ASTA
AQUA OLIVE SPUR
RUTS LILAC PECK
EIGHTDAYSAWEEK
STU ASS SENDAK
SYNCH DATE IWO
OOH OBI TEAS
JUNEINJANUARY
DUPE DUO GTO
ANT GETS USHER
SCOPES TAR ALA
TWELFTHOFNEVER
JUNK RAITT GAVE
OREO OLLIE ONES
GERE METER SANT
```

24

```
UNCAP OATS COST
PEARL SCOT ORCA
CALCULATOR MEAN
STL RAY TEAPOTS
PAY THEDA
RUTHLESS PECANS
OLEO READ STROM
STAT SPREE DEVO
ERROR TILL INAT
NASCAR NAMESAKE
OMEGA ILK
STOPPER ARI MSG
HOPI FAXMACHINE
OKIE EDIE IBEAM
PEER REIN TONGS
```

25

```
CZAR  OATS  SPAKE
ROLE  BLIP  OLSEN
AWES  LONI  FATED
BIRTHOFANATION
SET  ANT  ADIN
    PIG  ELIE  GBS
IDIOT  ANTE  FILE
LIFEISBEAUTIFUL
LEFT  AARP  EXTRA
STY  DRNO  APE
   JOAD  ODE  PCT
 DEATHONTHENILE
BORNE  NOTE  AQUA
ANGER  EVER  RUES
MASTS  DARE  CEDE
```

26

```
ZINC  PLAN  CRAVE
ESAU  RAGA  LAPEL
TAPEDEYEGLASSES
AYE  OWED  AMPERE
    CZAR  BTUS
DEALER  GRIP  ARE
RAVEN  CHIN  SLED
OVERSIZEBOOKBAG
PERK  GENE  PIECE
SST  SECT  CADETS
    MATH  FAQS
ARMANI  TOFU  UFO
POCKETPROTECTOR
SAXES  IOTA  EARL
ODIST  EDEN  OHMY
```

27

```
EBON  EDNAS  PLOT
ALSO  TRACE  OILY
ROLL  HENCE  SNIP
SCOOBYDOO  STEVE
   ELG  SPEARED
AROMA  EATING
CAVORT  NEO  EDEN
EVER  HINDU  DAYO
DERN  ENA  SAUTES
   INTUNE  NEEDY
IRANIAN  RAT
VOLGA  DERRINGDO
AMAD  DALAI  ARID
NAME  ATONE  TIED
SNOW  DENTS  OPTS
```

28

```
FARM  TRADE  SLAP
ALIA  REVEL  HALO
VOLLEYBALL  AWOL
ONEAL  SITE  KNEE
REDIAL  LANDED
    SNIP  USAGE
LUBE  BRIDGE  RLS
INA  CROQUET  TUT
ADD  LASSES  ASEA
ROMEO  STAB
   INTACT  ENRAGE
SING  CHET  DATED
TATA  HORSESHOES
AGOG  ESSAY  ANNE
GONE  DEERE  MEAL
```

29

```
COLA  SPRIG  STUD
OMAN  TRACE  LENO
SNIT  ROGET  ERIC
TIRAMISU  SMARTS
  CONE  PLAZA
TYPING  PROTECTS
HARD  ALIST  OOH
ALI  ALDENTE  TWA
RIM  SADAT  ITEM
PEAFOWLS  MEDALS
  DANCE  PETE
LIONEL  BELCANTO
ISNT  ERATO  MEOW
PENA  RABAT  AMEN
SEAN  KNELT  NODS
```

30

```
CRIMP  ALEC  ZINE
ATWAR  NATO  ENID
NEAPOLITANDANCE
ESS  PAMS  COLSON
    SOFA  DRNO
 EGGSFLORENTINE
SLATE  RATE  NEA
LABS  BEIGE  BARS
ATO  SOTO  MONDE
VENETIANBLINDS
   NELL  LORD
CRAZED  JAVA  LTD
HOLYROMANEMPIRE
ATOM  WORK  AARON
PETE  NESS  XRAYS
```

31

```
G L O B   G E M S   N A S A L
L A R A   A T O P   O P E R A
U S E R   L O N E   R E M I T
T H O R N I N O N E S S I D E
      E E L   D Y E
N E E D L E N O S E   B E D S
A T V   S O A K   S W I V E L
C H I N O   P A W   A B O V E
R E T I N A   P O P S   K I D
E L A N   S P I K E H E E L S
      A P R   R U G
D O Y O U S E E M Y P O I N T
U P E N D   F L E E   I D E A
P A T T I   A S T A   S L A P
E L I O T   B E A R   T Y P E
```

32

```
F L I P   S C A L P   Y U L E
R O B E   H O N O R   E V I L
O V E R   A M I G O   M E E K
  E X C U S E M E P L E A S E
      E N T R E   E O N
M A R I S A   A R T I S T S
T R O V E   G A L L   H O O
I M T E R R I B L Y S O R R Y
D O O   E B A Y   O P E R A
A R R A N G E   S W E D E S
    L A I   A S H E N
I B E G Y O U R P A R D O N
T O G O   N O S I R   O L A F
C Z A R   A M O R E   O G R E
H O N E   L O N E R   R A C Y
```

33

```
V I V I D   S S T S   W H U P
A R E N A   O P E N   I O N E
L A S T M I N U T E   L O S E
  P E N N Y D R E A D F U L
A Z U R E S   A R M   I R E
T I C   D I V A S   E A T E R
L O C I   D O T   A N T
  N I C K E L A N D D I M E
  E R R   R E V   T A X I
L I B R A   F I D E L   H I T
I D O   F H A   R E B A T E
Q U A R T E R M A S T E R
U N T O   M O U S E T R A P S
O N E S   P U T S   E N J O Y
R O D E   S T E T   R E A P S
```

34

```
K O B E   A D M I T   P S S T
I M E T   P A I G E   R E A R
W A S H I N G T O N   O T T O
I N S I D E   R O O S T E D
    C L A S P   R A I L
D E C A Y   O U T   S T E P S
E L U L   N U D I S T   M E A
L I T   B O R D E R S   E S L
H A T   I M E L D A   U N T O
I N L E T   D E Y   E L T O N
    E S T A   S E A M Y
S O F T E S T   R U S S E T
A R I A   P E R M I S S I V E
R E S T   E L I T E   E T E S
A S H E   N E P A L   S E N T
```

35

```
R E F S   S C O P E   Y I P S
A R L O   C A W E D   O N E I
G A E L S O F L A U G H T E R
S T E E P L E S   Y O L K S
    E D S   S O P H
F U S S E S   C O N S O M M E
A N T I C   A R A M   A A A
C Z E C H S F O R E R R O R S
T I E   P O W S   E E R I E
S P L I T E N D   O L D I E S
    R U E D   F R I
E C L A T   R E A S S U R E
B A S Q U E S I N T H E S U N
A N T I   A M O C O   R E L Y
N E S S   T A T E R   A R E A
```

36

```
P A L M E   A P E   A M A N
E L I E L   E M I L   L I L I
A L L A H   N A P A   A L O E
L I L L I A N H E L L M A N
E E E   P U L L   A O N E
    M A U I   I W O
W H E E L   O N O   K E E L
W E E W I L L I E W I N K I E
W E L L   A O L   K E E N E
    E M O   P H E W
  P H I L   K A L E   P A L
H O N O L U L U H A W A I I
I O W A   A P I N   L E M O N
A N I L   M O N K   M A P L E
N O E L   E N E   A L A I N
```

37

```
CORPS DONS  ARMS
ADOPT ALEC  LEIA
READYANDWILLING
MSS LEAST  ISNO
ESTHER OAK  DRJ
NASA  HOYLE  EKE
 USHER  EMCEED
 HUNTERSQUARRY
WONTON  OUTDO
AMI PRUNE  WHOS
XER GIN  MANANA
 TOGA CECIL VEY
MONOPOLYORCHESS
OWED PEEL  OATES
ENDS PSST  AMOCO
```

38

```
GAGA DORMS  SLUM
AXEL UBOAT  YIPE
PERM CORER  NEON
 MONKEYSAROUND
 SASS  TOP
CASTRO SEALSOFF
LIT CUTIT  LEVER
AMER TUTOR  SITE
STRAD TUNAS  NED
PONIESUP MAKEDO
 LEO  ASKA
BEARSWATCHING
ALDO HIERO  SOSO
GAZA ADREM  AREA
SLED TENSE  NEXT
```

39

```
BAND CASKS  AGED
OVER BLEAK  LAKE
MILA EMPTY  AMEN
BASILRATHBONE
ATONE YOO  PHI
YEN TABS  XFILES
 DELETE  CARA
ROSEMARYCLOONEY
IVAN  GERMAN
FACTOR SUNK  AWE
ELK DUO  ELDER
 RUEMCCLANAHAN
AJAR BEAUX  PEKE
MICA LARGE  IRES
ABEL ENDED  SENT
```

40

```
USSR RAMOS  MASS
TINA ASIDE  AMAT
IZOD MAXIE  NINO
LEWIS GIST  ONTO
 FORKINTHEROAD
ALL INV  SEQ
QUAD EEE  UHAUL
UNKNOWNVARIABLE
ATEAM ARE  MANN
 NOT  RAJ  NAT
SPANISHFORAND
MAZE AROW  MOOSE
OPUS GORKI  INEZ
KART ENTER  SEAR
EWES SEEYA  EDNA
```

41

```
OMAR PEARS  SAGO
ROPE ANGIE  TWAS
CROSSWORDCLUESS
HOSTESS  GRANDPA
 NEST  SEEN
 SLIP  TALKER
ASKS ACES  TONYA
WHATISACATEGORY
LATIN NINA  OXES
SHORTS  EGGS
 OTIS  PAPA
COASTED  ALAMODE
ONJEOPARDYTODAY
STAN IHEAR  RIPE
TORT NOTME  EATS
```

42

```
ALIVE MARC  ZIGS
ROPED ELIA  ETAL
LASTINLINE  NAVE
ONO BOOT  SAILED
 OLIN  MULTI
JASPER SUREHAND
IDEAS BORAX  NOR
BILL ARIAS  MILO
EEL SCULL  CACTI
DUSTPANS  PUREED
 COUNT  OISE
COHORT ICET  EKE
ABET HIGHROLLER
NEAL USER  MELTS
TYPE SATE  SKATE
```

43

```
S C A L D ■ P I S H ■ G A F F
P U R E E ■ O N T O ■ O V A L
A L I G N ■ T H I S ■ T E T E
S P L I T A P A R T ■ A C E D
M A S T ■ T I L ■ S I R ■
■ S H E E N ■ N O I S E
E M I L I O ■ R A P T U R E D
M E S E E M S ■ B E R N A R D
M A N D R E L L ■ R O D N E Y
A L T A R ■ Y O G I S ■
■ S A T ■ W O O ■ T A D A
W E N T ■ W I R E D A H E A D
O N O R ■ E L I S ■ B E R R A
R I V A ■ A L S O ■ U S I N G
D D A Y ■ K E E N ■ G E E S E
```

44

```
S O U S A ■ O T I S ■ C A S H
E A S E L ■ D A D A ■ O T T O
W R E A K ■ O X E N ■ U L A N
■ M A R R I A G E S A R E
S T E L L A ■ V I S E S
M A D E I N H E A V E N
A M I S S ■ I R V I N ■ C B S
R E F S ■ G R O A N ■ B O A T
T R Y ■ L O E S S ■ T E N S E
S O A R E T H U N D E R
I S A A C ■ O R I O L E
A N D L I G H T N I N G ■
M O O T ■ L Y R E ■ U N T I L
B O R E ■ I D E S ■ P L A T E
S P E D ■ B E E T ■ S Y N O D
```

45

```
S C A R F ■ H O P I ■ T R E X
T O R A H ■ A G I N ■ H A V E
E R I C A ■ S E N D ■ O P E D
M A D E L I N E K A H N ■
■ O C T ■ N A G G E D
F R I D A Y ■ R A G U ■ E D O
R U N O N ■ J A M E S C A A N
O S H A ■ S O B E R ■ A R M A
C H A K A K H A N ■ C R U E T
K E L ■ H I N T ■ C O R P S E
S E E R E D ■ B O P ■
■ I M M A N U E L K A N T
T O R T ■ A R A N ■ A L L O W
A T O Z ■ R I S K ■ N E A T O
J O E Y ■ K A T O ■ D E N I S
```

46

```
A V I D ■ A N T E S ■ B P O E
N O S E ■ M O U N T ■ A A R P
G I A N T P A N D A ■ S T E P
E L A T E ■ H E E L ■ E R G S
L A C I N G ■ A L T H O ■
■ S T U P O R ■ H I L D A
D U C T ■ A H A ■ O U T C R Y
A P R ■ W R I T I N G ■ A N E
S T O K E D ■ E V A ■ E R O S
H O S E A ■ T R Y I N G ■
■ S Y N C H ■ R A G T O P
D A W N ■ R O B S ■ T R O L L
E R O O ■ O R E O C O O K I E
B E R T ■ O P E N S ■ L A V A
S A D E ■ K E N Y A ■ L Y E S
```

47

```
A G E S ■ A T O N ■ E P I C S
M E E K ■ L O N E ■ N O T I T
T E R I ■ L O M B ■ R I O T S
S K Y M A S T E R S O N ■
■ O L E O ■ A L T M A N
D O N V I T O C O R L E O N E
E P E E S ■ H A G S ■ T O P
S T I R ■ T E A S E ■ S E R A
I S M ■ P O L L ■ F A T A L
S T A N L E Y K O W A L S K I
T O N I E R ■ W A R T ■
■ M A R L O N B R A N D O
B L A B S ■ I D E A ■ W O R N
E A G L E ■ A I R S ■ A N A T
A S T E R ■ M E S H ■ Y O Y O
```

48

```
B A L I ■ S W A G ■ M I M E D
A S I N ■ C E L L ■ I T A L Y
N I T A ■ A B L E ■ S A G A N
J A R J A R B I N K S ■ N N E
O N E A L ■ N O O S E ■
■ M I X E R ■ P U L S A R
A W L ■ V A I N ■ R A I S A
C H I C H I R O D R I G U E Z
T O K Y O ■ S T A B ■ M A E
S P E A R S ■ S K I E S ■
■ S N I T S ■ G E E N A
S P A ■ Z S A Z S A G A B O R
W A L D O ■ V E E P ■ D O P E
A C O R N ■ V E R A ■ O N U S
N O T U S ■ Y S E R ■ G Y N T
```

49

```
BATS . ERECT . SALT
ALOT . SOLOS . TROY
TONI . QUICKQUACK
ONICE . LEO . UNTIE
NECKTIE . AGE . .
. . SORTS . RESEWS
FOOTNOTE . INPART
ALTA . NEARS . ISEE
LITCHI . RETICENT
LOOKON . SALVE .
. . MGS . BEESWAX
AMAZE . TIS . SPADE
MINORMANOR . ALAN
ELAN . ULTRA . CLIO
NOTE . GLOBE . EARN
```

50

```
BLURB . JULIA . PAC
OUNCE . IRATE . ELL
TRIALBLAZER . ALA
HEX . FULLY . AFROS
. CAM . STILTS
RIALSPLITTER .
ASCOT . ECRU . EGAD
KITS . AVIAN . SULU
ESSE . HELM . HIRES
. DIARYPRODUCT
ENLIST . ATE .
PIANO . LYONS . TWO
OCT . BRIANTEASER
CHI . AISLE . AGAPE
HEN . ROPES . TORTS
```

51

```
TIPS . AVERT . EDGE
ONEA . MILAN . XENA
ILEFTITONTHEBUS
LEVEE . AND . ARTSY
STERNUM . OBIT .
. SKIMMER . IRA
HOLE . UNO . ADIDAS
ABURGLARSTOLEIT
REGGAE . ETS . LALO
DYE . SLALOMS .
. CBER . WEATHER
ALOHA . CSA . IRANI
MYDOGCHEWEDITUP
PRIM . LEGAL . PERU
SEEP . XRAYS . PREP
```

52

```
TECS . WRAY . REALM
ARAT . AONE . EAMES
RICA . SLOG . USING
SEARCHENGINE .
ISOBARS . SISKEL
. ASA . TOTO . IMA
FLASHGORDON . ROY
RODE . DIE . DOTE
ORE . SPOTREMOVER
ZAP . KART . NOG
ENTAIL . ERASERS
. FLOODCONTROL
APRIL . BULB . AIDE
THESE . IRAE . ICED
LIGHT . TATS . LAOS
```

53

```
BIAS . TRAP . POPUP
EDIT . HORA . IBIZA
LIMP . ABET . REGIS
LOSEONESHEAD .
AMATI . KNIVES
. TELLTALEHEART
. SPORE . ANNIE
FOGG . STRAY . TENT
ALERT . EASES .
TIMEONMYHANDS
ANSARA . ERIES
. TOYOURHEALTH
ARLEN . TREE . MINE
ROAST . TANS . ACAD
PESTO . OLDS . SASS
```

54

```
AUTO . FREEH . SLIM
IHOP . EARLE . TARA
ROBERTZIMMERMAN
SHERATON . DIANE
. EVER . BLIP .
TASTER . BOOS . RIC
ERAT . PLANO . ENO
MRTAMBOURINEMAN
POI . ARLES . NINA
OWN . LIES . MITTEN
. SLED . MASH .
ORATE . FORMULAE
DULUTHMINNESOTA
EBAN . IRATE . EROS
SENT . ESTER . DEPT
```

55

B	A	S	S	I		W	A	D			A	B	B	A
A	D	O	P	T		A	V	I	D		F	L	A	B
B	A	L	L	O	F	F	I	R	E		G	U	R	U
A	N	T	E		R	E	V	E	L		H	E	A	T
R	A	I	N	I	E	R			I	T	A			
		D	O	T		H	I	G	H	N	O	O	N	
M	A	S	O	N		M	O	S	H	E		U	N	E
A	F	A	R	E	W	E	L	L	T	O	A	R	M	S
R	E	A		S	A	N	T	E		R	E	S	E	T
V	E	R	A	C	R	U	Z		M	E	R			
		M	O	P		R	E	M	O	R	S	E		
J	A	V	A		A	L	T	A	R		S	E	E	R
I	N	E	Z		G	A	R	Y	C	O	O	P	E	R
L	E	N	O		E	Z	I	O		S	L	O	M	O
T	W	I	N		Y	O	N		A	S	T	E	R	

56

A	L	S	O		E	S	T	A		E	S	S	E	N
L	O	I	T	E	R	E	R	S		E	N	U	R	E
A	U	R	O	R	A	A	U	S	T	R	A	L	I	S
S	T	E	E	R		L	E	N	O		R	T	E	S
			O	A	S			A	R	E	A			
	S	I	L	L	S		T	A	T	I		N	E	E
A	T	N	O		T	O	O	T		L	E	A	S	T
R	U	S	S	I	A	N	R	O	U	L	E	T	T	E
T	N	U	T	S		T	O	I	L		R	E	E	S
S	T	L		E	S	O	S		N	O	O	S	E	
		A	S	E	A			O	A	R				
A	L	T	E		L	E	N	A		A	L	L	I	N
T	R	I	N	I	T	R	O	T	O	L	U	E	N	E
R	O	O	S	T		T	E	E	N	S	I	E	S	T
A	N	N	E	S		E	L	S	E		S	S	T	S

57

C	O	S	T		I	R	A	N		D	I	J	O	N
O	P	I	E		M	A	G	I		E	R	E	C	T
P	E	C	K	I	N	P	A	H		S	A	R	A	H
I	N	K		R	O	S	S	I		S	E	E		
E	L	E	M	I			P	L	I	E		M	I	A
D	Y	N	A	S	T	Y		D	R	A	I	N	S	
			S	H	E	E	R		A	T	L	A	S	T
L	E	A	H		S	A	Y	A	H		S	H	O	O
U	P	B	E	A	T		E	N	O	L	A			
R	I	D	D	L	E		A	S	O	C	I	A	L	
E	C	U		C	R	A	M		V	E	N	U	E	
	L	O	O		R	I	C	H	E		A	R	C	
A	L	L	A	H		M	A	H	A	R	A	J	A	H
N	E	A	T	O		O	M	I	T		D	A	T	E
E	T	H	Y	L		R	I	P	E		A	M	E	R

58

S	A	R	I		C	H	A	P		F	A	T	S	O
H	E	E	D		R	O	M	E		A	B	H	O	R
A	R	I	A		U	S	E	R		S	L	I	D	E
H	I	G	H	E	S	T	B	I	T	T	E	R		
S	E	N	O	R	A		A	L	I		D	J	S	
			A	D	O		P	A	R	R	O	T		
A	R	G	O		E	V	I	L		D	I	A	N	A
C	O	R	P	O	R	A	T	E	L	A	T	T	E	R
I	D	E	A	L		L	O	G	O		Z	E	S	T
D	E	A	L	E	R		O	N	E					
S	O	T		A	S	K		G	R	U	D	G	E	
	B	U	T	T	I	N	G	G	E	N	I	U	S	
S	C	E	N	E		Z	E	R	O		A	X	E	S
O	R	A	T	E		E	L	A	N		R	I	S	E
B	Y	R	O	N		S	T	Y	E		M	E	T	S

59

B	E	E	F		E	M	I	T		S	T	O	A	T
A	L	P	O		R	A	N	I		A	O	R	T	A
R	A	I	L		A	N	T	E		U	T	T	E	R
T	I	C	K	E	T	T	O	R	I	D	E			
A	N	A		T	O	R		N	I	M	B	L	E	
B	E	L	C	H		A	C	I	D		A	U	K	
		O	N	E		A	M	I	C	A	B	L	E	
	T	A	C	I	T	A	P	P	R	O	V	A	L	
P	I	N	O	C	H	L	E		A	M	I			
O	T	T		A	P	S	E		E	D	G	A	R	
P	O	I	S	O	N		N	A	T		A	G	E	
	T	O	E	R	R	I	S	H	U	M	A	N		
T	O	R	A	H		Y	O	G	I		R	I	T	E
L	O	I	R	E		E	M	M	A		A	N	E	W
C	O	D	E	D		S	P	A	N		L	E	S	S

60

S	M	A	S	H		S	H	O	E		I	F	F	Y
A	O	R	T	A		W	A	R	N		N	A	L	A
G	R	E	E	N	B	E	R	E	T		B	L	U	R
E	E	N		G	O	A	D		R	O	U	S	E	D
S	L	A	M	M	E	R		B	E	R	L	E		
		O	A	R		B	L	A	C	K	H	A	T	
S	U	D	A	N		M	E	A	T	S		O	R	O
T	H	E	N		D	E	B	B	Y		C	O	I	N
E	O	N		P	E	S	O	S		T	O	D	A	Y
W	H	I	T	E	C	A	P		C	R	O			
		G	O	R	E	S		S	H	E	L	V	E	D
A	T	R	I	U	M		G	L	U	M		A	L	A
F	O	A	L		B	L	U	E	B	O	N	N	E	T
A	N	T	E		E	A	R	P		R	A	N	G	E
R	E	E	D		R	O	U	T		S	T	A	Y	S

61

```
GOSH . VARY . FIRMA
RATE . EROO . ASIAN
ATOR . LILY . RABID
SEWARDSFOLLY . .
PRELATE . . AESOPS
. . DISNEYSFOLLY
BABEL . . NEST . EIN
AWED . SADTO . BANC
NFL . MISO . . BONKS
FULTONSFOLLY
FLYING . . BOOSTER
. . GREATSUCCESS
VIDEO . DIES . ONTV
ADORE . ELSE . UTEP
LOESS . NESS . TOSS
```

62

```
BANK . HOLEY . KILT
UVEA . AMORE . ONEA
SEEYALATER . STOP
. CRATERS . BORNE
. . KOS . AUREVOIR
MAGENTA . SOLO .
OPED . . TOALL . ASP
PEN . GOODBYE . LYE
EST . ARNEL . RANT
. . DUCE . ESSENCE
SAYONARA . PED .
EVENT . STRANGE
RANK . TAKEITEASY
BITE . ADELE . CITE
SLAY . BADER . KNEW
```

63

```
SWIPE . LARD . CHAR
LINER . OGEE . OATH
AFIRE . COMMUNITY
BETA . LANIER . KIM
. IMPEL . TRADUCE
ARABIA . STILE .
ROTUND . CAT . THOR
KNELT . NIL . PEEVE
SADA . DUO . BARREN
. TRAIN . ORIENT
PIGEONS . TAROT .
AVE . SCALER . RIPS
CONTAINER . FACET
ERIE . NCAR . ITALY
DYED . GENE . TELEX
```

64

```
RIFF . TASK . CABAL
INRI . OLLA . ORATE
STIR . MOIL . RIDES
QUEENOFMEAN . .
URN . ERTE . RETAKE
ENDEAR . AMASSED
. ATONAL . HEED
. HIGHWAYMEDIAN
DUAL . DEALER .
ARMENIA . ENTRAP
STATOR . GAPS . OUR
. DEPECHEMODE
PETRI . ESTA . AMIS
TORIC . ETON . LETT
SNIPE . PERT . ORSO
```

65

```
FOLDS . DISH . SKIP
ABOUT . ECHO . CODA
TENDERFOOT . ORES
EYE . POINTS . TEAS
. . IDOL . ENCASE
PRIVATEBEACH .
LAZED . ROTO . JAM
UFOS . PLANS . LENA
STD . ERIN . WIDEN
. SWEETCHARITY
CACHED . LEDA .
AGEE . ASSURE . CBS
LOCK . THUMBSCREW
ERIE . OOPS . IPANA
BALL . ROSY . NUTTY
```

66

```
SALT . ODETS . TOM
ALAI . LOGIC . BAKE
FULLLENGTH . EXIT
EMOTE . STOOLIES
. . SAGA . LOLL .
BIB . RUSSELLLONG
LOAF . LIP . AARON
ANSA . LALAW . BARA
NIELS . ALA . STAT
CALLLETTERS . EDS
. LIRA . STEW .
MEDITATE . LEAVE
IVAN . STILLLIFES
MIRE . ELROY . GRIP
ELK . REESE . HOLY
```

67

```
H A S T . L A P . T B O N E
A L T O . C O L O . W O M E N
L I A R . H A L L . I O N I C
V E R O N A . A E O N . I L E
E N S . E R A . S U B S .
. P O I N T . T E E T E R
. A P O . O T O S . D A I L Y
S L A P . T I R E D . T E L E
I L I A C . C A N I . E D S
M I R R O R . H O L E R
. T M A N . R E D . A C T
S T R . P E A S . M A S T E R
O U I D A . T A S M . T I N Y
U N I O N . A R E A . E M T S
S A S S Y . L A W . P E S T
```

68

```
B A S H . D I N G . I M A G E
O R C A . O R E O . N O M A D
W E O W E L O W E . C R A Z E
E N O . V O N . S W E E T E N
R A P P E R . C O H N .
. O N E T O N E S T O N E
A B L E . S O N . T E R R O R
L O O T S . A T E . D E A N S
S L U I C E . E S S . A L O E
O L D C O L D S C O L D
. T H A T . L E S T E R
C A L L S I N . A V E . E V A
A X I O M . I S S I S I S I S
F E N C E . S K I N . S L A P
E L T O N . H A N G . M A N Y
```

69

```
B E E F Y . D E B T . L A K E
A D E L A . A R L O . O X E N
L I L A C . R E I N . O L D S
I T S W H E N I T T A K E S .
. E T S . H O P I
L A R D . C A K E . I N G L E
A M A . W O R N . D E T A I L
L O N G E R T O R E C O V E R
A U G U S T . L I F E . E T O
W R E N S . S L O E . P L O Y
. G O A T . C A R .
. T H A N T O G E T T I R E D
J O A D . A L O T . B O O L A
A N T I . R I G A . A R M E D
B E E N . I D O L . T Y P E A
```

70

```
P A T E S . P O O L . C U T
E V E N T . A L I K E . A S A
C O T T O N B A L L S . R U B
K N E E W O R N . A S T R A L
. R E M A T C H . H O L E
A L B E D O . R O B O T .
W O O D . A N I M I S T I C
O N T . O T T O M A N . O N O
L E T S L O O S E . A P S E
. O D E O N . S A M S O N
E M M A . L E E T I D E .
T A L K E R . A R M O R E R S
U R I . L O T T O P R I Z E S
D I N . M O R A N . E G R E T
E S E . O M I T . R O A D S
```

71

```
C R E W . I N S E T . B E C K
H E R O . T O R R E . E L I E
E N G R . S T A R T E V E R Y
Z O O M L E N S . F E N C E
. H I L O . S A L L I E S
D A Y O F F W I T H A .
E X I L E . M O O T . B O A
L O P E . R E P A Y . R O B B
E N S . A O N E . A E R I E
. S M I L E A N D G E T
W E A R I E D . D R N O .
R A P I D . N I C O L A U S
I T O V E R W I T H . E T N A
T I R E . H A N O I . N E I L
E N T R . O H A R E . T E S T
```

72

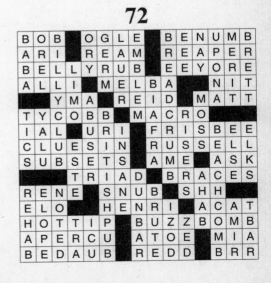

```
B O B . O G L E . B E N U M B
A R I . R E A M . R E A P E R
B E L L Y R U B . E E Y O R E
A L L I . M E L B A . N I T
. Y M A . R E I D . M A T T
T Y C O B B . M A C R O .
I A L . U R I . F R I S B E E
C L U E S I N . R U S S E L L
S U B S E T S . A M E . A S K
. T R I A D . B R A C E S
R E N E . S N U B . S H H
E L O . H E N R I . A C A T
H O T T I P . B U Z Z B O M B
A P E R C U . A T O E . M I A
B E D A U B . R E D D . B R R
```

73

```
H I V E D ■ M A C ■ A L L O W
A G O R A ■ O F A ■ L E E C H
D O U N I F O R M S I N T H E
J R S ■ R E D O A K ■ I T O N
■ ■ X Y Z ■ ■ R Y A N ■ ■ ■
S P E E ■ C L O D S ■ E B B ■
C A R N E G I E ■ I T A L I A
A R M O R E D D I V I S I O N
L E A N O N ■ O V E R C A M E
D D S ■ S T O N E ■ O N E S ■
■ ■ C E L L ■ ■ P A T ■ ■ ■
S I S I ■ E D U C E S ■ T A U
I N C L U D E T A N K T O P S
A D A I R ■ S A G ■ E R A S E
M O R A L ■ T H Y ■ D A T E D
```

74

```
R O L F E ■ S L A P ■ A J A R
O D I U M ■ R A S A ■ M A X I
T E N T O ■ S P Y S G I R L S
S A T U R N ■ P E T E ■ S E E
■ ■ ■ R Y E S ■ T A R ■ ■ ■
C A F E ■ P O I ■ A W A K E
A C U T ■ A R N E ■ R O L E S
T H R E E L E G G E D R A Y S
C O O N S ■ R O B B ■ S M E E
H O R S T ■ D D E ■ T O S S
■ ■ ■ A T E ■ F R E Q ■ ■ ■
E L F ■ T A X I ■ T R U I S M
S E I Z E F I R E ■ N A N C E
S A V E ■ F L A N ■ S I L A S
E K E D ■ Y E N S ■ T S A R S
```

75

```
C A L ■ C R E S T S ■ C A R P
A D O ■ L A C T I C ■ A M E R
M A R I O C U O M O ■ P A S O
E M E R G E ■ R E U P ■ P U P
R A T E ■ P E R R Y C O M O
A N T ■ R O A D ■ R O L E S
S T A R I N G ■ C H A R A D E
■ ■ E C C E ■ H O M O ■ ■ ■
P E R C H E D ■ I M I T A T E
I M E T A ■ A C E D ■ L I D
M A J O R D O M O ■ B A R I
E N O ■ D U M P ■ M A U M E T
N U I T ■ D O E S A P R O M O
T E C H ■ E R R A T A ■ D E R
O L E O ■ S E E D E R ■ E N S
```

76

```
S H E L F ■ A L T A ■ O T I S
L A M A R ■ L A I D ■ S A S E
O V I N E ■ U V E A ■ I K O N
P E G G E D M A R G A R E T ■
E A R ■ F U N ■ E L I S H A
S T E P A S I D E ■ A S T E R
■ ■ A L T ■ A L S ■ ■ E R A
■ B I L L E D W I L L I A M
M R S ■ R O N ■ E O N ■ ■ ■
M A N N A ■ A S S I S T I N G
E N T E R S ■ A G T ■ S E A
■ C H U C K E D C H A R L E S
T H O R ■ U T A H ■ R E A D S
H E M O ■ N O D E ■ T I T L E
E D E N ■ K N O T ■ S N E E R
```

77

```
M E C C A ■ S T A T ■ D A M P
A C O R N ■ A R L O ■ O R E O
D O D O D O M A I N ■ G E A R
A N E W ■ L E I ■ S L A N T
M O R B I D ■ P L A C E ■ ■
■ ■ A S S I S I S I G N O R
S T A R R ■ D E N I M ■ E M U
A R T ■ A S E ■ T A I ■ M I D
S I T ■ E T A G E ■ T N O T E
H O N O L U L U L U A U ■ ■
■ ■ R I N S E ■ F R A C A S
T U B A S ■ S R O ■ N O G O
O P E C ■ S O S O S O C I A L
G O A L ■ A R E S ■ D E L V E
A N T E ■ C E D E ■ E S S E S
```

78

```
M E C C A ■ A V O I D ■ S O D
A V A I L ■ M I N C E ■ A V E
C A R E F R E E E E L ■ G A S
A D E ■ R U S T I C ■ T A L K
W E D G E D ■ L O S E ■ ■ ■
■ ■ O D D B A L L L L A M A
B O U T ■ Y U L ■ D O L L A R
O R R I N ■ M O M ■ P A S T E
M A D D E R ■ H O P ■ L O T S
B L U E H A W A I I I I I ■
■ ■ A I D A ■ A N E M I A
F U S S ■ I R K I N G ■ A N N
O N E ■ T A B O O O O L O N G
R I G ■ A T L A W ■ T A R E S
E T A ■ G E E N A ■ S H I R T
```

79

80

81

82

83

84

85

Z	E	N	O		B	E	L	T		M	A	K	E	S
A	L	O	U		A	L	A	I		A	B	A	T	E
G	I	S	T		D	O	W	N		L	O	R	A	X
	S	H	O	P	P	I	N	G	M	A	U	L	S	
		F	U	R			L	A	I	T				
P	A	U	L	B	E	A	R	E	R	S		T	A	N
A	S	T	I		S	M	U		E	C	O	L	I	
S	K	I	N		S	A	R	I	S		E	W	A	N
S	E	L	E	S		A	B	C		L	I	M	E	
E	W	E		H	A	U	L	M	O	N	I	T	O	R
		P	E	L	T			F	A	B				
H	A	S	A	L	O	T	O	F	G	A	U	L		
H	O	L	S	T		P	E	W	S		T	S	A	R
I	W	I	S	H		I	D	E	A		E	T	T	U
S	E	T	T	E		A	S	S	T		S	A	S	S

86

M	O	S	E	S		A	V	E	R	T		O	D	D
C	H	E	A	T		R	A	D	I	O		R	A	Y
C	O	N	G	E	R	D	R	U	M	S		E	R	N
		T	E	P	E	E			S	C	A	L	I	A
H	A	I	R		A	N	T	A		A	S	S	E	S
I	N	N		O	R	T	E	G	A		W	E	N	T
S	T	E	E	R			M	A	T	T	E			
	E	L	V	E	R	S	P	R	E	S	L	E	Y	
			E	L	I	T	E			A	L	L	O	T
L	A	W	N		P	O	R	T	E	R		E	R	E
A	B	O	U	T		P	A	A	R		A	C	E	D
S	L	O	P	E	S			S	M	A	R	T		
S	A	D		T	H	A	T	S	A	M	O	R	A	Y
I	Z	E		R	O	S	I	E		E	M	O	T	E
E	E	N		A	P	P	A	L		S	A	N	T	A

87

D	E	V	O		C	H	E		A	S	S	U	R	E
E	L	E	V		O	U	I		S	T	A	T	E	S
F	O	R	E	G	O	N	E		T	O	R	E	A	T
T	I	A	R	A		C	I	A		P	A	R	L	E
		W	I	T	H	O	U	T	A	H	O	M	E	
S	H	E	E	N	A			T	I	T				
R	A	D	I	O	W	A	V	E	S		N	I	N	A
A	L	I	G	N		D	I	U		C	I	N	E	S
S	E	T	H		O	V	E	R	M	O	N	T	H	S
			J	O	E			B	R	O	L	I	N	
L	A	R	G	E	O	R	G	I	A	N	T			
O	T	H	E	R		B	I	D		E	C	L	A	T
C	R	O	O	K	S		D	I	D	A	H	O	R	A
H	I	D	D	E	N		D	O	A		K	O	O	K
S	P	E	E	D	O		Y	T	D		A	N	N	E

88

A	P	L	U	S		G	R	A	B		T	W	O	D
P	I	A	N	O		R	A	G	U		H	I	L	O
S	Q	U	A	S	H	O	N	E	S	H	A	N	D	S
E	U	R			A	S	K		D	U	N	D	E	E
S	E	A	M	O	S	S		S	E	E	K	S		
			E	S	P		S	U	P	S		C	A	V
I	N	T	R	A		I	P	S	O		C	A	P	E
F	O	R	T	Y	S	Q	U	A	T	B	U	L	B	S
A	T	O	Z		T	U	R	N		A	T	E	S	T
T	A	J		J	O	I	N		P	I	E			
		A	D	O	P	T		P	R	O	X	I	M	A
A	N	N	A	L	S		C	E	O			L	A	X
D	O	W	N	T	O	T	H	E	S	Q	U	I	R	E
I	V	A	N		F	E	E	T		E	M	A	I	L
N	A	R	Y		F	A	Z	E		D	A	D	A	S

89

A	J	A	R		S	L	O	T	H		Q	U	A	D
V	E	R	A		M	A	U	R	A		U	N	T	O
I	D	E	M		I	N	C	U	R		A	T	O	Z
D	I	S	P	A	T	C	H	E	D		S	I	N	E
			C	H	E			H	A	I	L	E	D		
B	A	I	L	E	Y		D	U	A	L				
R	U	B	E	S		D	I	S	T	E	N	D	E	D
A	D	I	N		S	A	V	E	S		O	R	L	Y
D	I	S	T	I	L	L	E	D		P	R	O	S	E
		F	A	I	R			P	A	M	P	E	R	
C	A	T	N	A	P		S	A	G					
A	L	O	U		D	I	S	T	R	E	S	S	E	D
D	O	N	T		A	S	P	I	C		W	A	X	Y
G	N	A	T		S	T	O	L	E		A	K	I	N
E	E	L	Y		H	O	T	E	L		B	I	T	E

90

M	O	R	N		E	L	S	A		U	L	T	R	A
A	B	O	O		B	O	O	B		H	I	R	E	D
D	O	N	S		B	A	A	L		U	S	A	G	E
F	I	N	E	A	S	F	R	O	G	H	A	I	R	
O	S	I	E	R		S	O	T			N	E	T	
R	T	E		M	A	R		M	O	P	P	E	T	S
			S	L	I	D	E		R	E	E	S	E	
	G	O	O	D	A	S	G	R	I	T	S			
C	I	L	I	A		S	I	E	V	E				
S	C	A	L	D	E	D		T	O	Y		U	P	C
T	E	D		L	I	N				T	Y	P	E	A
	D	R	U	N	K	A	S	A	C	O	O	T	E	R
S	T	A	K	E		D	Y	N	E		D	A	V	E
S	E	G	E	R		E	N	O	L		E	K	E	S
T	A	S	S	O		M	C	X	L		L	E	S	S

91

```
A M A T I   S U I T   Q U I P
S A L O N   O H N O   U R B S
T R A C T   P U L P   I D E S
I K N O W A S H O R T C U T
      M O M     W O R K
F E T E   B R A   W O O D S Y
L A O   D I A L S   U N I T E
I T S N O T P L U G G E D I N
T A C O S   T O R A H   T E T
S T A T I C   W E B   H O S E
      A D E E     O O O
M Y B O S S W O N T M I N D
S O S O   S T A R   H A N O I
E L E V   N E N E   E G R E T
W E R E   A R T S   R E E L S
```

92

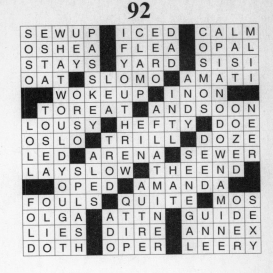

```
S E W U P   I C E D   C A L M
O S H E A   F L E A   O P A L
S T A Y S   Y A R D   S I S I
O A T   S L O M O   A M A T I
  W O K E U P   I N O N
  T O R E A T   A N D S O O N
L O U S Y   H E F T Y   D O E
O S L O   T R I L L   D O Z E
L E D   A R E N A   S E W E R
L A Y S L O W   T H E E N D
  O P E D   A M A N D A
F O U L S   Q U I T E   M O S
O L G A   A T T N   G U I D E
L I E S   D I R E   A N N E X
D O T H   O P E R   L E E R Y
```

93

```
S T E P   E K I N G   C H E
H I D E   A N N A L   C H A N
E R I E   S I T K A   H I N D
D E T R O I T R E D W I N G S
    S H E     D I A N
M A S   A R E S   O C A S E Y
O S K A R   N A C L   S A R A
C H I C A G O W H I T E S O X
H E R R   A S T I   B A S S I
A N T I C S   O C H O   Y E S
    M O S T     O N E
T O R O N T O B L U E J A Y S
R U I N   O K A Y S   E L M O
O I L Y   V E R N E   C O C A
Y S L   E D E N S   T E A K
```

94

```
C A S T   A D A M S   D A Z E
A C T A   F R A I L   O K A Y
P R O M   F O R M A   C A P E
P E P P E R W E I G H T
      S A N     B O S C S
C A V I T Y   A B N O R M A L
A R O S E   P L I E   E R A
P E T E R P O L L E N M A R Y
O N E   I L I E   E E R I E
T A R R A G O N   T E A S E R
E S S E N     B A D
    E I G H T I S S N U F F
J A I L   R O O T S   O G L E
A X L E   A B A T E   S L O T
W E L D   M O D E L   H Y P E
```

95

```
F A I R   N U M B S   C A R R
E M M E   O P E R A   A K I N
R O P E   T O R A H   M A M A
G U E S S I N G G A M E
I N L E T   E A R A C H E S
E T S   A D Z   A G L A R E
  S T O O G E   N O T A X
  Q U I E T O N T H E S E T
T U R N S   S P R I T E
W I N G I T   E P I   A T M
I T S A D E A L   S P R A Y
  P E R F E C T M A T C H
E X P O   R O D E O   S I T E
D I O R   O R I N G   H E I R
T I D E   R E N T S   A R C O
```

96

```
G A N G   S M A   E S T A T E
E M E R I T U S   A M O R E S
L A Z I N E S S   R E A R M S
    E T A   I L L   O P A
T R A V E L S S O S L O W L Y
O I L E R   T A U   U S E S
T O O   V O O M   P B S
  T H A T P O V E R T Y
A L T   V A N E   I A N
A R C H   P A S   A M P L E
S O O N O V E R T A K E S I T
S A Y   N E W   V I E
E M O T E R   F R A N K L I N
R E T A I N   D A N S E U S E
T R E B L E   A N T   R I T E
```

97

```
K I W I   S P A T E   O P E D
E R I N   C E C I L   N A P E
M A S S M A R K E T   E T E S
P E P T A L K   O N S P E C
    E Y E   S A N C T A
O O M P H   C C I   R O U T S
S R A   E T H E R S   P L E A
R O I   M A A N D P A   S N L
I N D Y   S P I R A L   E L I
C O M E T   I C Y   M S N B C
    A S I A N S   C O L
E N R O L L   E L N O R T E
M E I R   P A S S E D P A W N
M E A N   H O S T A   E N I D
A R N O   A K R O N   D I G S
```

98

```
L O C O   B R E A   G A I L
I C O N   A I T S   A O R T A
B E V E R L Y H I L L S C O P
R A E   E T A   N U L L
A N T A C I D S   L O O K T O
    D O C H O L L Y W O O D
A G A I N   D E E S   A X E
L A C T   G U A R D   F L I T
I B E   V I S C   F L A N S
B O R N I N E A S T L A
I N B U L K   N O R E T U R N
    B I G D   V I A   N A E
C A L I F O R N I A S U I T E
I T A L Y   O N E G   T O E D
D A V E   P E T E   A N D Y
```

99

```
A S P E N   A N K H   V A N E
S A L S A   P O O R   I L E A
T H E P E O P L E S C O U R T
A L A R   F R A N   O L M O S
    I A G O   I O N E
A I N T L O V E G R A N D
S N O   I D E A   I N C O M E
I C B M   S S T   E V E L
T H E A S P   E E R O   E R S
    T H E Y A L S O S E R V E
    J E E R   T W O S
G E T O N   G A T E   T H A I
I T S N O T Y O U R F A U L T
B R A G   C L U B   A T L A S
B E R G   M E T E   M E A N Y
```

100

```
P A P A   A M E N S   P O K E
A C E S   R E L E T   O B I S
S T O P P I N G B Y W O O D S
T A N C R E D I   L A R E D O
A S S A I   I N R E D
    S U N   O S S I C L E
J A R   O F G A B   B O O R
O N A S N O W Y E V E N I N G
A N N E   A E R O S   L E O
N O T W E L L   T W P
    C A L I F   R I N S E
S T J O H N   G R A I N I E R
T H E R O A D N O T T A K E N
L O S E   I R I S H   N O T E
O U T S   S Y S T S   E N O S
```

101

```
O S C A R   E L S   L I T H
L E A N O N   L E I   A S E A
I M N O T Y O U N G   I T L L
V I A   S E A S O N   C H E T
E T R E   F I R S T   A V E
S E D U C T I V E   A S T I R
    D O U S E   C L O S E S
E N O U G H   T O K N O W
S T E R N S   S E R T A
C A R A T   T U N A O N R Y E
R I V   S T R A D   T E A M
I L I A   R A V E N S   F R I
B E E R   E V E R Y T H I N G
E R S T   E E L   C O O L E R
S S T S   S L Y   W I L D E
```

102

```
S E T H   T H I G H   S H A W
A Q U A   H O W I E   K A L E
C U R R I E R A N D D I V E S
K I N D N E S S   G E T O U T
    C A N E   D E C O C T S
B O W A N D D A R R O W
R A I S E   I N O R   L I Z
I T C H   T U R O W   F I D O
T S K   H A T E   A A R O N
    C A K E S A N D D A L E
N A T U R E S   C E D E
O M E R T A   K I E L B A S A
H E A V E N A N D D E A R T H
O B O E   A V A I L   C I A O
W A R D   P E R C E   K A T Y
```

103

```
WAS  ADAM EDNAS
EMT  URDU YEASTS
DOR  DAHS ELYSEE
SEEDAGE ABU  IAM
 BEECOMPLEX  SRI
 ATEIN ALAE TAT
  DTS  RIM COTE
SPRAY TON DUNES
ARAY TEL PIE
REM SEVE LETGO
ASS KAYERATION
WAH ABE HISPEED
AGOUTI TOTO TRI
KERNEL ODED HUD
 SNARL VERA ENO
```

104

```
SAAB PERCE ATRI
OKRA EQUAL CHAN
NIGHTNURSE TETE
 MONACO TAP MIR
  LEILA IDIOT
GAMAL DINNERS
AHERO GEE AFT
GONEWITHTHEWIND
 YIN CAT GETTO
 NACELLE GESSO
DOWSE LYMAN
RAH EAU EROTIC
ITIS CLARKGABLE
FETA CARGO MAXI
TREY THIEF ERIN
```

105

```
BAJA ARRAY WISH
ALUG SAUTE ONTO
ROGETSTHESAURUS
KEG SUER SILENT
 EVERS BIRD
SPRITE VARY HAL
MANES MATE MODE
ISAWESAUHESAWME
THUS TILE ORDER
HAT WANT ONIONY
 KITE BRINY
ONFIRE ZINC OAF
BORDELAISESAUCE
EGAD ACTOR IDEA
YOYO WHINY MOST
```

106

```
AGENT ODDS ARLO
DANAE LOUT LAIR
DRDRE DRAINTILE
ONEINAMILLION
NEAT TASSEL COW
STRAITS SOOTH
 MUTISM RATA
TWOLANEBLACKTOP
HONE ERMINE
REPIN CINEMAS
USA OXTAIL TORA
 THREEONAMATCH
STROMBERG ALOHA
PROW ETTU AIRER
YELL CHAP MASSA
```

107

```
CHIS POSED APSE
LAST ADLAI ROAN
ALSO REARM LOUD
SOURGRAPES OHTO
SEEYA DUD PER
YDS BEAM MAJORS
 OFFDAY NOONE
 MAKESOMEOFTHE
ARILS SALVOS
SPRATS SPAR SKI
HEB SOP TWEEN
CARS BESTWHINES
ANAP ESTAR POPE
NUKE ICAME ERIC
STEW TITAN RANT
```

108

```
BACH DEAF SNAPS
ELLA INCA QUIET
NIETZSCHE ULTRA
TEACUP REELSIN
 HBO DOSE
NEA ISPIETZSCHE
ORDINALS ETHAN
HILT LYCRA LILT
OCALA APPROVER
WHILESARTRE ESE
 RUDD EAT
ARTFORM STOATS
GURUS ISSMARTRE
ALAMO TOTO STEW
REPEL SOLI ONES
```

109

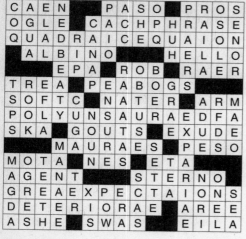

```
C A E N   P A S O   P R O S
O G L E   C A C H P H R A S E
Q U A D R A I C E Q U A I O N
  A L B I N O     H E L L O
    E P A   R O B   R A E R
T R E A   P E A B O G S
S O F T C   N A T E R   A R M
P O L Y U N S A U R A E D F A
S K A   G O U T S   E X U D E
    M A U R A E S   P E S O
M O T A   N E S   E T A
A G E N T     S T E R N O
G R E A E X P E C T A I O N S
D E T E R I O R A E   A R E E
A S H E   S W A S   E I L A
```

110

```
T W O S   R O T O S   E D A M
A R N E   A D U L T   U R S A
R I L E   N O B L E   R U N T
S T O R M D R A I N S   N E T
A H A   A I S L E   L A K E R
L E N O X     P A R A D E
  B I C Y C L E T I R E S
M O S E   L E H A R   O D D S
A R M Y F A T I G U E S
S P E E D Y     L O V E S
S H A R I   P R E S S   I N A
E A R   C A R E X H A U S T S
U N I S   M I M E O   R I I S
S E N T   A Z U R E   I N R E
E D G Y   T E S T S   S E E D
```

111

```
E G G O   I C E T   W H I P S
N O R A   N A V E   R E C A P
M O A T   G M E N   E R I C A
A D Z   P A I R O F S O C K S
S W I S H   S T R U T   L E M
S O A N D S O   S E L L E R S
E R N O   A L P   L E E
  D O U B L E C R O S S E S
  T R I   S U I   S A K I
C A U S I N G   S L O E G I N
I T T   G A R T H   H E L P S
T W O B A S E H I T S   E L I
R I P E N   W I N O   M E A D
I L I A D   U N T O   T Y N E
C L A M S   P E O N   V E E R
```

112

```
L O C H   T A B O O   J O B S
I N R E   A S I A N   E V E R
L E A P   K I L T S   R A R A
  A B C D E F G H I J K L M
    A E C   E S T A
F A S T C A R   E G R E S S
O S U   R A N G   G E N I E
L F I X L E V I R H Y O L D M
D I T K A   E L I E   A L I
S T E E L E   N A S T I E S
    A N N S   D E I
  Z Y X W V U T S R Q P O N
S I A M   I R A T E   O K E D
E T R E   E S S E S   F R A U
M I N N   D E I S T   F A T E
```

113

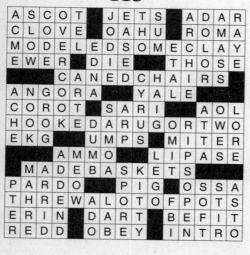

```
A S C O T   J E T S   A D A R
C L O V E   O A H U   R O M A
M O D E L E D S O M E C L A Y
E W E R   D I E   T H O S E
  C A N E D C H A I R S
A N G O R A     Y A L E
C O R O T   S A R I   A O L
H O O K E D A R U G O R T W O
E K G   U M P S   M I T E R
  A M M O   L I P A S E
  M A D E B A S K E T S
P A R D O   P I G   O S S A
T H R E W A L O T O F P O T S
E R I N   D A R T   B E F I T
R E D D   O B E Y   I N T R O
```

114

```
A S H E   I P A N A   I S L E
S E E K   R O T O R   T O A D
A G R E E K S T O I C S A I D
P O B O X   T Y R O L   P R Y
      U A R     S A M
T H A T M E N S H O U L D B E
H A D   B A T E   S K E I N
I G O   G A R O T T E   L L D
E A R T O   C R U E   H B O
F R E E F R O M P A S S I O N
    D I E     R A N
C P L   S N E A D   G A L A S
H E Y W H A T D O E S Z E N O
A N N A   T E E M S   Z I O N
W A X Y   A S N O T   Y A N G
```

115

```
P G P O N G   ■   B O U N D U P
S E E S A W S   ■ U K R A I N E
C O R O N E T   ■ M I G H T N T
H R H ■ A N O D ■ N E U T E R
E G A N ■ S P R I G ■ M O R E
R I P U P ■ S O D ■ ■ E V E
■ A S T O R ■ P I A ■ A D E
■ S L E E P G B A G ■
■ C R Y ■ O R G ■ E T H I C
T H E ■ O O H ■ T A R O T
A I N T ■ S O F A S ■ S O M E
I N T O I T ■ F R A T ■ N P R
L O A N E R S ■ D R U M M E R
S O L A R I A ■ C A N T A T A
P K S L I P S ■ H E N N E P
```

116

```
E R I ■ C H A ■ S T E P S U P
M E N A C E S ■ R E L A P S E
A F A R C R Y ■ S T A P L E R
I L L A T E E E ■ S T A I R
L E I ■ H I T S ■ E S T ■
S W E D E ■ S A L ■ P R E
■ I D E M ■ C A L I P E R
T E E N A G E ■ C L A M P O N
A R R O Y O S ■ T O Y S ■
B A N ■ S H Y ■ S O N A R
■ I A M ■ E S A I ■ I T E
■ L E T U P ■ S T R I P T T T
B E L A T E D ■ E R I T R E A
B I L L E R S ■ N O O S I N G
C A L L S T O ■ O W N ■ C D S
```

117

```
S H A H ■ A W A K E ■ L I F T
H E D Y ■ R O S E S ■ O N E S
E M O P H I L I P S ■ C A S K
I M N O T A F A T A L I S T ■
L E A S T ■ A Y E ■ N I P
A R I ■ P O U L T ■ O L I V E
E S S O ■ A T E ■ E X E T E R
■ B U T E V E N I F ■
O B S E S S ■ E L O ■ T A T I
V A N Y A ■ H E I S T ■ M O C
A D O ■ I W O ■ A P P L E
■ I W E R E W H A T C O U L D
A D D S ■ I D O A B O U T I T
S E A T ■ S A B R A ■ R E N E
K A Y E ■ S H O E R ■ S E G A
```

118

```
W A G E R S ■ A M P ■ V E E
E P I L O G ■ L O A D I N G
I N V E S T ■ G I V E I T T O
R E E V E ■ G I V E A D A R N
D A R E ■ G I V E I N ■
■ I N L O V E ■ T S K T S K
O W S ■ I D E A ■ G A T E
J E E P S ■ R N D ■ O S K A R
A L T O ■ D R A W ■ E R R
I D O I D O ■ T A L E N T ■
■ I N T A K E ■ O H S O
B Y M I S T A K E ■ R H E T T
O V E R T A K E ■ J E E R A T
W E N T A P E ■ U P L A T E
L S D ■ L E N ■ T O P P E R
```

119

```
L I S T S ■ P I S ■ R A M S ■
A N N O Y ■ A C T ■ O P I N E
B J O R N F R E E ■ A R S O N
R U R ■ C E L I N E D I J O N
A R T S ■ C A N O N ■ L U T E
T E S T R U N ■ S E C ■ D I A
■ O U N C E ■ R A G E D
■ F J O R D E X P L O R E R ■
V I O L A ■ T H I N E ■
E V A ■ L A G ■ O P E N I N G
L E N T ■ C O S T A ■ A M O R
M O J O S H U P O R K ■ E T A
A N E Y E ■ P O P I N J A Y S
S E T O N ■ T R I ■ O A S E S
■ S T U D ■ O T C ■ T R Y T O
```

120

```
A M E N ■ E S T E S ■ C A T S
S A L E ■ C H I M E ■ A M O I
S Y M B O L I C U N K N O W N
A B E R R A N T ■ E A R N S
M E R ■ D I S A S T E R ■
■ A A R ■ C H A N D L E R
I R A N I ■ A T O M ■ O R O
R A T I N G F O R A D U L T S
A G T ■ R I E N ■ H A L E Y
Q U A G M I R E ■ M A W
■ R E P E N T E R ■ U M P
P S H A W ■ D I A M E T E R
S I M P L E S I G N A T U R E
S L O E ■ P A N E L ■ T R I P
T O S S ■ A N G R Y ■ A N T S
```

121

```
B A B A   F A S T B   B B O Y
E D I T   E L L I S   A R T E
A L B S   R I A N T   N E O N
N I L E   G E N   A D D L E S
B B E A R I N G   T I C
      O E R   R E P H A S E
B C O C K   A D O   S A L L Y
S A G A   C E L     I S E E
U S E R S   E E L   S N O W B
P E E R E S S   S L O
    Y E T   D R O P T H E B
C A S T R O   O O O   W I N G
A N K H   O K A Y S   A N D A
A T I E   P O N C E   I D E M
N E T B   B P E E N   N U D E
```

122

```
B A H T   B O A R D   O S S A
A L E E   O L S E N   S K I N
S T A R C L I P L A P C A R D
H A D R I A N S     O U T E R
    K I T S     M A R L E N E
B E E B E   P R E X I E S
I D Y L   D E A D O N   C C S
B A S E R U N N I N G F O O T
B M I   O P T I C S   I R M A
    D E M E A N S   I N E P T
A B E L A R D     F L I P
R E W O N   T E L L S A L L
C L A P S N O W D A S H S E A
E L S E   A W A I T   E T O N
D A H S   B E S T S   S E N D
```

123

```
A M P E D   M A A M   P A L E
G U A V A   E L I A   E V A N
A S Y E T   L O O T   R E B S
T H E L A P O F L U X U R Y
E Y E   E N T I R E   A R C
    S L A B   A D A G I O
S T E P S   A M A T   G I N A
C A M O U F L A G E P A N T S
O L E O   O L E G   E I G H T
W E R N E R     R A I N
L O G   S E N S E D   A D A
    F E T C H I N G O U T F I T
A W N S   A S E A   H O T E L
S O C K   N E A T   O M E G A
K E Y S   D I K E   H E R O S
```

124

```
A L T A R   C L E A T   C P A
M O R T E   R A N C H   H A N
F R O F F T O N I C E   I R T
M I D I   O W E D   R O C K S
    R O D     I M O K A Y
K R I S T O N E R S O F F
N I T T I   A D A M   S L O B
O P S   S T O G I E S   I R A
B E T A   A M E S   N I C E R
    O F F S I D E K I C K O N
S P O R T S     E T E
C O L O R   C O E D   P E A S
A B A   O N O F F S W I T C H
L O T   O P C I T   A C U R A
A X E   P R O D S   S K I E D
```

125

```
S U M A C   J E T S   P O E T
I T A L O   O B I T   O S L O
P E R T H   N A N A   W R E N
    T H E R I Y A L T H I N G
    E I E I O     A C A C I A
D I N A R A T E I G H T
O L E   S N E A D   R A P I D
H A T H   S A R I S   N O D E
A T S E A   S L O O P   N E W
    R U P E E T U E S D A Y
A L K A L I     N O T E S
G U I L D E R R A D N E R
L E N D   R O A R   I R O N Y
O G E E   C A N T   E N S U E
W O R D   E D D Y   S A A B S
```

126

```
I S H   R O C K E T   M C M L
R C A   A T H O M E   I L S A
I R T   S T A R T S   C A T W
S E A S H O R E   T S A R
H A R E   M W A N D C H I L D
W K I N D     O R A   S A O
    S I R   A N I L   S Y N
    W H E N A M L O V E S A W
R A E   N Y S E   E N C
T W A   E L O     E A S T M
E A T D R I N K M W   N C A A
    S O S O   R U L E S O U T
M T E L   T S U R I S   O R E
G O A T   T O P E K A   T U E
O W L S   A B A S E S   S S S
```

127

```
M O D E L T █ I D E E █ M T V
A N A R C H █ L O R D H O W E
D E R I D E █ L O N D O N E R
C A N E D █ A B S S Y S T E M
A D E █ I M R E █ █ N A T E
P A R K S I T █ T R A I N E E
S Y S O P S █ R I O T █ A R R
█ █ P L E O N A S M S █ █
G O G █ A R C S █ I M A G E R
A N A L Y S T █ S T A N L E E
S E R A █ H U A C █ A R N
P I N N U M B E R █ H A D I T
I D E C L A R E █ T I L D E S
P A T E N T E D █ I N G E S T
E S S █ A H A S █ L E A N T O
```

128

```
S A D A T █ S T A B █ G A L A
E L O P E █ L A V A █ I M A X
U T T E R █ E X E C █ B Y T E
S H E R R Y P I C K E R █
S O R T O U T █ L L A M A S
█ U R L █ D R A I N A G E
S C A R █ C O A S T █ C A N
T A K E I T O N T H E S H I N
U R I █ G R A T E █ L U N A
F O R F E I T S █ E L I
F L A U T A █ D E E P S E A
█ D A N G L I N G S H A D
W I N G █ G O A T █ A H A R D
A C R E █ L A P S █ T O N T O
R E A D █ E D D Y █ O D E O N
```

129

```
S P I N E █ A U J U S █ V S O
A L O O F █ S K O S H █ A I L
M A N O F T H E W H I R L E D
E N S N A R E █ L E R O U G E
█ █ C I N E █ R E S E E N
O U T S E T █ A R I S E █ █
W H E T S E A S O N █ B E A T
E U R O █ C I A █ U R S A
S H I P █ W H E R E S D O W N
█ S L A Y S █ M A S S E S
C O P I E R █ T W I T █
O R I G A M I █ A L I A S E S
S T A N D I N O N E S W H E Y
T O N █ T N O T E █ F E E L S
S N O █ O G R E S █ Y E A S T
```

130

```
C A M S █ S N A P █ R A T O N
O P E C █ N A D A █ E L E N A
T E R R █ O N A N █ F E N C E
T E C I R C U M F L E X T E
A K I M B O █ █ U A R
█ P I N T I L D E A T A S
A T L █ S E A N █ S E T O U T
S H U T █ O P E █ M O R E
O R L E S S █ U T A H █ L A W
F U U M L A U T H R E R
█ A L P █ T R I O D E
F A C C E D I L L A A D E S
S L I C K █ A M I E █ L E I S
H E N C E █ T I E S █ T O T E
E A T I N █ E N D S █ O N Y X
```

131

```
O U R █ T O U R █ H A S P
U S E █ P A N Z A █ E I E I O
T H E P R O M I S E D L A N D
R E D R O S E █ H A D █ F E D
A R I E L █ P A R A D I S E
C I T Y O F G O D █ E R O S
E N S █ G A I T █ D W E L T
█ P U R G A T O R Y █
A L F I E █ G A L A █ P P K
L E O N █ P E R D I T I O N
T A R T A R U S █ N O N C E
A R K █ G A P █ I V A N H O E
I N F E R N A L R E G I O N S
R O U G E █ T E A S E █ L O U
█ F L O E █ E A S T █ E S P
```

132

```
G C L E F █ F L O E █ S H E D
I R A T E █ L O O K █ H O P E
G O W H E R E T H E I O N I S
S P A N █ H A T █ O N D E C K
█ B I B I █ C U T █
P R I C I N G C A T H O L I C
L A D █ D O R I C █ E L I S E
A D I N █ S U L K S █ E V A N
T I N T S █ M I L E R █ E A T
H I G H I M P A E R O B I C S
█ T O Y █ G M E N █
D R A W U P █ R O E █ A M A S
D I S A P P E A R I N G A C T
A S I S █ E V I L █ A L I N E
Y E A H █ D E N Y █ B E D E W
```

133

```
X R A Y S P E C S ■ G I Z M O
M A D E W A V E S ■ A T E A R
A T O N E T I M E ■ T O R S I
S T R ■ E E E E ■ M O R O S E
E L E C T S ■ N O O R ■ H E N
S E R A I ■ C T N S ■ P O U T
■ ■ R E P O S E S ■ R U S E
J A N S S E N ■ D E S I R E D
O L E O ■ A N A G R A M ■ ■
K L A N ■ R I C E ■ M A T E S
E A T ■ A L E C ■ F E L I N E
S L E E P S ■ O P A H ■ M G T
T O N E R ■ Q U I T E A B I T
E N E R O ■ I N T E R V E N E
R E D O N ■ N T H D E G R E E
```

134

```
I T T A K E S A V I L L A G E
C H O C O L A T E C O A T E D
B O A R D O F T R U S T E E S
M U T E ■ ■ E H S ■ T E A S E
■ ■ S E T ■ E E C ■ M E L
S P A ■ T W A D D L E R ■ ■
H A L F H O U R ■ O N A P A R
E S P R E S S O M A C H I N E
A S S E N T ■ P A K I S T A N
■ ■ T E A R O P E N ■ A T E
L I Z ■ R E F ■ D O I ■ ■
E W E L L ■ D A H ■ ■ S O L D
P O P E Y E T H E S A I L O R
U N P A R L I A M E N T A R Y
S T O R E D E T E C T I V E S
```

135

```
P O L I T I C A L S Y S T E M
O V E R I M A G I N A T I V E
M E A T T H E R M O M E T E R
E R R ■ T E N O N ■ M A H R E
R E N T E R S ■ O M E L E T S
A M E E R S ■ S L U R S ■ ■
N O D E S ■ L O O T S ■ B I B
I T O N ■ B A D G E ■ B A M A
A E F ■ C A D D Y ■ W A S P S
■ ■ P O B O Y ■ L I N E R S
V A P O R E D ■ T A L K S U P
C L A S S ■ G A R T H ■ E D A
H O S T I L E T A K E O V E R
I N S E C T R E P E L L E N T
P E E R A S S E S S M E N T S
```

136

```
G O T O F F ■ C A R P E T E D
A P O G E E ■ A L A C A R T E
S T O R E D ■ G E T S R E A L
B I L E ■ O B E S E ■ S A G A
A M A ■ O R O ■ ■ ■ D E N
G U T ■ P A N A M A ■ T O R E
S M E A R ■ E V E N M O N E Y
■ ■ C A T S I T T E R ■ ■
W O D E H O U S E ■ N O O S E
E N O S ■ S P O O K S ■ I L L
N E O ■ ■ U N A ■ L O G
T A R T ■ A O R T A ■ A P E R
A D D I T I V E ■ V I S A G E
P A I R E D U P ■ E T H N I C
E Y E E X A M S ■ S A Y S N O
```

137

```
C O L L E C T I O N P L A T E
A H O O S I E R H O L I D A Y
I M P R O V E O N N A T U R E
N Y S E ■ N E O N ■ L O S
■ N A M E S ■ ■ O T T ■
R P M ■ T O M ■ H A D A ■
E L A B O R A T E D E T A I L
P O T E N T I A L E N E R G Y
O P T I C A L I L L U S I O N
■ G E L S ■ N E D ■ A R N
■ A P E ■ R O S E S ■ ■
E L O ■ T A C O ■ A B B A
P E R S O N A L O P I N I O N
P U T O N E S F O O T D O W N
S T O P S T H E P R E S S E S
```

138

```
F U Z Z Y W U Z Z Y ■ J A M S
T R A U M A T I Z E ■ A C U T
C O M B A T A N T S ■ I T S A
■ ■ B I S ■ C O N F L I C T
C H I N U P S ■ P O T H O L E
T E A ■ M A A S ■ S O N E S
S A N T A C L A U S ■ U S S ■
■ ■ O C T U P L E T S ■ ■
■ C R O ■ S T O N E H E N G E
S O A K S ■ R A T E ■ E E R
O U T S I D E ■ R O S S S E A
B R A T P A C K ■ ■ T A S ■
E S T E ■ C L E A R A S M U D
R E A P ■ H A N D I N H A N D
S S T S ■ A T T E N D A N C E
```

139

```
P I P E S T E M   P O T A G E
O N E L L A M A   O P E N E R
S N A K E P I T   T A N N E R
E S C H E A T   M E L D E R S
      H A T S   D I N E R
E N T R Y   C E S T S I B O N
D I R T   S A N T A C L A U S
I C E   U P S T A T E   S T Y
C H E E S E C A K E   B E R N
T E S S E L A T E   P E R E C
      C R U D E   S U L U
R O S A N N E   L A M I N A L
A N O R A K   S I X P E N C E
H E L P M E   A L O E V E R A
S A S S E R   P A N D E R E R
```

140

```
D O S S I E R   T H E R M A L
I N T H R E E   W O R D O N E
S T R A I N S   E U R A S I A
C H A R S   C H E S S S E T S
R E I D   M A I Z E     S A T
E N G   C A L L E D U P
D O H   A X E L S   C H R I S
I S T H M I     P O D U N K
T E A S E   C H U R N   M C I
      T O R E O P E N   B I L
A S H   E L W A Y   D A D O
S T E A D I E S T   R A K E D
P O I S O N S   R I O T I N G
I K N E W I T   E S S E N C E
C E Z A N N E   E M E R G E S
```

141

```
  S N A P A T   Q U I C H E
P E O N A G E   U N M E A N T
H A S T I E R   A C O L Y T E
O F T E N E R   R A K E S I N
B O R N E   A P T S   S E T S
I W I N   A Z I Z   S T E L E
A L L A B U Z Z   S U E D E S
      C R O Z I E R
R U A N D A   A D H E R E T O
A N N E E   E Z E R   E N O L
T H E M   P U Z O   S I D E D
T I M E L A G   G R A N U L E
E R O S I V E   R A M E S E S
D E N I Z E N   A R M R E S T
  D E S A D E   M E S S R S
```

142

```
D O U P   B E G O F F   V I P
E R N E   B A R R E L   I N A
M A I N S Q U E E Z E   O H S
E N S U E   G A Z E L L E S
A G E L E S S   D E C I A R E
N E X T Y E A R   S E T T E R
      O C T A L   H E N S
  B E A U T Y C O N T E S T
S E L L   R E S A Y
W A I L E D   D E P R A V E S
E N C O R E S   R E A L E S T
E P I T O M E S   N O N C E
T O T   D O N T G O T H E R E
O L E   E D D I E D   A T O P
N E D   D E A R M E   S O W S
```

143

```
S L A P D A S H   T R O W E L
E A S E I N T O   B I L O X I
T R I A S S I C   A B D U C T
H A T C H E C K   R A D N E R
      H U L K   L A D L E
S W E E P   S H O D D Y
H A Y S   T H E F A R S I D E
A W E   C H I N T Z Y   D I D
H A S S L E F R E E   C O V E
      W E N T I N   D Y L A N
A T S E A   T E E N
P R E E N S   G I L L I G A N
L A P T O P   I M B E C I L E
U S T O U R   L E O T A R D S
S H A N T Y   A S W E L L A S
```

144

```
O N C R E D I T   A M T R A K
M A H A R A N I   B A H A M A
E V A P E R O N   U S E F U L
R E T I C E N T   T S E T S E
      E T R E   C A S E S
C Z A R S   S C U B A S
O I L S   S C A M A R T I S T
I T E   T H U M B E D   T E A
F I X E R U P P E R   C O E D
      C E N S O R   K O R D A
P S A L M   T H I N
A U D I O S   C O A M I N G S
T E M P L E   A E R O F O I L
E D I S O N   S C E N E O N E
R E T E S T   T O M O R R O W
```

145

P	U	B	L	I	S	H	■	W	R	I	T	E	U	P
A	P	R	I	O	R	I	■	H	O	S	A	N	N	A
S	T	A	N	N	I	C	■	A	L	A	D	D	I	N
S	E	L	E	S	■	K	I	T	E	S	■	U	F	O
O	M	E	N	■	F	T	D	I	X	■	T	R	I	P
U	P	S	■	A	L	O	O	F	■	A	R	E	E	L
T	O	S	S	D	O	W	N	■	C	L	A	S	S	Y
■	■	■	C	O	U	N	T	M	E	I	N	■	■	■
I	N	D	E	B	T	■	K	I	C	K	S	O	F	F
C	A	I	N	E	■	A	N	N	I	E	■	N	O	A
E	T	R	E	■	A	B	O	I	L	■	M	E	R	C
C	A	N	■	B	R	A	W	L	■	N	I	P	A	T
O	L	D	S	A	L	T	■	A	G	E	S	A	G	O
L	I	L	A	L	E	E	■	B	A	W	D	I	E	R
D	E	S	C	E	N	D	■	S	O	S	O	R	R	Y

146

M	O	H	S	■	O	L	D	■	I	C	O	N	I	C
A	T	E	M	■	T	O	O	■	N	U	M	E	R	O
T	O	R	A	■	T	A	I	■	C	R	A	V	E	D
T	O	O	L	S	O	F	T	H	E	T	R	A	D	E
E	L	I	T	E	■	■	Y	E	N	■	■	■	■	■
S	E	C	O	N	D	M	O	R	T	G	A	G	E	S
■	■	■	E	A	U	■	I	R	I	T	I	S	■	■
H	O	M	E	I	M	P	R	O	V	E	M	E	N	T
I	N	E	S	S	E	■	S	U	E	■	■	■	■	■
C	A	R	P	E	N	T	E	R	S	L	E	V	E	L
■	■	■	T	E	L	■	■	A	R	E	N	A	■	■
K	I	T	C	H	E	N	F	L	O	O	R	I	N	G
A	D	O	R	E	D	■	E	E	R	■	A	L	E	E
N	O	D	E	A	L	■	R	A	G	■	T	E	A	R
S	L	O	W	L	Y	■	S	K	Y	■	A	D	D	S

147

A	D	D	S	T	O	■	S	A	T	C	H	E	L	S
C	O	A	L	E	R	■	P	T	O	L	E	M	Y	I
T	O	T	A	L	S	■	L	A	L	A	L	A	N	D
S	R	A	■	L	E	G	I	B	L	Y	■	I	D	E
O	F	F	■	E	R	A	T	O	■	G	L	A	D	■
F	R	I	A	R	■	S	U	I	T	O	R	■	■	■
G	A	L	L	■	A	P	P	L	I	C	A	T	O	R
O	M	E	L	E	T	■	■	D	A	P	H	N	E	■
D	E	S	E	R	T	R	O	S	E	■	P	E	T	S
■	■	■	G	E	N	E	V	A	■	M	A	C	H	O
U	R	G	E	■	■	V	E	R	S	O	■	R	E	N
S	E	A	■	I	B	E	R	I	A	N	■	I	R	A
A	L	S	O	R	A	N	S	■	I	G	O	T	I	T
G	A	S	R	A	N	G	E	■	L	O	U	I	S	E
E	X	Y	A	N	K	E	E	■	S	L	I	C	E	D

148

S	E	M	I	P	R	O	■	C	R	I	S	P	E	R
U	R	A	N	I	U	M	■	H	O	T	L	I	N	E
G	A	R	D	N	E	R	■	A	B	O	U	N	D	S
A	T	E	U	P	■	I	S	T	O	■	S	K	A	T
R	O	S	C	O	E	■	A	R	C	■	H	E	R	R
■	■	■	T	I	P	■	R	O	O	F	■	R	O	I
P	O	M	O	N	A	■	C	O	P	A	■	T	U	N
A	P	A	R	T	■	D	A	M	■	T	H	O	N	G
R	E	N	■	E	C	U	S	■	S	T	A	N	D	S
T	R	I	■	D	O	L	T	■	O	U	I	■	■	■
R	A	C	E	■	M	C	I	■	D	E	R	M	A	L
I	G	O	R	■	P	I	C	S	■	S	N	A	R	E
D	O	T	E	S	O	N	■	A	L	D	E	N	T	E
G	E	T	C	U	T	E	■	N	E	A	T	N	I	K
E	R	I	T	R	E	A	■	S	A	Y	S	Y	E	S

149

A	C	C	R	E	D	I	T	■	A	D	U	L	T	S
T	H	I	E	V	I	S	H	■	S	A	F	I	R	E
B	U	T	T	E	R	M	I	L	K	D	O	N	U	T
E	R	R	A	N	T	■	S	I	M	S	■	G	M	T
S	N	A	G	■	R	I	F	E	■	R	E	P	O	■
T	U	T	■	A	N	I	S	E	■	F	A	R	E	S
■	■	P	E	A	C	E	N	O	B	E	L	I	S	T
■	■	■	D	I	A	G	N	O	S	I	S	■	■	■
■	■	F	R	O	N	T	A	L	A	T	T	A	C	K
G	E	O	R	G	■	B	Y	T	E	S	■	A	N	S
E	L	L	E	■	P	E	A	S	■	F	R	O	M	■
N	I	L	■	D	O	L	T	■	M	A	L	A	W	I
O	N	E	C	E	L	L	E	D	A	N	I	M	A	L
M	E	R	I	N	O	■	S	A	N	D	P	I	L	E
E	S	S	A	Y	S	■	T	H	E	S	S	A	L	Y

150

O	N	E	S	P	O	T	■	C	I	T	R	I	C
R	E	S	P	I	G	H	I	■	O	N	E	I	D	A
E	X	T	E	N	D	E	D	■	A	V	A	L	O	N
S	T	O	C	K	E	R	S	■	L	A	M	E	N	T
■	■	■	T	I	N	E	■	■	L	U	S	T	S	■
O	U	T	R	E	■	T	H	E	S	I	S	■	■	■
W	H	O	A	■	C	H	E	A	P	D	A	T	E	S
L	O	N	■	C	L	E	A	V	E	S	■	A	G	O
S	H	E	P	H	E	R	D	E	D	■	T	R	I	M
■	■	■	L	I	M	E	Y	S	■	E	R	A	S	E
G	A	S	U	P	■	■	D	I	D	I	■	■	■	■
A	N	I	M	A	L	■	P	R	O	W	L	C	A	R
T	A	R	A	W	A	■	M	O	N	A	L	I	S	A
O	M	E	G	A	S	■	S	P	I	R	I	T	E	D
R	E	D	E	Y	E	■	S	A	D	N	E	S	S	■

151

```
A M B A S S A D O R S H I P S
M A R R I A G E L I C E N S E
P R O T E S T S A G A I N S T
  T Z U       F O N G
    R C A   S S R   H A M S
S P O O L I N G   S T R A P
P A S T O R A T E   K O A L A
I M P O S E D   T R A F F I C
T E R S E   A B O U T F A C E
E L E C T   U N H E A T E D
S A Y A   A H S   R D S
    N A M E       H M O
M A R I T I M E N A T I O N S
O P E N A C A N O F W O R M S
B E E I N O N E S B O N N E T
```

152

```
L E T T   I V A N P A V L O V
A X O N   N I N E O N E O N E
I C O N   G O T O P I E C E S
D I K   M O L E     T R A I T
A S H   O D E S S A   E L L S
S E E I N     T U T T E D
I T A L I C   P O T S   S O S
D A R K T A N   P I T C H I N
E X T   O B O E   C U P O L A
      E R O D E S   A L E C K
B T E N   T E L L E R   S H E
R O A R S   L I V Y   T A E
I N G O O D T I M E   P O N Y
T I E B R E A K E R   U R G E
S C R E E N T E S T   B E E S
```

153

```
A W S H U C K S   S A M I A M
C O P A P L E A   O V E R D O
C O U R T I E R   M E N S A L
U L M   O N P A P E R   A M A
S E E N   T O L E   S T U B S
E N D U P   N E E   I D E S
      D E B E E R S   T I D E
H I S N I B S   P I R A T E S
A C T I   S H A R P E N
B E A K   E S E   L I P I D
A B Y S M   A S S N   C A M E
N O S   A D D I S O N   M A C
E X P O S E   S U P E R E G O
R E U B E N   T R A V E L E D
A S T E R S   S E R E N A D E
```

154

```
R U N S D R Y   S T E R E O
A L O H A O E   B O O L E A N
M A T I L D A   I S O L A T E
A N A N I A S   G O T   L I S
D O T E   N T W T   S A I N T
A V E R T   S O A K   A S T A
S A S S E D   E L E V A T O R
        T R O I K A S
W R I T E U P S   N O D I C E
H E N S   G U M P   P A N A M
E T A P E   L E A H   T A T E
R A F   M M E   D E F A M E R
E X U R B A N   R A I S E R S
T E N C E N T   E R N E S T O
O S K A R S   S T E T S O N
```

155

```
S H O T S   T I E S   E R G O
M I N E O   O L D T I M E R S
E N T R Y   B L U E D E V I L
A D A M   S O U   E L N I N O
R I P I N T O S H R E D S
    T O A T E E   S I L O
O R I E N T   D A R C   T A O
W I N S O U T   L O U S E U P
L O T   S E E P   A T O D D S
S T E P   E R A S E R
  G R O W M I S T Y E Y E D
A B R A D E   M T S   H I D E
M E A T E A T E R   G E E S E
P E T E R N E R O   P A L E R
S P E D   S A S S   A D D L E
```

156

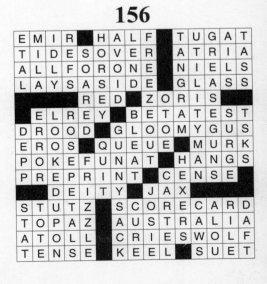

```
E M I R   H A L F   T U G A T
T I D E S O V E R   A T R I A
A L L F O R O N E   N I E L S
L A Y S A S I D E   G L A S S
        R E D   Z O R I S
  E L R E Y   B E T A T E S T
D R O O D   G L O O M Y G U S
E R O S   Q U E U E   M U R K
P O K E F U N A T   H A N G S
P R E P R I N T   C E N S E
    D E I T Y   J A X
S T U T Z   S C O R E C A R D
T O P A Z   A U S T R A L I A
A T O L L   C R I E S W O L F
T E N S E   K E E L   S U E T
```

157

```
OPTICALACTIVITY
KEEPATADISTANCE
APASSAGETOINDIA
YSL  KTEL  SSE
SISI   RAJ   STLO
   DJS  IOUS  AID
AGREETODISAGREE
CLOSEONESEYESTO
HEATPROSTRATION
OAR  SEUL  SHA
ONKP  RAM   TAFT
   AMP  MOOG  PRO
SUPPLEMENTATION
ITSALLINTHEGAME
BETWEENTHELINES
```

158

```
MIGRATE  PRIMACY
ENROBES  RUBELLA
ACETONE  OBERLIN
TRYOUT  APEX  EEK
HEART  LEES  DYNE
EARS  BURR  PASTE
ASE  CANONLAW
DEADASADOORNAIL
    OVERRULE  IDI
PRIZE  MONA  PROF
HERE  MOMS  LISLE
ADO  GONE  PENPAL
SENTOUT  MEDIATE
EYEWASH  PRINCES
SEDATES  HUNGERS
```

159

```
PCCLONE  STRIDES
ROLODEX  EATDIRT
ONETIME  ELEANOR
DNA  NEMESES  ETA
DONG  APLUS  ISIT
ETUIS  LAP  ERICA
REPROVAL  ELENA
   DOOR  SPEC
  JOLTS  QUICKFIX
DOPEY  CUR  TORME
ICED  JOINS  NOIR
SUR  RAWDATA  GTO
ALAMODE  MIRAMAX
RANOVER  ELEVATE
MRDEEDS  STAINED
```

160

```
TOPPRIZE  ACTSON
ONELINER  SLYEST
ATTAGIRL  TURTLE
TOETOTOE  ABATES
   ERSE  SNORT
IOTAS  SALOON
THOU  YINANDYANG
CIA  MINORCA  QUA
HODGEPODGE  LUTZ
   LIENEE  CEASE
ASIAN  SHEA
BUDDHA  SCANDALS
ASLEEP  PASTORAL
THEYRE  ALTEREGO
HIDERS  NEAREAST
```

161

```
PALLID  TRUEBORN
AVIATE  RESTAREA
LENNON  AVONLADY
MRED  TAN  ALTS
STUFF  PQRS  SOTO
 SPIRITUALS  ROI
  LEN  INAT  IRS
NOPLACELIKEHOME
EVE  KIWI  ERO
EEK  STATEROOMS
DROP  ENYA  LLOYD
 TERI  BRA  ITNO
MOTOROLA  LEGION
ANEMONES  PRAVDA
SEASNAKE  SANEST
```

162

```
DIST  JOKEWRITER
ENTO  ITALIANICE
AHEM  THRUSTUPON
DOES  NEALE  SILT
SNL  HERO  DENIS
POMPEY  KATO
ORION  BEWITHIT
TOLLBAR  ELEANOR
 FLEABAGS  DRDRE
  NATO  SOPORS
CANWE  OPEN  NIT
AREA  HADES  LEDA
NEWSREPORT  YSER
ONTHEFENCE  LIST
EASYSTREET  EATS
```

163

I	D	I	G	R	E	S	S	■	J	O	S	T	L	E
N	E	L	L	I	G	A	N	■	U	S	U	R	E	R
A	L	L	I	N	O	N	E	■	M	I	N	U	T	E
S	M	U	T	■	S	T	E	P	P	E	■	E	T	C
E	A	S	T	S	■	E	R	R	O	R	■	L	E	T
C	R	E	E	L	S	■	E	I	N	■	S	O	R	E
■	■	R	A	T	E	R	S	■	S	E	V	E	R	■
C	L	E	A	V	E	R	■	M	A	L	T	E	D	S
H	O	S	T	S	■	M	I	S	S	E	S	■	■	■
A	C	T	I	■	M	I	C	■	E	D	U	C	E	S
G	A	R	■	L	I	N	E	N	■	S	P	R	A	T
A	T	A	■	U	N	E	A	S	Y	■	S	E	R	E
L	I	N	A	G	E	■	G	Y	M	K	H	A	N	A
L	O	G	G	E	R	■	E	N	C	L	O	S	E	D
S	N	E	A	D	S	■	S	C	A	M	P	E	R	S

164

C	A	S	H	F	L	O	W	■	A	B	L	U	S	H
A	L	L	A	L	O	N	E	■	S	C	O	N	C	E
S	E	A	L	A	N	T	S	■	T	O	W	C	A	R
S	K	Y	L	I	G	H	T	■	I	M	G	A	M	E
■	■	■	E	L	S	E	■	P	E	P	S	I	■	■
S	T	A	Y	S	■	F	A	L	A	L	A	■	■	■
H	U	B	S	■	■	D	E	S	I	D	E	R	A	T	A
A	T	L	■	J	U	N	K	F	A	X	■	T	E	N
Q	U	E	B	E	C	C	I	T	Y	■	T	O	R	N
■	■	L	A	T	E	N	S	■	G	I	Z	M	O	■
T	A	L	O	N	■	■	A	S	E	C	■	■	■	■
A	R	E	N	A	S	■	S	H	O	O	T	S	A	T
L	E	A	D	U	P	■	H	A	R	D	A	L	E	E
E	N	V	I	E	R	■	O	N	R	E	C	O	R	D
S	T	E	E	L	Y	■	O	D	Y	S	S	E	Y	S

165

S	T	R	O	B	E	■	A	L	B	A	■	M	U	M
C	R	A	N	I	A	■	G	O	E	S	L	O	N	G
Y	O	D	E	L	S	■	E	V	E	N	I	N	G	S
T	W	I	N	K	I	E	D	E	F	E	N	S	E	■
H	E	A	D	S	E	T	■	Y	A	W	■	T	N	T
E	L	L	■	S	H	O	A	L	■	V	E	T	O	■
■	■	M	I	T	E	R	■	O	V	E	R	L	Y	■
A	S	W	A	N	■	R	A	P	■	A	S	S	E	S
S	P	E	N	D	S	■	T	A	U	N	T	■	■	■
T	I	R	E	■	T	H	E	U	N	■	L	E	V	■
I	C	E	■	P	O	O	■	L	I	S	S	O	M	E
■	E	R	G	O	N	O	M	I	C	C	H	A	I	R
O	T	I	O	S	I	T	Y	■	O	R	A	N	G	S
R	E	C	O	I	L	E	R	■	R	E	V	E	R	E
B	A	H	■	T	Y	R	A	■	N	E	E	D	E	D

166

S	O	I	T	■	P	A	P	E	R	S	O	V	E	R
I	N	R	E	■	A	D	A	M	A	N	D	E	V	E
G	E	O	L	■	W	I	R	E	H	A	I	R	E	D
N	O	N	L	I	N	E	A	R	■	P	U	N	N	Y
P	R	I	S	M	■	U	P	I	N	■	M	A	L	E
O	T	C	■	P	E	S	E	T	A	S	■	L	Y	S
S	W	A	Y	E	R	■	T	U	T	T	I	■	■	■
T	O	L	E	D	O	S	■	S	T	A	M	M	E	R
■	■	■	S	E	T	H	S	■	E	S	P	A	N	A
I	T	S	■	D	I	E	T	E	R	S	■	C	A	T
N	O	L	O	■	C	R	A	T	■	E	L	E	M	I
A	K	I	N	S	■	I	N	H	O	N	O	R	O	F
R	O	P	E	L	A	D	D	E	R	■	B	A	R	I
O	R	O	N	O	M	A	I	N	E	■	A	T	E	E
W	I	N	D	T	U	N	N	E	L	■	R	E	D	S

167

G	R	A	S	S	F	R	O	G	■	R	A	S	T	A
L	E	M	O	N	S	O	L	E	■	E	X	P	O	S
U	N	P	L	O	T	T	E	D	■	P	E	R	E	S
I	O	U	■	B	O	O	M	■	A	L	L	U	D	E
N	I	L	S	■	P	R	I	O	R	Y	■	C	A	N
G	R	E	A	T	■	S	C	I	■	C	E	N	T	■
■	■	T	A	B	A	S	C	O	S	A	U	C	E	■
A	V	O	I	D	E	D	■	U	S	U	R	P	E	D
C	I	N	N	A	M	O	N	R	O	L	L	■	■	■
A	T	T	Y	■	I	R	E	■	K	O	R	D	A	■
D	A	H	■	O	N	E	W	A	Y	■	S	O	I	T
E	M	E	R	G	E	■	W	R	E	N	■	M	M	E
M	I	L	E	R	■	D	A	L	A	I	L	A	M	A
I	N	A	N	E	■	O	V	E	R	T	O	N	E	S
A	C	M	E	S	■	M	E	N	S	S	T	O	R	E

168

S	N	O	W	J	O	B	S	■	A	V	A	N	T	I
C	A	S	H	E	D	I	N	■	P	I	G	E	O	N
O	P	P	O	S	I	T	E	■	O	N	H	O	L	D
F	A	R	■	T	E	P	E	E	S	■	A	L	L	I
F	L	E	A	■	A	R	A	T	■	S	O	F	T	■
■	M	Y	D	E	A	R	■	R	R	S	■	G	R	E
■	■	H	A	F	T	■	S	O	P	P	I	E	R	■
C	O	H	O	R	T	■	P	R	I	C	E	S	■	■
O	R	A	C	L	E	S	■	S	H	E	A	■	■	■
N	P	R	■	S	R	O	■	K	E	E	N	E	D	■
T	H	A	W	■	H	O	P	I	■	O	N	E	G	■
R	A	S	H	■	O	T	E	L	L	O	■	G	L	O
I	N	S	I	T	U	■	S	L	O	W	B	U	R	N
T	E	E	T	E	R	■	T	E	L	L	A	L	I	E
E	D	S	E	L	S	■	S	T	A	Y	S	F	O	R

169

```
 C H E S T S   N I C K E D  
S H O T P U T   I N H A L E D
C O R D O B A   G R A N U L E
U R N   R A N C H E R   S I T
B A S T E   D O T   D R I V E
A L I I   K O L A S   E V E R
S E N D M E N O F L O W E R S
      I M P O R T U N E      
M A K E M I N C E M E A T O F
A R E S   S E A R S   V A S E
R E N T A   S S N   C E N S E
C O N   C A T T I E R   S U B
E L E C T R O   G L A C I A L
L A T R I N E   H E N N E R Y
  S H O V E S   T E E N S Y  
```

170

```
J U G B A N D   R E F I L M
A M R A D I O   M O R A V I A
S P A N D E X   T I A R A E D
P I N K   C O D A   E N D O
E R D E   E L O P E D   H O N
R E A D   O N O N E S O W N
  S M U   M G S   G A L E N A
    P L A Y   M E D O
S H O O I N   P A L   P R Y
C A N N O N E E R   P E A S
A V E   N A V A J O   Y M C A
R E I D   I R O C   J O H N
C O D I C I L   R A G O U T S
E N A M O R S   A L I E N E E
R E S E T S   M A E S T R I
```

171

```
M I S S T E X A S   S A L S A
A N T H O L O G Y   A M A H S
O V E R T A X E D   L A V A S
I O W E   T O N   P E T I T E
S K E W   E X T R E M I S T S
M E D I C   O R E N   S H E S
    S H A   Y A P S   E R E
S A C H E T S   M A T I S S E
O T O   T W A S   L A D  
A T M S   O A K S   T E D D Y
P O P E M O B I L E   C R E E
D R O N E D   D E A   L A S S
I N U I T   P L U G S A W A Y
S E N O R   T I T L E R O L E
H Y D R O   A D H E R E N T S
```

172

```
L O N G S H O T   R E G A R D
I B E L I E V E   E V E N E R
B L U E E Y E D   P E L A G E
R I T E   R I S E R   G A S
A G R   S W U N G   A R T S
R E A P   P I M A   A D A T E
Y E L L S A T   P A J A M A S
    O A T H   S L A P    
S L O W I S H   T A R T A N S
C A N E D   E L H I   S L O P
A Y E R   A L I E N   A N O
L S D   B E D E W   E C H O
E L I N O R   S H R U N K E N
R O M E R O   T I E S C O R E
S W E D E S   O P E N S F O R
```

173

```
D U K E I T O U T   S P E C S
E V I L T W I N S   N I X O N
R U S S I A N R O U L E T T E
A L M A S   K E N T   T E T E
T A E   I C E A G E S   R O Z
E S T E   E R D A   P E N N E
    C P A S   S T O M A T A
S O P O R S   O C E L O T
S P A N I E L   B A K E
M E L O N   O D A S   R V E R
I N O   T R U A N T S   I T E
N C O S   D I C K   T I D E D
N A K E D A S A J A Y B I R D
O S A G E   A P O L L O O N E
W E S A Y   S O B S I S T E R
```

174

```
L A T C H K E Y   A G A W A M
O N E H O R S E   C O R O N A
C E R A M I C S   H E A R T S
A M E N   P A M P E R   K I T
L I S   S P A R   S U R G E
  C A S E   E N O S   P O O R
    A L B A   F A S T O N E
S C H M E A R   I N H U M E D
C L I P A R T   T E A R  
R E A L   D I S C   G N A T
O A T E S   S T E M   G A M
U N U   I N T U N E   C A L I
N E S T L E   A T H L E T E S
G R E E K S   R E T I C E N T
E S S A Y S   T R A V E S T Y
```

175

```
B E A N S A L A D ▪ B I L K
A A B A T T E R Y ▪ M A M I E
S T I M U L A T E ▪ A N A M E
H S T ▪ P A C E ▪ D R A G O N
▪ M E S H ▪ C H I N E S E
T H R I F T ▪ G H A N A ▪
H E A D Y ▪ A R A B E S Q U E
A R I D ▪ B L I N I ▪ P U R R
W E L L B E I N G ▪ A L I G N
▪ E A S E D ▪ P R I Z E S
T H I C K E N ▪ B U T T
H A M L E T ▪ M O L D ▪ A S P
U N B A R ▪ P E R S E C U T E
M O U S Y ▪ A R E A C O D E S
P I E S ▪ T E R R O R I S T
```

176

```
B R E A K D A N C E ▪ G R E G
W I G G L E R O O M ▪ L O A N
A G G R E G A T E S ▪ I L S A
N O B ▪ E A R E D ▪ I N L E T
A R E A ▪ S A P I E N T
▪ A R M ▪ T A T U M ▪ S E W
T I T I A N ▪ D E L A W A R E
E L E A N O R ▪ D E T E N T E
A I R S T R I P ▪ R E S T E D
R E S ▪ R A G E S ▪ S E A
▪ L A D A D O G ▪ R C M P
R E G I S ▪ T A U R O ▪ L E A
A L E G ▪ C O N T E S T A N T
N O A H ▪ O N T H E H O U S E
D I R T ▪ M I S S K A N S A S
```

177

```
H A L L P A S S E S ▪ A J A R
O R A T O R I C A L ▪ C U R E
S E N D S A N O T E ▪ E S S E
E T C ▪ T M E N ▪ E A S T O N
R H E E ▪ W E E P S ▪ A N A
S A R I S ▪ E S T O P ▪ S I C
▪ D E A D ▪ E V I L E S T
A S T E R N ▪ E R E C T S
C H E R V I L ▪ T R E E ▪
T E X ▪ I T A L Y ▪ D R O L L
A R T ▪ C A M E L ▪ S H O O
L A U R E L ▪ V E R B ▪ M A V
O T R O ▪ O P I N I O N A T E
N O E S ▪ O U T O F S I G H T
E N D S ▪ S T Y L E S H E E T
```

178

```
R U B A D U B D U B ▪ S A S H
O N E M A N A R M Y ▪ A L T O
U S C I V I L W A R ▪ P E E P
N E O ▪ I T B E ▪ D A P H N E
D A M E S ▪ O L D S C H O O L
S L E D ▪ S A B E ▪ C O U P E
▪ D A I S Y M A E ▪ S A S
T H E Y L L ▪ S P E E D S
S O C ▪ C O W P A T T Y ▪
A M O C O ▪ E L S A ▪ R E P S
R E N O V A T E S ▪ G E N R E
I M O G E N ▪ A I D E ▪ D I E
N A M E ▪ D I S G U S T I N G
A D I N ▪ O P E N S T A N C E
S E C T ▪ R O D S T E I G E R
```

179

```
K N O C K O F F ▪ W A S H U P
N E W C O M E R ▪ O P P O S E
A L L I N O N E ▪ N E I M A N
C L E ▪ G O C A R T ▪ N E T S
K I T E ▪ E K E D ▪ M O I
S E S A M E ▪ E N O L ▪ A D O
▪ G O U R D E ▪ A I D A N
D E C L A R E ▪ G U R N E Y S
E L L E N ▪ S W E R V E ▪
A D A ▪ S E T H ▪ L A P S E D
N O M ▪ N U I T ▪ T A P E
S R O S ▪ A P P E A R ▪ L I P
H A R L E M ▪ S A V E F A C E
I D E A T E ▪ A S O N E M A N
P O R T A L ▪ W E N T W I L D
```

180

```
H A L ▪ W E S T M I N S T E R
A N I ▪ I L T R O V A T O R E
R O N ▪ P L A I N S P O K E N
P I O N E E R S ▪ R E C T
I N C O U R T ▪ T A L E N T S
S T U M P Y ▪ D R S E U S S ▪
T E T E ▪ T O E T A P ▪
S D S ▪ O C O N N O R ▪ C V I
▪ S T A G E D ▪ O L A N
▪ L A O T I A N ▪ T A P E R S
B O S T O N S ▪ C A R A M I A
O A T H ▪ G A L I L E A N
S T R E A M L I N E S ▪ N N E
C H A R L I E R O S E ▪ C C S
H E Y N I N E T E E N ▪ Y E T
```

181

```
SHOWSUP ■ TIARAED
MANHOLE ■ ASPERSE
ONTOAST ■ LAPLACE
RDA ■ STICKY ■ SLAP
EBRO ■ ETRE ■ ■ SPF
SAID ■ READE ■ BEER
■ GOES ■ COMEEASY
■ SNACKFOOD ■
PRISONED ■ NEWT
RENA ■ TNOTE ■ WHOA
FCC ■ SWAN ■ SAND
IRES ■ TONICS ■ USE
RUNOVER ■ LINEDUP
MISFILE ■ ONALERT
STEAMED ■ RAPINES
```

182

```
KINGKONG ■ ARAMID
ONELITER ■ SAFARI
ALLOTTEE ■ SITSON
LILA ■ SLATED ■ ENG
ANIT ■ YSER ■ RED
SEESAW ■ EAT ■ DADO
■ BEATS ■ EATON
PULLEDTHESTRING
ISAID ■ MERIT ■
NANA ■ WOW ■ BURSAR
GTD ■ ASHE ■ ETNA
POE ■ INTEND ■ LECT
ODDEST ■ EVAMARIE
NAUSEA ■ LOWSPEED
GYPPED ■ SINGSONG
```

183

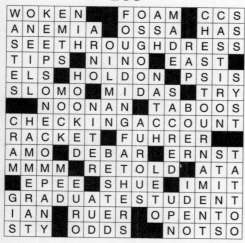

```
JACKSUP ■ MISLEAD
ONLEAVE ■ ASSAYER
ENIGMAS ■ TOTTERY
BUMS ■ LEMANS ■ SOD
LIB ■ UTAH ■ HOBO
OTIS ■ EATAT ■ ERIC
WYNNS ■ CREWNECK
■ OUTSHINES ■
SHOWEDUP ■ TOSCA
TYNE ■ SPLAT ■ NEAL
IDED ■ PALE ■ ARB
GRO ■ RELYON ■ ABLE
MANMADE ■ HUSKIER
ATTIMES ■ ATHIRST
SEALANT ■ SOANDSO
```

184

```
PAPERS ■ LIOTTA
IVORIES ■ WALTHER
TIPOFTHEICEBERG
MASSE ■ AXLES ■ CRO
ETTE ■ MITES ■ COIN
NOH ■ LITRE ■ BOLES
■ RETINAE ■ SAVOR
■ QUEENMOTHER ■
TUNIS ■ ELEANOR
SHEEN ■ MCDVI ■ FOL
LESS ■ LEASE ■ AMBI
OUT ■ FATSO ■ ABOOK
PRIVATEENTRANCE
EGOISTS ■ GALLEON
SENATE ■ POLYPS
```

185

```
WOKEN ■ FOAM ■ CCS
ANEMIA ■ OSSA ■ HAS
SEETHROUGHDRESS
TIPS ■ NINO ■ EAST
ELS ■ HOLDON ■ PSIS
SLOMO ■ MIDAS ■ TRY
■ NOONAN ■ TABOOS
CHECKINGACCOUNT
RACKET ■ FUHRER ■
AMO ■ DEBAR ■ ERNST
MMMM ■ RETOLD ■ ATA
■ EPEE ■ SHUE ■ IMIT
GRADUATESTUDENT
IAN ■ RUER ■ OPENTO
STY ■ ODDS ■ NOTSO
```

186

```
MADAM ■ UGHS ■ CALI
AMITY ■ PRIM ■ HMOS
COLOR ■ SOLITAIRE
SIENNA ■ CAROTENE
■ TEARJERKER ■
LOTS ■ EERY ■ HOSED
ANA ■ COTY ■ HOOPLA
PINHOLE ■ PALMIST
POTALE ■ CARD ■ NIE
SNERD ■ SOIR ■ ADES
■ PECCADILLO ■
INCISORS ■ SOCCER
FIRSTRATE ■ GOTTA
FLAT ■ OPEL ■ IVORY
YEWS ■ TERI ■ CERES
```

187

```
POREOVER ■ SLALOM
INATRICE ■ IODINE
TAKEABOW ■ GUMMED
CDE ■ LENIENT ■ ESL
HASH ■ SORTA ■ PATE
ERIES ■ ENL ■ ODAY
DENIMS ■ DABBLERS
■ RUTS ■ SOUL ■
FIRETRAP ■ XRATED
AVES ■ ERR ■ SCONE
CAMS ■ TEEUP ■ KOHL
ENA ■ OCEANID ■ TAU
SHILOH ■ MAKEKING
IONIZE ■ PRESENCE
TESTED ■ SYRINGES
```

188

```
POSEN ■ STA ■ SHEB
ARENA ■ AWAD ■ MODE
WINDSHIELDWIPER
ABSOLUTECEILING
TIER ■ ESP ■ DDE ■
■ SPY ■ STTERESA
ADIEU ■ VERA ■ RIP
FORENSICEXPERTS
ALI ■ OTOE ■ ENSUE
RESTEDON ■ SEA ■
■ ULA ■ DYE ■ MEGA
PENCILSHARPENER
CLASSICALBALLET
BESO ■ MANE ■ CEASE
SCAN ■ ETD ■ TRIES
```

189

```
SWINGIT ■ OTHELLO
AAMILNE ■ NOUVEAU
MRSPOCK ■ CEMENTS
PRO ■ WOWSERS ■ DIT
LARS ■ GATOR ■ LIME
ENROL ■ RIV ■ DINER
■ TYROS ■ REHANGS
■ COLDFRAME ■
■ OPENAIR ■ HODAD
EVERY ■ SIS ■ NUMIC
DENY ■ SPENT ■ PISH
URN ■ ATEDIRT ■ STE
CLATTER ■ FAUSTUS
TAMMIES ■ FINEART
SPECTRE ■ STANDBY
```

190

```
OPAQUE ■ PLOY ■ LPS
GROUTS ■ AINU ■ EAT
LIKEASISTER ■ SPA
EXIT ■ EASE ■ IFSAY
■ ZINGERS ■ OILS
LIMAS ■ ORATORS ■
ATOLLS ■ STUNTMEN
TINCANS ■ INSHORE
ESTONIAN ■ SIERRA
■ PADDIES ■ TRESS
FRET ■ ELMTREE ■
LILLE ■ BEAU ■ COLA
ALI ■ FROSTFLOWER
GEE ■ THAI ■ FOREST
SYR ■ SOTS ■ SYDNEY
```

191

```
IGLOOS ■ BADEGGS
CAYUSE ■ MADEFREE
ELITES ■ EDENTATA
BIN ■ SAME ■ NEW
ELGAR ■ NONACTIVE
RETREAD ■ VESTEE
GOOFFTHEDEEPEND
■ COLOR ■
THESHOWMUSTGOON
RUSHES ■ BEELINE
INCONTACT ■ TOLET
ETA ■ CUSS ■ WAL
SEPARATE ■ OVIEDO
TREMOLOS ■ VILLAS
ESSAYER ■ SALLYS
```

192

```
HARDBARGAIN ■ CAR
ANALOGOUSTO ■ ITE
LIVINGYEARS ■ TAD
ETE ■ RASPY ■ NANA
RADICALS ■ CETYL
■ NAVE ■ CLARICE
SHASTA ■ OPENDOOR
COMPETESAGAINST
ONPAROLE ■ WRESTS
FOLDERS ■ RADS ■
FRIED ■ BURSTERS
EATS ■ CHASM ■ RHO
DRU ■ TOOTHENAMEL
AID ■ DOMOARIGATO
TAE ■ SPORTSCASTS
```

193

```
LOSE  ONESTEMPER
ONEMOMENTINTIME
LETITALLHANGOUT
ANGLO LAE  EENS
  DOE    CLASS
   ZED EEC  KOS
SALOME SNUFFOUT
ITALICS STIRFRY
RATATATS ELOISE
EDS  DOH  REN
   SCENA    THE
 ALOU ENC EPODE
ALEUTIANISLANDS
GETTINGONESGOAT
ONTHEFENCE ERSE
```

194

```
CARLOAN SCALARS
ONEACRE PANACHE
ROUGHIT ARTSHOW
LITERAL RAISINS
ENTRENOUS   EDU
OTE   SPEEDTRAP
NERD ASARULE
EDSELS   RICHES
  CATERTO HAVE
WORKSOVER   NAE
ARE  EXITSIGNS
PIASTER PROVOST
NOTLIVE POLENTA
ELAINES EVERTOR
RESTART REASONS
```

195

```
CHICKFLICK RSVP
RESPIRATOR ILIE
ALLANADALE PINS
FLA DUEL PHEDRE
TENT EDIBLEROOT
ENDRUN ALAR USA
RESET ANECDOTES
  VEAL SHED
TVDINNERS RIPON
EAU SARI ASLOPE
AIRFILTERS EPPS
SNARLY MESS TOT
EENY STATEHOUSE
RSTU TINATURNER
STEP SONGSTRESS
```

196

```
BEATSME STRIDES
IMBORED ARIDEST
GASMASK BATISTA
MIO SHOWBIZ PAR
ALLA CHAT  TATE
NEVIL HIT ARIES
 DERAT THECARS
  PROTESTED
QUARREL CRETE
CURRY RIN BURNT
HICK ARNO PARA
ACH PRIESTS NOM
SKIPOLE HEADSUP
TENONER ENDNOTE
ENSIGNS STEAMED
```

197

```
ASCAP  POGS  SAV
STARE FERRO EVE
TONGA RABIN MER
INTERFACING IMA
NEONLIGHTS TEAL
  TINGES BARRY
 SPINELS RAKEIN
CHINESEAMERICAN
HALEST NOCENTS
ELLAS ADDING
ELAN ACCEPTABLE
TOG CHARLESSLAW
AWE RIDEA STIPE
HER ALIAS EAGER
SRS GLAM ABELS
```

198

```
FAIRCATCH SLANG
ATLEISURE SABER
CLOSEINON WORSE
TAVI ASIF  TATA
ONEG ROSEBUSHES
ITIN ONE ICEAGE
DATE ORDEAL MGR
  DEFY AGAS
ACE ADESTE ACAP
SARTRE HEN TARO
PLAINCHANT ISAW
ELSE KYRA AULD
COUPS POWERBASE
TURIN ENAMELLER
STENO SAYSAYSAY
```